framed spaces

INTERFACES: Studies in Visual Culture

EDITORS: Mark J. Williams and Adrian W. B. Randolph, Dartmouth College

This series, sponsored by Dartmouth College Press, develops and promotes the study of visual culture from a variety of critical and methodological perspectives. Its impetus derives from the increasing importance of visual signs in everyday life, and from the rapid expansion of what are termed "new media." The broad cultural and social dynamics attendant to these developments present new challenges and opportunities across and within the disciplines. These have resulted in a trans-disciplinary fascination with all things visual, from "high" to "low," and from esoteric to popular. This series brings together approaches to visual culture — broadly conceived — that assess these dynamics critically and that break new ground in understanding their effects and implications.

For a complete list of books that are available in the series, visit www.upne.com.

Monica E. McTighe, *Framed Spaces: Photography and Memory in Contemporary Installation Art*

Alison Trope, *Stardust Monuments: The Saving and Selling of Hollywood*

Nancy Anderson and Michael R. Dietrich, eds., *The Educated Eye: Visual Culture and Pedagogy in the Life Sciences*

Shannon Clute and Richard L. Edwards, *The Maltese Touch of Evil: Film Noir and Potential Criticism*

Steve F. Anderson, *Technologies of History: Visual Media and the Eccentricity of the Past*

Dorothée Brill, *Shock and the Senseless in Dada and Fluxus*

Janine Mileaf, Please Touch: *Dada and Surrealist Objects after the Readymade*

Monica E. McTighe

framed spaces

PHOTOGRAPHY AND MEMORY IN CONTEMPORARY INSTALLATION ART

Dartmouth College Press   Hanover, New Hampshire

Dartmouth College Press
An imprint of University Press of New England
www.upne.com

Manufactured in the United States of America
Designed by Mindy Basinger Hill
Typeset in Minion Pro and Myriad Pro
by Integrated Publishing Solutions
5 4 3 2 1

University Press of New England is a member of the Green Press Initiative. The paper used in this book meets their minimum requirement for recycled paper.

Library of Congress Cataloging-in-Publication Data

McTighe, Monica E.
Framed spaces : photography and memory in contemporary installation art / Monica E. McTighe. — 1st [edition].
pages cm — (Interfaces: studies in visual culture)
Includes bibliographical references and index.
ISBN 978-1-61168-205-2 (cloth : alk. paper) —
ISBN 978-1-61168-206-9 — (pbk. : alk. paper) —
ISBN 978-1-61168-251-9 (ebook)
1. Art and photography. 2. Installations (Art) —Themes, motives. I. Title.
N72.P5M38 2012
709.04′074 — dc23 2011051354

contents

acknowledgments

This project could not have been completed without the help and support of many people. First, a great debt of gratitude is owed Howard Singerman, my mentor and advisor, whose persistent and generous support of my work has helped me in countless ways. In addition, I am grateful to the professors in the Department of Art History at the University of Virginia who helped me develop this project, providing financial support and guidance. Thanks are owed as well to the Department of Art and Art History at Tufts University and the Faculty Research Awards Committee at Tufts University whose generous moral and financial support of my work has helped me complete this project. In particular, I need to thank my colleague, Eric Rosenberg who has been a steadfast and generous mentor throughout my time at the university. Thank you to the *künstlerhaus büchsenhausen* in Innsbrück, Austria, which provided me with a fellowship that contributed to the work in this book. Additional thanks are due to my colleagues Gregory Williams and Benjamin Carp, who read drafts of the chapters, Leslie K. Brown, and Richard Pult and Amanda Dupuis of the University Press of New England. And much gratitude goes to the artists and others who have been so generous with their time, knowledge, patience, and support, including Tony Cokes, Renée Green, and Javier Anguera, Ann Hamilton, and Louise Lawler, as well as Janelle Reiring at Metro Pictures. Thank you to David Karp, who has been by my side through thick and thin. And last but not least, thank you to my family, especially to my father, E. James McTighe, and my sister, Michele Kendall, who have helped me in innumerable ways to complete this work. This is for you.

Monica E. McTighe

SOMERVILLE, MASSACHUSETTS, 2011

framed spaces

introduction

Across the dark space, two transparent silk chambers float side by side above oily cement floors in the recently vacated spinning mill. Through the silk panels of each chamber, the observer can see the silhouettes of two long tables. On each table, video projectors, mounted on a turning mechanism, cast on the thin silk the image of a line being drawn by a pencil. The space is large, covering a half-acre with a ceiling supported by metal columns arranged in a grid pattern. The projections sweep around this vast space — sometimes chasing each other, sometimes crossing each other. An image falls on the silk screens, splits into two, converges with the second projection, and shatters into four. As the viewer stands there, the sound of the pencil hissing on the paper fills the humid Virginia air and the pencils sweep across the viewer's body, the forest of metal columns supporting the ceiling, and finally the cinderblock walls of the empty spinning mill.

Later, when the viewer sees photographs of this installation, *ghost: a border act* (2000), in a retrospective catalog of the artist Ann Hamilton's work, they do not capture the complexity of her experience of the installation. The reproduced photograph, thin, bounded clearly by its edge, and difficult to read because of the dim light in the space, seems to bear little relationship to the installation that the viewer saw and experienced. Photographs, however, are necessary for a historian of site-specific installation art, as her object of research once exhibited often no longer exists, having been disassembled and stored, or dispersed. Fortunately, many installations are photographed, and in the course of their research historians study these photographs carefully.

Although installation art is often assumed to be an art of direct experience, it is often mediated by photography. If installation art requires the presence of a viewer, what does it mean when the majority of viewers see them only in photographs? As scholars have found, the history of ephemeral art objects and events, such as installation art, is filtered through the memories of the people who saw them first hand. These memories are often solidified or distorted by the documentation that is published alongside the work. Photographs mediate memory; history is a representation often constructed from these bits of evidence.

For instance, with Ann Hamilton's *ghost: a border act*, the viewer went on to write about this installation. A television show titled *Art: 21, Art in the Twenty-First Century* was broadcast on the Public Broadcasting Service in the United States and showed videotape of the installation, as well as interviews with the artist. These fragments of the work of art may then end up in a textbook via the circuitous routes of memory, word of mouth, art review, and brief catalog description. The few photographs and videotapes of these events are often embroidered by memory, which transforms the work into myth, distancing it from the history of the event. A student in an art history lecture hall is provided with a distilled and perhaps distorted verbal description with a single photograph of an art installation. In one of the earliest accounts of installation art as a category, Julie Reiss advocates careful consideration of historical sources to counteract the transformation of history into myth. She encourages scholars to critically analyze personal accounts, press reviews, interviews with artists, and archival evidence, such as photographic documentation.[1]

This book examines ways in which installation art, photography, and memory are intertwined with one another. Photography has shaped our understanding of history and memory since the nineteenth century. In the last forty years, a time in which the issue of memory has become of great interest in art practice and society in general, the theory of photography and photographic practice has become even more important in contemporary art.[2] At the same time, installation art has become one of the ubiquitous, often criticized, métiers in contemporary art practice.

Ephemeral installations that are concerned with the physical limits and material qualities of a site and interested in the viewers' perceptions would seem to elude representation through photographs. It is natural to think then that photographs of these works are both lacking and supplementary to the work itself. However, most installations are photographed. Amelia Jones notes that ephemeral art practices, such as body art (and I would add installation art), require documentation to gain symbolic status.[3] As Miwon Kwon notes of site-specific art, "The documentation of the project will take on another life within the art world's publicity circuit, which will in turn alert another institution for another commission."[4]

One focus of this book then is to analyze discrete examples of photographs of installation art in catalogs and books to demonstrate how these have shaped our understanding of the work. A second focus of this book is to examine the different ways contemporary installation artists have used the installation format, with its similarity to photographic archives, collections, and even cinema spaces, to examine how contemporary society cultivates memory and constructs history. For instance, in Renée Green's installation *Partially Buried in Three Parts*, there is a bank of video monitors, on one of which we see Green flipping through a book with the photographs of Robert Smithson's site-specific work *Partially Buried Woodshed* of 1970. *Partially Buried Woodshed* was destroyed, and the remains decayed into the earth at Kent State University decades ago. Therefore, the images in the book are one way for Green, who was a young child when the *Woodshed* was made, to access this moment in history. In her work *Partially Buried in Three Parts*, Green avails herself also of the personal memories of herself and others, as well as artifacts, television reports, and books to uncover a network of associations and connections threaded through Smithson's 1970 piece. In the process, Green reveals this moment in history to be a complex of overlapping events, memories, and experiences that connect her personally to the history of the year 1970 and to Smithson's woodshed.

The connection to history and memory through photographs and objects is one of the themes of the site-specific installation *Partially Buried in Three Parts*. The work is an archive focused on this network of connections and events in the 1970s. Installation art and photography often overlap in the practice of archiving and collecting, which has increasingly been used by artists in the questioning of memory and history in contemporary art practice in the last thirty years. And now, there are numerous installations that question history and memory through collections of photographs, films, videos, and other objects. As Hal Foster notes, these works are part of an "archival impulse" that I believe is connected to a growth of interest in the issues of history and memory in the last few decades of the twentieth century.

Aura and Experience

Cultural critic Walter Benjamin's examination of experience, memory, and photography, and art critic Craig Owens's essays on postmodernism, photography, and representation served as the starting point for this project. Benjamin's essays from the mid- to late 1930s, including "The Work of Art in the Age of Mechanical Reproduction," "On Some Motifs in Baudelaire," and "The Storyteller," provided basic questions to guide the research. Benjamin's essays describe the way that experience has changed in modernity by examining how these forms of memory have been conditioned by new technologies, specifically photography. In Benjamin's argument, experience has been fundamentally changed and even degraded in the shift from preindustrial to industrial modes of production. The change is reflected in the duality of memory that he describes as "the decline of aura." The following summary simplifies Benjamin's thinking about memory and aura but will provide the background for the theoretical issues in this book.

In Benjamin's classic essay, "The Work of Art in the Age of Mechanical Reproduction," he lays out the relationship between the traditional work of art and its reproduction. An air clings to unique, handmade objects bound to a particular place and time. These objects have "lived" a history that their contemporary viewers have not, and they bear the marks of that history in their material form. Take a centuries-old painting by Rembrandt. It bears the unique marks of its maker, who laid on brushstrokes in a distinctive manner to catch the textures of textiles and other things. The paint and canvas bear evidence of having been made in the seventeenth century. The work is a fragment of a different time and has survived centuries in the possession of various owners before it appears before the curious viewer in the museum. For Benjamin, the encounter with this object can be described in terms of *aura*. Aura bloomed in the viewer's face-to-face encounter with the work of art. "If we designate as aura the associations which, at home in the *mémoire involontaire*, tend to cluster around the object of a perception, then its analog in the case of a utilitarian object is the experience which has left traces of the practiced hand."[5] In this quotation, Benjamin connects aura to *mémoire involontaire*, which is the memory that erupts from the unconscious and engages the subject in a vivid, bodily recollection of the past. He connects this vivid, bodily experience of memory with the hand knowledge of the person who uses a tool.[6] Aura also lends the work a kind of presence that resembles in certain respects the presence attributed to sacred images and figures. In the encounter with a sacred image, a sense of distance springs up between the viewer and the object.

However, the photograph eliminates the aura of the work of art, removing distance and making it accessible, bringing the work to the masses. Benjamin aligns the photograph with a different kind of memory, *mémoire volontaire*. He offers as an example of *mémoire volontaire* the French writer Marcel Proust's dissatisfaction with his memories of Venice, which he compares to a collection of dry photographs.[7] The snapshot produced by the mechanical action of a camera represents the one-touch, instantaneous action of the modern world that is designed to accommodate the masses. The photograph is flat and thin, reducing experience to a set of visual information locked in a frame. Memory as photographic reproduction and archival materials, in repressing certain kinds of sensuous information, marks the stark divide between the past and the present, between memory that consists of visual data and memory that engages more of the senses. The transformation of memory practices generated both excitement and crisis. As Mary Ann Doane writes, in photography and film, "Time is, in a sense, externalized, a surface phenomenon, which the modern subject must ceaselessly attempt to repossess through its multifarious representations. The rationalization of time ruptures the continuum par excellence and generates epistemological and philosophical anxieties exemplified by Henri Bergson, in his adamant reassertion of temporal continuity in the concepts of durée."[8]

Henri Bergson, the early twentieth-century philosopher, had used the relationship of the photograph to lived experience as a metaphor for the way science describes the vital world. Bergson argues that we experience the natural world as a fluid and shifting continuum. However, modern science has difficulty grasping the complexity and vital quality of "life" and tries to break it down into manageable units. Bergson compares this analytic quality of science to the way that photographs and films still and fragment the visual world.[9] He already had an image of this in the work of Eadweard Muybridge's motion studies, which broke the movements of bodies into snapshots.

The American scientist and efficiency expert Frank B. Gilbreth then applied these tools to the study of workers' motions and produced films that he used to render the gestures of people in factories and offices more efficient.

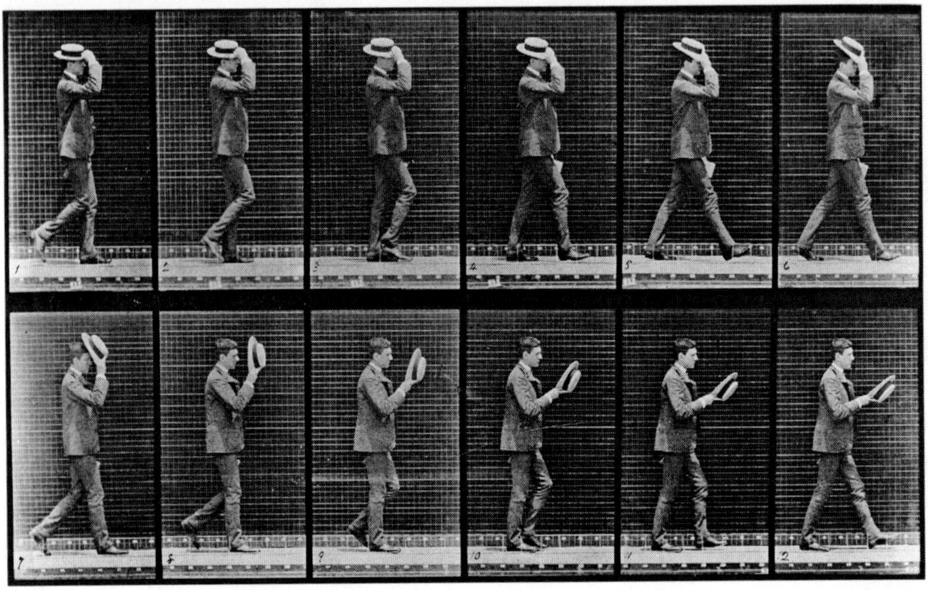

FIGURE I.1 Eadweard J. Muybridge (1830–1904), Plate 44, Walking Taking Off Hat, Animal Locomotion, 1887, Volume VII, Males and Females Draped and Misc. Subjects, 1885. Collotype on paper, 8⅛ in. x 13½ in. (20.64 cm x 34.29 cm). *Gift of the Edwin J. Beinecke Trust, Addison Gallery of American Art, Phillips Academy, Andover Massachusetts, 1984.6.463.*

These activities were part of the rationalization of time that Doane describes. These photographs used in sciences and industry become the model for certain conceptual artists in the 1960s who draw on the direct uninflected treatment of the photograph and the form of the grid in their work. The serial structure of these photographs is taken up as a mode of presentation in the work of figures such as Douglas Huebler, Bernd and Hilla Becher, and Hollis Frampton. By the end of the twentieth century, the scientific discourse that incorporated photographic images as evidence in the nineteenth and twentieth centuries had become an object of criticism for theorists who ask how these images produce meaning and have effects in the real world in the context of sexual and racial discourses. Photographs in this view reduce the complexity of experience to easily organized categories and bits of visual information, and I will argue that some installations, such as Green's, draw precisely on these photographic practices, structures, and critiques. The problem of the rationalization of time in the early twentieth century is analogous to the problem of photographing an installation that focuses on the viewer's internal experience of the site. Something is lost, and other aspects of bodily experience are distorted in the recording.

Installation Art and Experience

The relationship between the authentic work of art and its photographic documentation that Benjamin describes in terms of aura is suggestive when considering the relationship of installation art to photography. Installations often have a certain atmosphere and seek to engage viewers through more of the senses than vision. Installations are also often specific to the time and place in which they are exhibited. All of these qualities suggest that the components of aura can be found in some way in contemporary installation art. Perhaps we can say more accurately that direct or bodily *experience* takes the place of aura in contemporary installation art.

The interest in experience in art or experience *as* art is not new or exclusive to installation art. It seems to have emerged in the course of the twentieth century in discussions of the role of modern art in society. The interest in art as experience perhaps reflects a "hunger for experience" that the historian Craig Ireland observes to have emerged in the last decades of the twentieth century.[10] Even Clement Greenberg writes in his 1939 essay "Avant-Garde and Kitsch" that the reception of modern painting should differ fundamentally from the experience of the everyday object.[11] A decade later he suggests that the all-over painting responds to a sense in modern culture that there is no longer a hierarchy of values in society — and that the ultimate difference is between "the immediate and the un-immediate."[12] Modernist painting strived to achieve immediacy. His protégé, Michael Fried, would go on to describe this distinct, immediate visual experience as the "presentness" of modernist painting. For Fried and Greenberg, modernist painting was the pinnacle of aesthetic experience, which must be preserved by modern culture.[13] In other realms of art production in the 1960s, there was, by contrast, an emphasis on art as durational, everyday experience — experience outside the museum and gallery space. The members of the Fluxus movement; those associated with John Cage, Robert Rauschenberg, and Merce Cunningham; Allan Kaprow; and the Minimalists advocated art as a situation that includes objects, performers, audience, durational time, and perception. These "live" art practices of the 1960s, in contrast to the modernist art in museums, were often events and installations that encouraged viewer participation, everyday temporalities, and included social interaction. Carrie Lambert-Beatty describes the work of Yvonne Rainer in these terms. Rainer incorporates everyday gestures into the structure of her dances to balance two different modes of time: the unstructured contingent intervals of everyday gestures within the formal time period of the performance.[14] And the live event of performance art and body art also emphasizes the viewer and the performer's direct bodily experience.

Installation art can be counted as one of those ephemeral art practices that emerged in the 1960s. Claire Bishop traces a chronology of installation from the mid-1960s to the present based on the idea that the viewer's direct experience of the work is one of the defining features of installation art. The chronology ranges from Allan Kaprow's *Happenings and Environments* to the social gatherings in the 1990s that Nicolas Bourriaud named "relational aesthetics."[15] Bishop frames her inquiry by asking what type of experience and by extension what subjects of this experience are produced by various installation spaces.[16] Her categories constitute four "modalities of experience." One modality derives from the phenomenological subject described in the work of philosopher Maurice Merleau-Ponty. Merleau-Ponty posits a subject fully enmeshed with the space it experiences, so that perceptions of self and world continually condition each other. Rather than having a stable and certain viewing position, the subject in this modality is continually prompted to examine and reflect upon its changing perceptions. According to Bishop, these spaces address an embodied viewer who is continually made aware of her or his perceptions. The historical model for this type of work is, of course, Minimalism. Another category of installation addresses not a single viewer but the audience as a community, producing viewers that are activated politically. As an early example, Bishop points to Brazilian artist Hélio Oiticica's installation works, which provided tactile experiences of different materials such as sand, water, and straw. She defines Oiticica's work in these terms in order to shift "relational aesthetics" into the realm of installation art, although relational aesthetics also has close ties to performances and Happenings in the 1960s. These works grouped under the rubric "relational aesthetics" all require the active, real-time engagement of participants in a certain time and space.

Because of the interest in face-to-face communication, direct experience, and active engagement in Bishop's criticism of installation, there is an iconoclastic emphasis that infuses her work, as well as Nicolas Bourriaud's. "Relational aesthetics" is the term that Bourriaud coined to describe work that frames not an aesthetic object but rather the interaction among individuals and objects as designed by an artist. Bishop distinguishes "relational antagonism" from Bourriaud's relational aesthetics as an interaction that emphasizes not utopian and inevitably temporary connections among participants at a Tiravanija opening but rather the real world tensions and antagonisms that are brought out in communities. Despite Bishop's criticism of relational aesthetics, both her ideas and Bourriaud's are founded on the notion that direct face-to-face interaction and experience is better for political and social systems.[17] These works of art downplay the role of photography, as well as present challenges to documentation. In situating relational aesthetics in the realm of installation art, Bishop suggests that installation art has important similarities to performance and body art.

Photographs as "Memories" of Ephemeral Art Practices

The issue of documentation has been explored in body art and performance, especially in the work of Amelia Jones. In Jones's discussions of the documentation of performances, she argues that critics writing on body art have focused too much on the value of the unmediated presence of the artist in the work. However, Jones is doubtful that body art is unmediated, and using the term "supplement" from Jacques Derrida, she notes not only that the photograph is a supplement in the way Derrida defines it but also that there are many points of deferral of the artist's immediate presence in body art. "The sequence of supplements initiated by the body art project—the 'body' itself, the spoken narrative, video, and other visuals in the piece, the video, film, photograph, and text documenting it for posterity—announces the necessity of 'an infinite chain, ineluctably multiplying the supplementary mediations that produce the sense of the very thing they defer.'"[18]

In fact, Jones claims that performance art and its photographic documentation are mutually dependent. She writes, "The body art event *needs* the photograph to confirm its having happened; the photograph *needs* the body art event as an ontological "anchor" of its indexicality."[19] The photograph frames the ephemerality of the event. In the twentieth and twenty-first century, we seem to be fascinated by the ephemeral, by things that will disappear, and there seems to be something poignant and pleasurable in viewing a photograph of a work or an event that one did not witness first hand. Barbara Clausen describes it as "a moment that can be desired only in its non-existence."[20] She as well as others have suggested that ephemeral art practices need to be considered not only as specific and discrete events in time but also in terms of their reception, of which photographs are often an important part.[21] The status of photographs and supplementary documents is also one of the themes of Martha Buskirk's *The Contingent Object of Contemporary Art*, in which she argues that certain photographs of performances have become iconic to the point where the viewer, in an art history class, for instance, does not question the origin and meaning of the image. The image comes to stand for the work in a way the artist never intended.[22] Others have also commented on this problem in ephemeral artworks.[23] Photographs both solve and create problems when we are trying to understand the past.

This book does not attempt to be a survey of the practices of memory in contemporary art in general.[24] The chapters that follow explore how photography and the related media of film and video have helped to shape our understanding of history and memory in the context of works of installation art. Many of the works described in this book help viewers to understand the way photographs and other kinds of recordings have been used to construct memory and history in the realm of art practice and beyond. Others try to resist the flattening effects of photography by producing installation to provoke a bodily memory. Like Jones's work, this book too uses Derrida's notion of the "supplement" and seeks to question the way we read photographs as documentation not just of installation art but also as part of history and memory.

Site-Specific Art

The writing on postmodern theory and site-specific art that has taken place in the United States and Europe in the last thirty years is important in this discussion. In this body of art criticism, the photograph as a theoretical object takes a much larger role. Art historian and critic Craig Owens's work, inspired by Walter Benjamin, includes photography in discussions of site-specific art. For instance, Owens writes about Smithson's work in the Great Salt Lake titled *Spiral Jetty* (1970), which he said included not only the earthwork but also the film documenting its production and Smithson's essay titled "Spiral Jetty" published in *Arts of the Environment* in 1972. In his articles, "Earthwords" and "The Allegorical Impulse: Toward a Theory of Postmodernism," Craig Owens draws on the writings of Benjamin to argue that there is an equivalence between Smithson's site-specific pieces, his writings, and his photographs of these works in his site/nonsite dialectic. The nonsite, as writing about or photographs of the site, points to the site, and the site points back to the nonsites.[25] The work does not stay put but circulates among the various elements, never wholly present in any of them.

In part 1 of "The Allegorical Impulse: Toward a Theory of Postmodernism," Owens makes the connection between photography and site-specific art by saying, "The site-specific work becomes the emblem of transience, the ephemerality of all phenomena; it is the *memento mori* of the twentieth century."[26] He then notes that photographs of temporary works of art always seek to fix the ephemeral. Photographs are supplemental to the work but absolutely tied to it at the same time. They in a certain respect double the work. The term *supplement*, as Jacques Derrida uses it, however, has two senses. Derrida describes the frame of a work of art as outside and supplementary to it, but it also, he says, marks an absence at the heart of the work. The absence is indicated by the fact that the work requires some kind of frame. Smithson's work and to varying degrees other works of site-specific art have this dimension. As Owens notes, the presence of photography in Smithson's notion of nonsite adds a new dimension to the notion of site-specific art.

In the more recent writing of art historians and theorists Nick Kaye, Miwon Kwon, and James Meyer, there is an agreement that there is something more than the type of site-specific art that is built in place, is temporary, and requires the presence of the viewer who experiences it directly. These art historians argue for another type of site-specific art that is characterized as "discursive" per Kwon, "functional" in Meyer's words,[27] and in Kaye's writing by the notion that site is unstable due to the viewer's performance in and production of the space.[28] According to Kwon,

> The "work" no longer seeks to be a noun/object but a verb/process, provoking the viewers' critical (not just physical) acuity regarding the ideological conditions of that viewing. In this context, the guarantee of a specific relationship between an artwork and its "site" is not based on a physical permanence

> of that relationship (demanded by Serra, for example), but rather on the recognition of its unfixed impermanence, to be experienced as an unrepeatable and fleeting situation.[29]

Among these descriptions of varieties of site-specificity an interesting parallel emerges with the description of memory in the twentieth century—between bodily internal memory, presence, and direct experience, and archival or photograph memory, which makes memory fragmentary, mobile, and subject to discussion and questioning. Photographic documentation is key to the mobility and instability of site in Smithson's work. The photograph as nonsite is that which renders the site something parallel to language, which can circulate through publications, galleries, and museums, and be a part of discourse. Both Meyer and Kwon link this aspect of site-specificity to photography and to an expansion of the notion of site to include fields of knowledge and inquiry. In this way, memory and history become part of the discourse of site-specificity.[30]

Memory and History in the Art World of the 1980s and 1990s

Memory was perhaps the epistemological concern of the late twentieth century in the academic world, as many have argued. Artists and curators had also begun to examine memory in the context of art and culture. The debates and questions about memory and history seeped into art exhibitions and writings, perhaps influenced by the work of Jean Baudrillard in the book *Simulacra and Simulation* and that of Fredric Jameson in his article "Postmodernism, or the Cultural Logic of Late Capitalism," in the *New Left Review* in 1984. Jameson's piece was subsequently republished as a catalog essay for an exhibition titled *Utopia/Post-Utopia* at the Boston Institute of Contemporary Art in 1988. In it Jameson worries about the loss of memory.[31]

Modernism in Fredric Jameson's characterization is the time of grand narratives that propel the modern subject through a coherent sense of development and progress. In postmodernism, Jameson claims time is subordinated to space and memory disappears.[32] "At any rate, from this nostalgic and regressive perspective—that of the older modern and its temporalities—what is mourned is the memory of deep memory, what is enacted is a nostalgia for nostalgia, for the grand older extinct question of origin and *telos*, of deep time and Freudian Unconscious . . . and for the dialectic also."[33]

Jameson links this materialization of time to the decline of modernism, and in fact, he writes about these issues in the context of that essay on the exhibition of installations at the Institute of Contemporary Art in Boston. There is a link between the sense of the decline of modernism, installation, and now materialized memory. The sense of depth provided by history, memory, and even, as Jameson argues, the unconscious are emptied and made thin in his description of postmodern space. This space is where postmodern subjects lose their sense of historical orientation and any ability for community or collectivity.[34]

For Baudrillard, the age of simulacra produced rather than reflected reality. In a desperate scramble to recover memory, whatever remained of the past was preserved in what he perceived to be a museum culture. "The same holds true at Cruesot, at the level of the 'open' museum where one museumified in situ, as 'historical' witnesses of their period, entire working-class neighborhoods, living metallurgic zones, an entire culture, men, women, and children included—gestures, languages, customs fossilized alive as in a snapshot. The museum, instead of being circumscribed as a geometric site, is everynow, like a dimension of life."[35]

Baudrillard's ideas were influential in the New York art community in 1983 and 1984. Artists, such as Ross Bleckner, Peter Halley, and Philip Taaffe, all painters in the Neo-geo movement, as well as commodity artists such as Haim Steinbach and Jeff Koons, regarded these ideas as critical endorsement.[36] Neo-geo, with its smooth, machine-tooled paint surfaces and cool, hard-edge abstract forms, and Koons's vacuums and Steinbach's digital clocks with their hard, shiny, plastic surfaces were claimed as perfect examples of art as simulacrum. Others perceived the work of the Neo-expressionist painters of the 1980s and even the work of Sherrie Levine to be linked to his ideas.[37] Critics, such as Thomas Lawson also noted a revival of previous avant-garde movements in Neo-surrealism and Neo-pop, and the re-creations of Judson Dance theater performances, Happenings, and Fluxus events.[38]

In many critics' perceptions of the art world in the early 1980s, there was a general sense that art movements and avant-garde gestures—art history—were simply being recycled, with retro fashion and nostalgia extending across the realm of pop culture. Thomas Lawson associates the sense of repetition with a completion of the hegemony of American power. He writes in *Artforum* in 1984, "This linear belief system has begun to fade, its practicality replaced by a more effectively repressive concept of progress as eternal return, the cyclic time of myth in which culture no longer evolves but simply revolves. In this 'post-Modern' world, history is no longer a tool of self-identification, and ultimately of autonomy, but is instead merely an instant commodity."[39] Lawson describes the situation of the "continuous present" in terms of both a lack of creativity and an inability to conceive of a future. Other critics, such as John Howell and Lisa Liebmann, regarded the return to history as a way to digest the innovations of the past and to engage in a playful sort of decadence. Kate Linker describes the culture in terms very similar to Baudrillard and Jameson."[40]

In terms of art, this resurrection of history took the form of dehistoricizing art historical styles and practices such as Expressionism, Dada, Surrealism, and turning them into signs to be used at will in making a work of art. Critics and artists at this period nevertheless seem to be unable to decide whether the phenomenon of repetition is a form of market-driven cynicism or simply nostalgia.[41] As Hal Foster observed, these appropriations could be either a form of cynicism or an apt form of criticality for the time.[42] It could be, as well, that this is a form of working through traumatic events—the rapid changes of the twentieth century. History or art history, if not memory, becomes a problem for artists to work on in the late 1970s and 1980s.[43] It is because of photography and other recording media that artists were able to remake notable performances, use images from historical works of art in their work, or appropriate historical images and outmoded fashion.

An exhibition organized around this perception of memory was *The Art of Memory: The Loss of History* at the New Museum of Contemporary Art in 1985.[44] The artists included Judith Barry, Adrian Piper, Louise Lawler, Martha Rosler, René Santos, Troy Brauntuch, and Hiroshi Sugimoto. The writers for the exhibition, William Olander, Abigail Solomon-Godeau, and David Deitcher, are concerned about the commodification and reification of memory in the form of mass media images. This process of reification, they argue, results in a loss of history, or the suppression of alternative historical discourses, as well as the loss of individual control over memory itself. The photograph is perceived in this exhibition, therefore, as an ambivalent critical tool.[45] It can be used to support dominant power structures or to undercut them. The essayists characterize memory in the 1980s as fragmentary. William Olander goes so far as to assert that this fragmentary memory is one of the chief preoccupations of art in postmodernism.

Most of the artists who made work for the exhibition drew their images specifically from the mass media. Martha Rosler's video installation *Global Taste* used television advertisements taken from around the globe. Richard Prince re-photographed scenes of leisure from magazines, and Christopher Williams's site-specific photo installation *On New York II* combined a media image of an execution in Bangladesh, performed for the cameras, with a stock tourist image of New York City. The artists in the exhibition also made histories from these collections of images that undercut official histories, such as Sarah Charlesworth's *détournement* of a month of the *Herald Tribune*. In this project, she removed all of the text and left only the masthead and photographs of a month of the newspaper. Bruce Barber's *Remembering Vietnam* combined an advertisement/tribute by United Technologies to the soldiers of Vietnam with a description of a war crime from an official government investigation. Finally, Hiroshi Sugimoto exhibited photographs of natural history museum displays and empty theaters, while Louise Lawler showed photographs of a storage room at the Rude Museum in Dijon, emphasizing the artificiality of the museum effect. The exhibition displayed memory as representation, and the artists critiqued the social codes in images.

Whereas the work in that exhibition centered on the loss of immediacy, presence, and connection in memory through photography and video, *Places with a Past* arranged in Charleston in 1991, was organized around the notion of the immediate presence of history and memory. The curators of *Places with a Past* invited artists to come to Charleston and create site-specific works that engaged the history of the place. A wide range of artists participated, such as Ann Hamilton, Christian Boltanski, Chris Burden, Cindy Sherman, Lorna Simpson, Alva Rogers, and David Hammons.

In her catalog publication, Mary Jane Jacob emphasizes the idea that the works created used narrative in order to recover repressed or marginalized histories.[46] The artists were expected to deal with some aspect of Charleston's history. Most of the pieces were constructed in historic buildings in downtown Charleston and drew on the atmosphere inherent in these old buildings.

The memory evoked in these works is body-oriented memory that utilizes the historic sheen of a city like Charleston. Miwon Kwon argues that this exhibition neutralized the critical capabilities of site-specific work:

> While site-specific art continues to be described as a refutation of originality and authenticity as intrinsic qualities of the art object or the artist, this resistance facilitates the translation and relocation of these qualities from the artwork to the place of its presentation, only to have them return to the artwork now that it has become integral to the site. . . . Conversely, if the social, historical, and geographical specificity of Charleston offered artists a unique opportunity to create unrepeatable works (and by extension, an unrepeatable exhibition), then the programmatic implementation of site-specific art in exhibitions like *Places with a Past* ultimately utilize art to *promote* Charleston as a unique place.[47]

Kwon's critique suggests that memory can easily become a type of commodity that bolsters rather than critiques the system into which it is placed.

The exhibition *Doubletake* at London's Hayward Gallery in 1992 took the theme of collective memory. Lynne Cooke wrote a chapter titled "The Site of Memory" in which she observed in the early 1980s an interest within popular culture and literature in the idea of a fabricated memory that produced a convincing type of authenticity. She used the example of the film *Blade Runner*, in which one of the main characters, a genetically engineered clone, is convinced that she is human because of the vivid memories that have been implanted in her brain.[48]

Cooke observed that a distinction exists between organic, genuine memory and artificial memory in Philip K. Dick's original novel. The distinction does not exist, however, in William Gibson's "cyberpunk" fiction of the same period. Citing Howard Singerman, Cooke argued that collective memory now has effectively been taken over by mass cultural material and media-produced memory, which has colonized private memory.[49]

Memory and mourning surfaced in artwork in the late 1980s and early 1990s in the context of AIDS as well. In 1994, Simon Watney writes that, for a community that was experiencing an overwhelming number of AIDS deaths, "the questions of seeing and remembering take on a very special significance in relation to AIDS."[50] Douglas Crimp argues in "Mourning and Militancy" that, because the gay community had been so discouraged from mourning and, in fact, encouraged to hide the devastation of AIDS from the greater public, mourning was in fact a type of militancy.[51] Because many artists had experienced AIDS on such a personal level, they found that the appropriate response was in the form of intimate photo diaries of friends' illnesses and deaths, AIDS portraits, and individual sculptural memorials.[52] A different response was the public action posters, such as were shown in the exhibition *On the Road: Art against AIDS*. The traveling show included posters designed by artists such as Barbara Kruger, Gran Fury, and Cindy Sherman. The annual *Day without Art*, organized by the group Visual AIDS, and founded by curator Thomas Sokolowski, curator Gary Garrels, critic Robert Atkins, and curator William Olander, began in 1989.[53] The organizers requested that arts organizations close one day a year in memory of AIDS victims. At the same time, Group Material's AIDS timeline was published in various art publications and served both as a memorial and wake-up call for a public and government determined to ignore the urgency of the AIDS crisis. Other AIDS memorials, such as the NAMES quilt, and various other activities such as vigils and personal memorials, also served as embodiments of memory and loss.

Two more books on art and memory need to be acknowledged before I describe the structure of the current book. Lisa Saltzman's *Making Memory Matter: Strategies of Remembrance in Contemporary Art* discusses the work of several contemporary artists who use various strategies for memorializing.[54] Saltzman organizes the work she discusses around various forms of indexes that have been made for centuries in art. Taking as her starting point the legend of the Corinthian maiden who traced the shadow silhouette of her departing lover on a wall, Saltzman focuses on contemporary versions of shadows (i.e., video projections), silhouettes, and casts. Saltzman argues that contemporary art in many ways employs the strategy of the index as absence to bear witness to atrocities and everyday life alike.

Joan Gibbons's *Contemporary Art and Memory: Images of Recollection and Remembrance* categorizes various works of contemporary art via different ways of remembering. These range from personal remembrance or autobiography to postmemory—those who contend with events that took place before they were born—and to archives and museum collections as memory. Both Saltzman and Gibbons acknowledge one of the premises of this book, which is that memory and history have become significant themes in art since the 1970s.

Installation Art as Heterotopia

Installations provide a space to think critically about contemporary experience. For the book *Installation Art in the New Millennium*, the authors engaged Jonathan Crary to write the preface. In it he claims, "Aesthetic debates dependent on notions of 'medium' are out of touch with contemporary actuality."[55] Installation, for Crary, is not directed so much to the development of aesthetic experience as it is a response to an "epistemological crisis." Previous to the late nineteenth century, Crary claims, a balance existed between the human "sensorium" and the conditions of perception. However, with the transfer of vision, hearing, memory, and thinking to machines, the human faculties of perception were overwhelmed by the bewildering amount of new information available. Crary claims that installation is important because it provides a means to cope with the immense changes in perceptual conditions in the late twentieth century, by testing and presenting new means of experience. "Memory work" in contemporary art deals, perhaps, with the overwhelming transformations of contemporary society. I will take up both these arguments with regard to installation art. Installation art provides a way of coming to grip with the changes in the present but also a means to reflect on the past.

Michel Foucault describes the materialization of memory via his notion of genealogy.[56] In genealogy, memory settles into material, resting in the document, the statement as spoken, written, or remembered.[57] It clings to the surfaces of bodies, materials, and objects. Thus, in Foucault's writing of the 1960s, memory is materialized, fragmented, and dispersed. For Foucault the sense of history as progressive had faded as well. Therefore, in the era of material memory it is necessary to map sites. His discussion of mapping sites and the establishment of relations among sites is reminiscent of Robert Smithson's discussion of both geological time and site/nonsite. Foucault writes, "Site is defined by relations of proximity between points or elements; formally, we can describe these relations as series, trees, or grids. . . . The storage of data in the memory of a machine; the circulation of discrete elements within a random output (car traffic, the sounds on a telephone line); the identity of marked or coded elements inside a set may be randomly distributed, or may be arranged according to single or multiple classifications."[58]

Within these sites there are relations that can be figured, Foucault writes, in visual terms. By performing this type of mapping, Foucault is able to distinguish between quotidian sites and those he calls "heterotopias." Heterotopias are sites marked off from society that paradoxically connect to all other sites in society. They open out as well onto other times. Foucault names as examples the library, the museum, the cemetery, and the cinema. These are all spaces that are connected to the materialization of memory.

Installations can be described as another form of heterotopia, a place set off from society where different times and places intersect via objects, materials, and images. Installation seems to be a particularly appropriate practice for artists interested in memory and history because it can take on the form of these structures that are charged with keeping memory and history: the archive, the library, the museum collection, and even the stage and movie theater.

The "technologies of vision," such as film and photography, provided a way to materialize time.[59] Art practice provides a space in which to reflect on these technologies and the way we construct history and memory. There are at least two important dimensions of the relationship of photography to installation art. For temporary installations, the photograph is often the only thing left of the work. The ideal viewer would see the piece in person and have a direct, bodily or phenomenological experience of the site. When regarded in this manner, the photograph is a supplement to the installation, and it is read as if it were a visual document. The photograph may not be the ideal way to preserve a bodily experience, and it raises additional questions about how time is materialized in the photograph.

The second dimension focuses more on the photograph as something that frames a part of the visual world and makes it mobile, allowing it to be recontextualized, to become discursive. In the context of installation art, the photograph is investigated as a mediator of history and experience. Because it is a representation, it is already inscribed and shot through with meanings invested in it by its cultural context and the understandings carried by its viewers. The materiality of the photograph is an advantage in this kind of critical historical practice, as it seizes and holds time, disrupting its flow and making it possible to analyze it. Cutting the continuous flow of time and freezing it in object or photograph form, materializing it, enables this reconsideration of history. Benjamin had argued that the uncertain nature of meaning in the photograph "unsettles" viewers until they are provided with a caption. It is the unsettled quality of the photograph that enables the rereading of it and, by extension, the rewriting of history.

The Structure of This Book

This book discusses two dimensions of the relationship between installation art and photography. First is the notion that photographs of installation have shaped our memories and conditioned the histories written about these works. Second, some of the works in this book encourage us to consider how photography produces effects of memory and is used to construct histories via the installations of archives, photographic images, and objects. And during the passing of analog photography, the book encourages viewers to realize that photographs, film, and video are historical objects whose effects and status should be questioned.

This book's four chapters track a rough chronology, beginning in the late 1970s. The first two chapters deal with the archives of specific works of installation art. In the first chapter, that archive consists of a group of catalogs of exhibitions devoted to installation art in the 1970s. The chapter begins with a look at the role of photography in the exhibition catalog for *Rooms* at PS1 in Queens, New York, in 1976. *Rooms* invited artists to take the literal site of the exhibition as inspiration for the content of the work and resulted in many site-specific pieces that exist now only as pictures. The chapter considers the documentation of the work in the exhibition, the form of the catalog, and what work was included in the show as well as the works that were picked up in reviews. Gordon Matta-Clark was one of the participants in the exhibition. The role of his photographs of his own building cuts presents another twist to the issue of documentation. Chapter 1 examines Matta-Clark's artist book *Splitting*, focusing on the way his collages play with photographic space and their relationship to the bodily experience of his site-specific piece *Splitting* from 1973 to 1974. This chapter concludes with a discussion of an exhibition at Artists Space in 1978 that included the work of Adrian Piper, Cindy Sherman, Louise Lawler, and Christopher D'Arcangelo. Janelle Reiring, who later went on to co-found the gallery Metro Pictures helped organize the exhibition. It was her intention to present the work of artists who thought consciously about the way their photographs and installations were arranged and the way that viewers would see and "read" the work as a result. The work in this exhibition points to the art institution as a kind of frame but also causes viewers to reflect on their own habits of viewing and interpreting art. The catalog had few photographs; instead, language takes the place of photography in this exhibition.

In the second chapter, the archive is the Renée Green installation *Partially Buried in Three Parts*. Green's work examines her connection to Robert Smithson's *Partially Buried Woodshed* and engages with the way a work of art has been represented in its documentation and the memories of those who saw it. The piece goes beyond that to examine the myriad connections between personal memory, social history, political idealism, and the global art world. This chapter focuses on the films and installation associated with *Partially Buried in Three Parts*. Special interest is paid to Green's fascination with outmoded recording and presentation technologies such as film projectors and slide shows. Green's work also demonstrates her interest in the way systems of information produce categories and meanings. The photograph is a serial, infinitely reproducible object and is a modern means of organizing and communicating information. She plays with the serial nature of the photograph in order to encourage viewers to question how the "framing" of images and of information shapes our understanding of it. Viewers become critical readers in her installations and other archive-type installations.

The last two chapters focus on bodily memory in installation art, that is, how artists use objects and materials to evoke sensuous memories. Photographs of these installations are problematic because they don't capture the complexity of the work. However, photographs and films in installations in the era of digital media, as historical objects, have become a spark for bodily memory.

The third chapter examines a recent work by Ann Hamilton, a prolific installation artist who has made monumental atmospheric installations comprised of organic materials, sound recordings, mechanical elements, and videos since the 1980s. Hamilton is interested in perception and the body and considers the viewer's experience of primary importance in her work. Her installations mostly appear to the greatest number of interested viewers, however, in the form of beautifully composed, richly colored photographs. Photographs of Hamilton's work, as well as other installations that focus on the viewer's bodily or phenomenological experience, raise questions about the relationship between experience and image. What is lost when an installation is reduced to a photograph? Chapter 3 examines this question in the context of her 2001 installation *the picture is still*, which I was able to see in Japan. This chapter also looks at Hamilton's series of photographs called *face to face*, which I argue is a way of infusing bodily experience into the photographic image. These are pinhole photographic portraits that Hamilton made using her mouth as a kind of camera. Hamilton's work and others focused on perception seek to provide a way for viewers to engage in a reflection on experience and memory grounded in the body and senses.

The final chapter examines video and film installation and the use of sound in installation art at a moment when analog film and photography is becoming outmoded. Each of the artists addressed in this chapter made projected films or video installations that reflect on how the film projector and image preserved and shaped memory. The recent film installation by the British artist Tacita Dean titled *Kodak*, the video *Headphones* incorporating found footage by artist Tony Cokes, and the film installation *Situation Leading to a Story* by Matthew Buckingham raise different questions about the relationship between images and experience in the context of changing recording technologies. Chapter 4 will examine these artists' interest in how photography and film and sound recording have been incorporated as part of the practice of memory in the twentieth century.

Installation is not a medium but a multimedia practice. I argue that, from the late 1970s to the present, photography has come to pervade the practice of installation and become the unacknowledged foundation of this now ubiquitous métier. The installations in this book bear a relationship to the photographic archive. This book examines the different ways that photography and installation art reinforce, enrich, and contradict each other. Each chapter explores different ways that photography is involved in memory in the context of installation art, examining not only what is lost in the photographic documentation of installation art but also how, in the context of installation art, photography and memory produce new sorts of narratives and histories.

ONE

expanding the frame

INSTALLATION ART IN THE 1970S

Installation Art and Modernist Painting

> Most museums and galleries are designed to show masterpieces; objects made and planned elsewhere for exhibition in relatively neutral spaces. But many artists today do not make self-contained masterpieces; they do not want to and do not try to. Nor are they for the most part interested in neutral spaces. Rather, their work includes the space it's in; embraces it, uses it. Viewing space becomes not frame but material. And that makes it hard to exhibit.
>
> —Alanna Heiss on the exhibition *Rooms* at PS1 in 1976

In the late 1960s, major art institutions in the United States had only recently and with a great deal of trepidation brought the new practices of installation and site-specific art within their walls. Simultaneously, there was a glut of artists who wanted places to exhibit and who, as Alanna Heiss asserts, were making work that challenged the conventions of the traditional art gallery. With the support of government funds, new exhibition spaces run by artists began to sprout all over New York City and other cities across the United States. These new spaces exhibited time-based, ephemeral art practices such as video, performance, and installation art.[1] These new forms of art and types of exhibition practices led artists and critics to question the values of the traditional art gallery devoted to exhibitions of modernist painting and sculpture.

This chapter explores three examples of installation art in the 1970s in New York that challenged these traditional art gallery practices. These projects include the exhibition *Rooms* at PS1 in 1976, Gordon Matta-Clark's piece

Splitting from 1973 to 1974, and an exhibition at Artists Space in 1978 of the work of Adrian Piper, Christopher D'Arcangelo, Louise Lawler, and Cindy Sherman. Using the idea of the "frame" as a pivot point, this chapter examines the ways these projects broke the conventions of the modernist art gallery. Two different dimensions of framing are examined. Taking the now commonplace notion that the exhibition space is a kind of frame for artwork, the chapter asks how these examples of installation art "broke" the frame and challenged the strictures of modernist art exhibition conventions. Second, because for the most part only the photographs and the texts that describe them survive these pieces, these projects will be examined via exhibition catalogs in an effort to understand how this type of representation conditions the historical understanding of these exhibitions.

Because of its ephemeral and motley character, installation, in contrast to painting, has been marginalized in writing on the history of contemporary art. Its marginalization parallels that of the modernist movements of Surrealism and Dada in the history of 1960s Greenbergian modernism, which is based on abstract painting.[2] As artists and critics had come to realize by the end of the 1960s, modernist art, painting in particular, required a certain kind of setting in order to achieve the sense of its aesthetic autonomy and visual purity. "The outside world must not come in, so windows are usually sealed off. . . . Unshadowed, white, clean, artificial, the space is devoted to the technology of esthetics. Works of art are mounted, hung, scattered for study. Their ungrubby surfaces are untouched by time and its vicissitudes. . . . The space offers the thought that while eyes and minds are welcome, space-occupying bodies are not — or are tolerated only as kinesthetic mannequins for further study."[3]

This is an oft-quoted paragraph from the trio of articles that artist and critic Brian O'Doherty (aka Patrick Ireland) wrote in the mid-1970s about the conventional modernist art gallery. As an artist who was exhibiting in alternative art spaces in New York in the late 1960s and early 1970s and as the director of funding for the visual arts for the National Endowment of the Arts, O'Doherty had an interest in the way art was exhibited. O'Doherty argued that the modernist gallery continued to serve as a kind of frame for the work that contained it and, along with a certain decorum for the viewer, dictated how the art was to be seen. Modernist painting is made for the eyes alone. Installation breaks the traditional frame of art, as exemplified by painting, and often engages more than the visual sense. O'Doherty regarded installation-type practices, therefore, as a rupture within the historical category of modernist sculpture and painting.

It is useful to get a sense of how the modernist art gallery was viewed in the early 1970s by summarizing O'Doherty's arguments from "Inside the White Cube." O'Doherty began his examination of the conventions of framing in the modernist institution by describing how paintings have been displayed. The first article gave a brief history of the hanging of paintings since the eighteenth century, making clear how the white gallery wall became more and more important over the course of the twentieth century. These developments, he argued, had to do with the ways in which the painting frame and the space within the frame changed with the development of modernism.

He points to a painting from 1831–33 by Samuel F. B. Morse of the interior of the Louvre in which paintings are hung in the typical salon style, crowded on the wall from floor to ceiling. In this setup, the space of the gallery wall is divided hierarchically, but other than that it is irrelevant to the paintings that are placed on it. It is irrelevant because each painting is a self-contained universe. With an illusionistic sense of space created by whatever optical devices the painter might employ, such as single-point perspective or atmospheric perspective, these paintings become spaces that open up to the viewer and ask to be explored by the eyes.

In these images, the frame is nothing more than a boundary marker. But once the flat surface of an image becomes a factor, O'Doherty argues, the frame takes on greater weight and places "pressure" on the surrounding wall. The relationship between modernist aesthetics and the frame as a formal device is more complicated. In modernist painting, the edge of the painting and the frame that formalizes it become a kind of problem. If the edge of the painting is emphasized, then the wall of the gallery becomes a factor in the display of the work. It was photography, O'Doherty argues, that sensitized viewers to the edges of images. In the photograph, the frame is an integral part of the work.

Installation art has been associated with the dissolution of the frame of painting and, by extension, the expansion of art into nonaesthetic realms, as Alanna Heiss's statement above implies. In the late 1960s and 1970s, as O'Doherty's writing indicates, the conditions that were questioned were those that dictated the exhibition of modernist painting. The challenge took a variety of forms. If the "white cube" modernist art gallery, which displays painting, excludes the passage of time, then installation would bring time into the gallery space.[4] If the modernist gallery excludes the body and focuses on the eye, then installation is oriented to the body.[5] If the gallery alienates spectators or viewers from their experience, then installation needs to bring viewers and experience into the work of art.[6] By using modernism as a foil, O'Doherty is able to historicize the exhibition space and, in so doing, both define the practice of installation and derive its genealogy. In its liberation from the modernist painting ideology and aesthetics, the wall of the white cube is punctured and the outside world is allowed in. The frame of the work of art is provisional and shifting in the practices that challenged modernist painting.

Jacques Derrida asks continually in his discussion of the "parergon," What is inside and what is outside the frame? If the frame defines in some way the actual work, how does it do so? He concludes that not only is the parergon a supplement to the work but also "it is the internal structural link which rivets them to the lack in the interior of the *ergon*. And this lack would be constitutive of the very unity of the *ergon*."[7] It is the lack that defines the work (*ergon*) and that calls for the parergon as a supplement. I propose that, if the frame of installation art is in some way external and held by the institution that shelters and sponsors, it is also internal. Installation always points to the conditions that frame it, and because those conditions vary among the different kinds of sites and institutions, installation also points to its mercurial identity.

The examples chosen in this chapter reflect different ways of dealing with installation as a kind of frame. John C. Welchman argues that, in the 1970s, the period of each of the exhibitions discussed in this chapter, interest shifted from the frame as a literal object or limit to what Welchman calls the metaframe or second frame of the institutional context.[8] Robert Morris argues that the "newer work" of the 1970s expands the frame to include not only the work but also the space in which it is placed and the relationship of the viewer to the work and to the space.

Most often, in recent installation art, the art institution has served as a kind of de facto frame or limit. Even the art institution as a literal frame of four walls is not necessary. It is the sanction of the art institution, as Martha Buskirk has shown, that is required. The institution provides the ground against which the installation becomes a form: "There is always a form on a ground, but the *parergon* is a form which has as its traditional determination not that it stands out but that it disappears, buries itself, effaces itself, melts away at the moment it deploys its greatest energy."[9] And this parergon or institutional frame can take the form of a photograph in an exhibition catalog. Given this, another dimension of installation art can be gleaned from examining the role of photography in the work. Documentary photographs of the work are usually seen as supplementary to the actual work of installation art. Photographs of installations, especially those that have appeared in exhibition catalogs, are one of the things by which installation art is framed and given "symbolic status," as Amelia Jones says.

Artists have already been thinking about the relationship photography has to their installation pieces. Because installation artists are often interested in engaging the body and the senses, one common attitude to the photograph regards the image as insufficient in relation to the experience of the work. For these artists, the photograph is marked by loss — a loss that can be signified in a variety of ways: as a sense of the passage of time, in terms of the limitations of the visual sense, in terms of the flatness and discreteness of the image, or the silence of the image. Bodily experience, in this outlook, always exceeds the frame of the photograph. In addition, photography has been examined with skepticism in poststructuralist texts because it is a visual medium that is rooted in Western notions of rationality and objectivity. Installation, in this sense, can be seen as a critique of the primacy of vision in Western art. Artists who are interested in this dimension of installation art have, therefore, carefully considered how their works are documented.

Installation, even as it lacks an essence and demands a frame, also internalizes that frame, pointing to the conditions that frame it and questioning them. This book examines various aspects of this tension between photographic documentation and direct experience of installation art. We will also examine how artists have incorporated photography into the content and structure of their installations, taking advantage of the photograph's air of objectivity and rationality, and its ability to map and articulate spaces, to render the visual world meaningful, and to produce its own orders of rational organization, time, memory, history, and knowledge.

PS1 and *Rooms*

In 1976, the PS1 arts space opened its present location in Queens, New York, in a neighborhood that commentators described as full of active factories and warehouses.[10] The PS1 building was a disused nineteenth-century school with two wings and three floors plus an attic and accessible roof. When the Institute for Art and Urban Resources, run by Alanna Heiss, learned that the building was slated for demolition, they negotiated a lease with the city of Queens for one thousand dollars per year for twenty years. The Institute, founded in 1971 under Heiss's leadership, took a mission to find abandoned spaces that could be renovated and used for exhibition and studio space for artists.[11] The Institute intended the old building to house artists' studios that could be rented cheaply, project spaces where artists could develop and exhibit long-term projects, exhibition spaces, and a performance space. PS1 was to be an arts center that could accommodate the new art of the 1970s, which its supporters argued required exhibition spaces that could be altered and "messed up" by the art that was often produced in and displayed in them. Martin Beck notes that such broken-down spaces were accepted as part of the aesthetic of post-Minimalist art in the mid- to late 1970s.

The inaugural exhibition *Rooms* at PS1 in Queens was intended to showcase the way such a new space could function. According to *Artforum* reviewer Nancy Foote, the exhibition was thrown together in a matter of months but managed to include the work of new and well-known artists from the East Coast and West Coast of the United States, as well as Europe. There were seventy-eight participating artists who chose among different spaces in the old school building, including classrooms, corridors, attic, roof, basement, coal bin, and playground. Because the building was only modestly refurbished to house the new arts center, it was the raw, crumbling walls and warped and debris-strewn floors that inspired the exhibition. Artists were asked to use the building for work that was built in place and responded to the material qualities of the structure.

Nancy Foote in *Artforum* and Rosalind Krauss in *October* were two reviewers of the exhibition in major publications at the time. Foote used the terms "project" and "gesture" to describe the work in the *Rooms* exhibition, which suggests the influence of Brian O'Doherty who had published two of his three articles on the "white cube" the previous spring in the same magazine. The final one would appear in the next issue of *Artforum*. Foote tends to focus on the best-known artists in the show, such as Joseph Kosuth, Gordon Matta-Clark, Richard Serra, Suzanne Harris, Carl Andre, and others. However, Foote discusses more artists than Krauss and emphasizes that the ways in which the seventy-eight artists used the building differed.[12]

Foote discerned a category including artists who focused on the surfaces of the old school building and made them part of the content of the art; she included Lucio Pozzi's panel paintings, Michelle Stuart's wall-rubbings, and Frank Gillette's photographs of various walls, corners, and other surfaces of the school. In another category of artists who used windows, Foote mentions Daniel Buren, who covered windows in the auditorium with stripes, and Doug Wheeler, who altered windows with coverings of darkened plastic that transformed day into night. In another category of artists who used the structure and materials of the building itself for their work, she included Matta-Clark, David Rabinowitch, and Jene Highstene. Rabinowitch's piece in the second-floor corridors cleared paint off large areas of the wall and then made circles in the plaster.[13] Highstene's sculpture used the floorboards from the classroom where he chose to exhibit the work. In this piece, he used the boards as part of a chicken-wire structure for a large mound covered in black concrete.

Although Foote included a greater variety of artists than Krauss, she ignored those who used the rooms in the building as empty spaces for sculptural scenes, as in Ned Smyth's re-creation of the *Last Supper* in the attic, or those who used the space to hang pictures, photographs, and drawings, such as Howardena Pindell's set of framed video stills titled *Video Drawings*. These don't seem to fit into the themes of site-specific abstract art that the review promotes. However, it is fair to say that these are different ways of dealing with the space of PS1. So, Foote's categories are useful in that they provide a sense of the variety of work in the exhibition, but they are also rather narrow in that they describe actions taken in relation to the physical structure of the building. Another set of categories could be created based on how artists considered issues of framing and emphasis.

Framing the Interactions between Artwork, Exhibition Space, and Viewer

It is helpful to develop a new set of categories in the *Rooms* exhibition based on a field of relationships between viewer, artwork, and space.[14] These relationships delineate situations produced in momentary interactions between the work, exhibition/cultural context, and viewer.

BETWEEN VIEWER AND ARTWORK: DENNIS OPPENHEIM AND COLETTE

These categories spring from the variations among the mutual relationships between artwork, viewer, and space. One category would include those installations in which the space acts as a frame for the relationship between the work and the viewer. These include installations that used the rooms at PS1 as empty spaces to fill with objects. In these works, the exhibition space (the walls, ceiling, and floor) becomes a kind of frame that must disappear in favor of what it frames.

For instance, Dennis Oppenheim's piece is a type of theatrical tableau in a room on the second floor of the building. Called *Broken Record Blues*, it is a scene of two dolls, one of which faces the corner of the room in a chair — like a child sent to the corner — while the other lies facedown on the floor. A mark on the floor connects the two. In Colette's *David's Wraith*, located in the attic, viewers pass through a corridor to find themselves in a room hung with silk and satin where in one corner a performer is tucked in an alcove of the room. The performer reclines dramatically like the French historical figure Marat in Jacques-Louis David's 1789 painting *Death of Marat*. In these installations, the walls and floor of the space, generalized and subordinated to the theatrical scene, serve as a setting. And while these works invite the viewer to complete the narrative of which the scene is a part, they do not point to the specific qualities of the building in any direct way.

BETWEEN ARTWORK AND EXHIBITION SPACE: SERRA AND RYMAN

Part of the *Rooms* exhibition were installations in which the relationship between the work and the space becomes the focus and in which the difference between the work and the space is so fine as to be indistinguishable. In these, the relationship of the work to the viewer is deemphasized. Artists such as Richard Serra used the surfaces of the space as a type of ground for a physical action. Richard Serra's untitled piece was located in an attic space with a steep, pitched roof. In this work, Serra cut a trench through a concrete floor and then sunk two steel beams in it, creating a dark diagonal line as it moved across the floor. One beam faced hollow side up and formed a trough, while the other had a solid side up and was positioned flush with the floor. As Richard Tuttle remarked, it was difficult to tell whether Serra was taking advantage of an existing structure in the space or if he cut a new channel, as the line

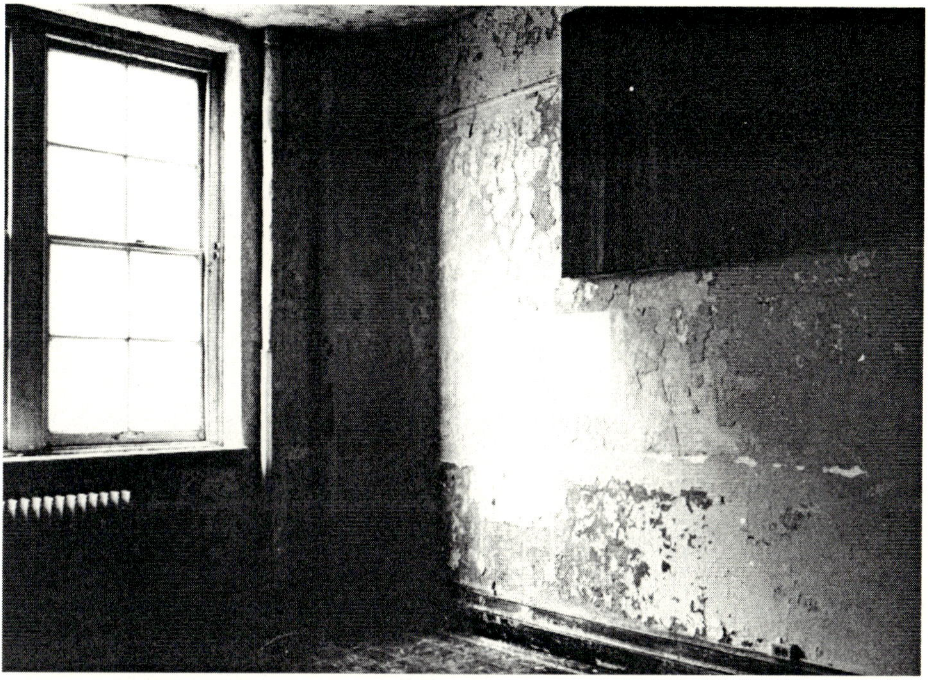

FIGURE 1.1 Robert Ryman, untitled from *Rooms* exhibition, PS1, 1976. *© 2011 Artists Rights Society (ARS), New York.*

of the trough extended from a channel in the wall to the spot where the roof beam met the floor.[15] Serra blurred the distinction between the work and its physical context.

Another piece similar to Serra's in its subtlety was Robert Ryman's untitled work located in a small, dark room on the first floor of the new wing that looked out on the inner courtyard. Ryman used its windows to illuminate two small, pale squares on the wall. In the photograph reproduced in the catalog, the two squares, out of line with each other, glow in the light of the windows. The artist removed any extraneous paint from the wall and adhered two pieces of paper covered with white watercolor to the wall's surface.

Serra's and Ryman's work frames the relationship between the work and the space. As site-specific postminimal work, it is far more difficult to articulate the limit of each of the elements (work and exhibition space) in that relationship, and both would have been destroyed at the end of the exhibition.

ARTWORK AS DOUBLE OF EXHIBITION SPACE: LUCIO POZZI AND MICHELLE STUART

There were installations in which the relationship between work and space was so tenuous that the work doubled some aspect of the space. This category of work is described by Krauss in "Notes on the Index." In part 2, she focuses on two of the seventy-eight artists in *Rooms* whose work exemplifies the notion of indexicality that she puts forth: Lucio Pozzi and Michelle Stuart. Pozzi placed paintings of various sizes in different areas along the corridors of the first floor. Depending on the direction that a visitor turned, the paintings could have been some of the first things that one saw when entering the exhibition. Pozzi's paintings, as Krauss discusses at length, were two-toned abstractions whose dividing lines and colors matched those of the old, peeling paint in the corridor. Michelle Stuart's drawings, which were rubbings of the wall and wainscoting hung on the wall opposite the site from which they were taken, were located in a corridor on the second floor.

BETWEEN VIEWER AND ARTWORK/EXHIBITION SPACE: PATRICK IRELAND AND GORDON MATTA-CLARK

Another category includes installations that engage the viewer's changing experiences of space as they walk around a room. Patrick Ireland (aka Brian O'Doherty) and Gordon Matta-Clark explored the way space can be experienced as either two or three dimensional. Ireland participated in the exhibition with an installation/drawing that dealt with embodied seeing and perspective. Ireland's *Rope Drawing No. 19* was located in room 201 in the old wing of PS1 down the hall from Matta-Clark's work. In an emptied classroom with its chalkboards intact, Ireland hung a series of ropes from the ceiling by threads and attached them to the floor. From a distance, they would appear as white lines drawn from the floor toward the ceiling, standing out as figures against the ground of peeling walls and dusty chalkboards. In her review, Foote describes moving through the space and watching the lines coalesce and scatter as she took different positions. Ireland used the format of the magic square, arranging the ropes in a 25 by 25 square on the floor, cutting

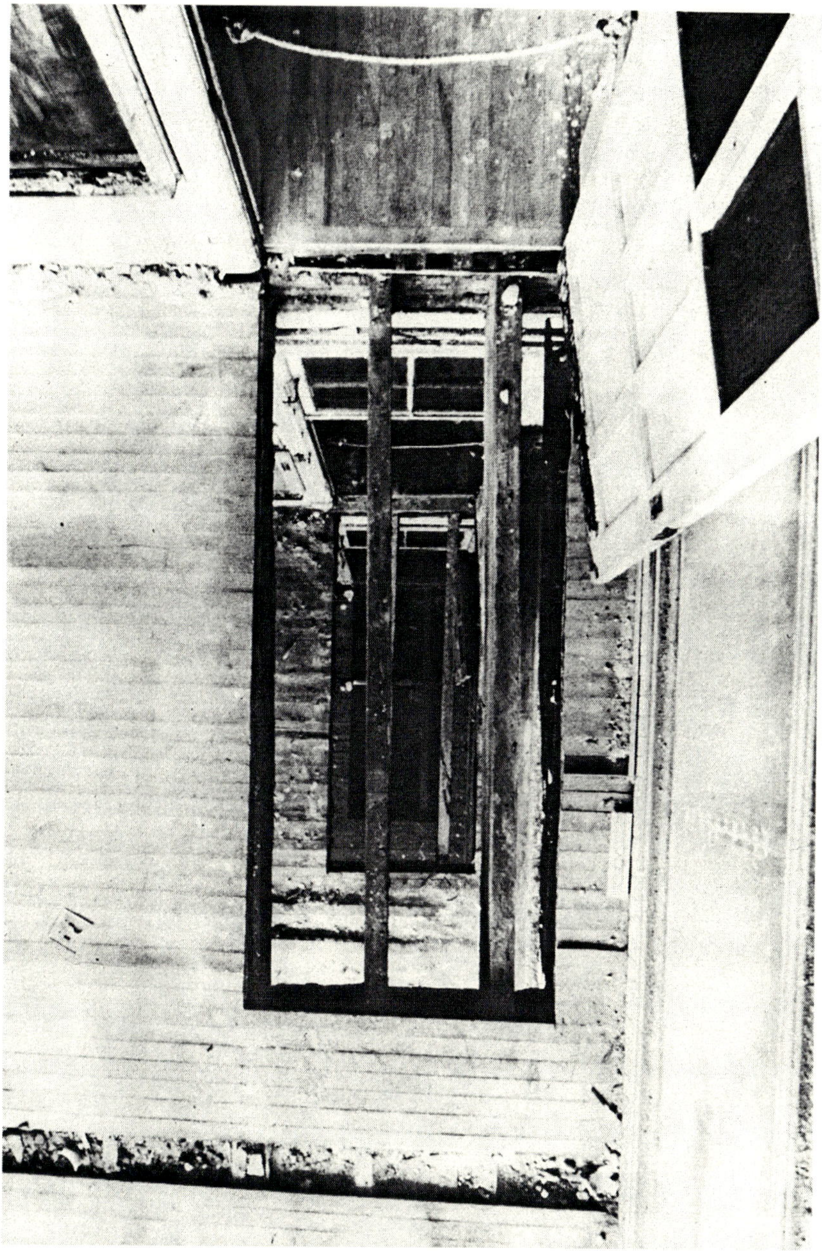

FIGURE 1.2 Gordon Matta-Clark, *Doors, Floors, Doors* from *Rooms* exhibition, PS1, 1976.

the ropes into various lengths and placing them in rows that in any direction also added up to 25 feet. It is interesting to think how this work responds to the artist's writing on the frame and the exhibition space in his trio of articles on the "white cube," as he makes a piece that in effect has no frame but maintains the important visual distinction of figure and ground and single-point perspective dependent upon the viewer's moving body.

Gordon Matta-Clark's work also changes in terms of the viewer's perspective and gains significance as an image. He took rooms 109, 209, and 309, which were located in a corner of the old wing of the school, facing the inner courtyard. He cut a piece that echoes the size and shape of the doors of each classroom out of the floors in front of the doorways of each classroom. And in each cut, the artist preserved the floor joists. The photograph published in the subsequent catalog suggests that the piece was playing with the notion of mirror reflections, as the shape of the cuts rhymes the doors. The photograph is taken from close to the ceiling and looking straight down into the cuts. It is hard to discern the separate cuts as they recede from the camera. And in this way, they resemble the reflections in facing mirrors, which become difficult to distinguish as they recede in the mirror.

Both Ireland's and Matta-Clark's work focuses on the visual interplay of three- and two-dimensional space. Their pieces changed as the perspective the viewer took of them changed. They made the building a presence by framing it but also focused on the viewer's body in the space. And the photographs of the work further elaborate these issues.

BETWEEN VIEWER AND ARTWORK/EXHIBITION SPACE: MARY MISS AND SUZANNE HARRIS

Another category of framing would include those installations in which the work and the space involve the viewer's bodily experience of the space. These installations use structural features of the building to guide viewers' awareness of their body and perceptions within the space. Suzanne Harris and Mary Miss made works of this sort. Harris's *Peace for the Temporal Highway*, a room-sized piece that functions as a framing and scale device, was built as a tunnel-like structure of cardboard whose roof descended from the room's ceiling at a sharp angle and whose walls also narrowed as they approached the windows of the room. Viewers entered the room and found themselves in the dark space of the structure whose opening framed the radiator underneath the windows. Ira Joel Haber and Sue Weil described being in and around the structure in terms of being large inside the structure and small outside it.[16]

In a large room overlooking the inner courtyard on the third floor, Mary Miss installed a simple wooden corridor that drew on the viewer's sense of perspective and her own body's scale in relation to the work. *Sapping* positioned the viewer to look from its entrance down its length. Judging from the photograph reproduced in the catalog, the viewer entered the classroom and had to walk around the structure in order to enter or see into the corridor. In this way, the work positioned the viewer and created a point of view. Artist Howardena Pindell describes it this way: "One feels, walking around and into *Sapping*, as if one has been edged into a symbolic dimension as Gulliver or a Lilliputian."[17] In each of these pieces, rather than being generalized, as in the theatrical works described above, the relationship between the viewers' bodies and the peculiar features of the room were called into play. In this sense, the installation framed that dynamic, momentary encounter.

The *Rooms* Exhibition and Photography

Although this set of categories does not exhaust the works that were presented in the show, it does give a sense of the variety of works included in the exhibition and that were overlooked in the contemporary reviews. In this brief survey of *Rooms*, there is a dichotomy between site-specific and sited installations that lend themselves to photographic documentation and those that elude photography. Some of these works, such as Oppenheim's, can be photographed without compromising the work, while in Harris's and Miss's works, something is lost in the photograph that must be made up with firsthand descriptions. Like the minimal object, these pieces depend on the more unpredictable element of the viewer's body and perception. Matta-Clark and Patrick Ireland's too depend on the viewer's body, but the works reference pictorial formats. These are "present-tense" works of art.

Mary Ann Doane, in analyzing the work of photographers, philosophers, and psychoanalysts in the beginning of the twentieth century argues that there was a sense in the twentieth century that it was impossible to grasp the present moment as it happened because of the limitations of the body.[18] There is a lag between physical stimulus and the brain's perception of the stimulus. Photography and film attempt to capture the present moment, which eludes human perception. She writes,

> But it is finally in the new representational technologies of vision — photography, the cinema — that one witnesses the insistency of the impossible desire to represent — to archive — the present.[19]

The longing to grasp the present is only partially solved by the photograph. It is photography's indexicality that makes it seem to offer "presentness." But even the photograph, which fixed a moment of time, always represents the past. In the photographs of the experiential installations of Mary Miss and Suzanne Harris, the "impossible desire to represent the present" is clearest. The photographs do not capture what the work is about.

Doane argues that modernity is characterized by the ephemeral, the chance moment. She describes this as "the contingent" and notes that it is a form of resistance to the rationalizing systems of time that developed in the last centuries. Chance represents a rupture with the rational organization of time in industrialized modernity. "Its lure is that of resistance itself — resistance to system, to structure, to meaning. Contingency proffers to the subject the appearance of absolute freedom, immediacy, directness."[20] Something similar seems to take place with installations that focus on experience and perception. They offer the possibility of chance encounters in the bodily experience of the space. It is in the failure to fulfill this desire to hold on to the contingent, to the present moment in its fullness, that the archival impulse emerges.

Rosalind Krauss's two articles published in *October* in 1977 are canonical essays in the literature of postmodernism. Her agenda in these articles was first to establish a connection to Marcel Duchamp in art practices after modernist painting and, second, to undercut the critical assertion by modernist critics that modernist abstract painting was a straightforward presentation of painting materials rather than a type of representation. She is only tangentially or perhaps not at all interested in "installation art" as such; it is a pretext for her argument. However, the argument Krauss makes about the work in *Rooms* illuminates some of the connections between installation and photography that this book seeks to describe. Krauss describes the relationship between site-specific art and photography in terms of the index. She begins her discussion with the linguistic term "the shifter," which indicates a word that gains its particular meaning by its circumstances.[21] She goes on to connect the shifter to the notion of an index: "In so far as their meaning depends on the existential presence of a given speaker . . . the pronouns announce themselves as belonging to . . . the index."[22] An index is the physical trace of something having been present, such as a footprint or a photograph that points at something no longer present.

However, photographs also seem to bring absent referents a kind of presence because of their nature as indexes. The light recorded in the photograph is reflected from the object that is photographed, creating a direct, physical connection. The photograph as index represents a limit — the closest that one can get to a moment as it happens. "In photography for the first time, an aesthetic or spatial representation could be made by chance, by accident, without human control. And it would still be a sign of something, perched precariously on the threshold of semiosis. As the sign most clearly connected to the present and presence, perhaps it is the ideal limit of the instant that is approached by the index."[23]

Doane distinguishes between two kinds of indices. One is the indexical trace — the fingerprint, the photograph, which always indicates a pastness — and the other is the deictic index: "the signifiers 'here,' 'now,' 'this,' 'that' — are inextricable from the idea of presence."[24] The index hovers between presentness and pastness. The frame and the photograph have similar positions. They point to something in the here and now but, in doing so, make it past, absent, or elsewhere. At this point in the argument, it is possible to pull in the thread of Derrida's discussion of the parergon and to connect it to the photograph's relationship to installation. "*One* wishes to go back *from the supplement to the source*: one must recognize that there is *a supplement at the source*."[25] The instantaneous photograph approaches presence, the fullness of a lived moment, but never quite achieves it and therefore points to a lack or absence at the heart of what it frames.

Krauss argues that, in the *Rooms* exhibition, "the ambition of the works is to capture the presence of the building to find strategies to force it to surface in the field of the work."[26] Krauss suggests as well that it is impossible to experience the fullness of presence in these works. She argues that, even as the presence of the building surfaces within the frames made by artists such as Matta-Clark, the framed material is filled with an incredible sense of time past: "the paradox of being physically present but temporally remote."[27] The representation, even as it resembles the original, points (as an index) always to the action of something in the past. The framing that takes place in these works, whether painting, drawing, or photograph, that bring the materiality of the building to the viewer's attention also suggests absence because they point to an action that took place in the past. The photographic archive emerges as a solution to the impossibility of grasping presence in site-specific installation art.

Photographs are at the same time contingent. A camera can be pointed in any direction; anything can fill the photographic frame. The photograph is replete with detail, which makes it difficult to develop a specific meaning from a photograph.[28] Mary Ann Doane describes this as "giving the spectator nothing to read."[29] Photographs therefore demand a caption, as Walter Benjamin noted, or an order that produces meaning. The silence of the solitary image leads to a desire to see the photograph of the moment before and the moment after in order to discover a meaning. A single photograph naturally leads to a series, which demands an order.

John Baldessari's *Alignment Series: Disaster Story Line (Getting It Straight)*, which appeared in the *Rooms* exhibition, is a wonderful example of this desire to produce order and meaning from contingency. It is a series put together by choosing a linear element in photographs of various disastrous situations: "(hurricanes, floods, explosions, landslides, drought, etc.)." These lines are then drawn on the photograph and aligned with a line produced by the wainscoting or dado of the wall. "Basically, an attempt to find a steady, straight, continuous line in a sea of muddledness," writes Baldessari.[30] The line is a way of producing order and meaning from contingency. Photographic series, sequences, narratives, and archival orders result from this desire to fill in absence, to make something meaningful from photographs.

Catalog as Narrative and Archive

We can turn now to one narrative, one photographic archive gathered for the *Rooms* exhibition: the catalog. The designers of the exhibition catalog for *Rooms* conceived of it as a kind of walk through the exhibition space with each page representing a different room. In this way, the exhibition catalog mirrors the exhibition space. The catalog and exhibition begin with a group photograph of all the participants and organizers of the exhibition and a shot of the exterior of the Romanesque Revival building's façade rising above the streetlights and a nearby Amoco gas station. Photographs of the entrances to the old school building, the more modest of which is labeled "Girls," follow these. The doors are an invitation to turn the page and visually enter the building. Waiting on the other side are not clean and renovated spaces but images of the classrooms before they had been cleaned up for the show. Floorboards are torn up and resting in corners. Paint peels from the wall, and old desks and chalkboards await removal. These pages represent what greeted the artists as they began to make their work.

The next few pages show artists working in each of their spaces. In one, John Baldessari leans against the wall of a corridor, bearded chin in hand, as he contemplates a series of photographs on the wall. In the next pages, we see people working on Jennifer Bartlett's piece, hanging up her enamel plates; Matta-Clark tearing up floorboards; and Jene Highstene regarding a chicken-wire and board structure covered with black concrete. These action shots are intended to demonstrate how PS1 differs from the traditional art gallery and museum space, which artists are not permitted to "mess up," by giving us a sense of how an artist goes through the process of making a work. They also suggest that the process of production and the site were to the work in *Rooms* as important as the final work itself.

The layout of the catalog is an attempt to solve the problem of representing the experience of a body moving through the space of the exhibition. The catalog uses the turning of pages to suggest movement from one room to the next. But the designers chose to give not just a diachronic sense of the layout but also a synchronic one with a nod to later art historians who would be interested in understanding the arrangement of the show. For each floor there is a list of participating artists along with the number of the room in which their work was exhibited and a ground plan showing the relative size of each space and its location in the building. In this way, the reader gets a sense of how the show was divided up and arranged.

It is the exhibition space that provides the ground for the narrative to unfold, while the photographs map that unfolding, and in this process, the space of installation becomes an articulated space that must be read. Nancy Foote speaks to this in her review as well. She argues that the arrangement of the show contributed to the content of the theme in which context becomes a kind of content. In the catalog and photographic documentation of the work, the space is laid out for the viewer, but there is also movement through time at different scales. In the individual photograph we have a sense of the temporal and temporary quality of the work due to the nature of the photograph, which records a moment in time, but also a sense of movement through the space of the exhibition as one turns the pages.

Foote makes the claim that each installation in the exhibition influenced the view of the next installation and that, because of this, an overall aesthetic issue became clearer: "Installations and projects are rarely called upon to socialize, since they usually have the place to themselves. . . . But as one picked one's way through the rubble from piece to piece, something of the same phenomenon began to occur. Installation itself, not individual projects, became the esthetic issue."[31] The issue that Foote describes can be stated as "How does one make an installation?" and when one considers this question, installation becomes a defined art form, such as sculpture and painting, rather than one that responds to its site. In focusing on this dimension of the show, the building recedes from our consideration of the work. Despite the emphasis on the old building and its qualities as a space for showing art, it remained relatively neutral as a frame for the art.

The photographs of these pieces and the catalog do two things in relation to the work in the exhibition. First, they map the space of the exhibition. This mapping made it possible for me to develop the categories of work that are outlined in the preceding paragraphs. Second, the sequence of photographs on separate pages provides a narrative thread through the show, which mimics a visitor's walk through the space of the PS1 building. The catalog acknowledges time as part of the works in the show, as an element of the work or in the ephemeral nature of many of the pieces, which in turn situates the exhibition as part of the genre of process art and site-specific art. The catalog demonstrates to the potential audiences at PS1 not only the quality and expanse of the exhibition space but also its curatorial mission. As Alanna Heiss noted, PS1 was started to nurture the new art practices that did not fit comfortably in the more established museums in the New York area. The exhibition and the production of the catalog have secured *Rooms'* place in the art institution and in art history. The photographs and the catalog itself serve as an archive for the show, giving it symbolic value, and rendering it an object of art historical classification and study.

Breaking the Frame: Gordon Matta-Clark's *Splitting*

> I like very much the idea of breaking frames — the same way I cut up buildings. I like the idea that the sacred photo framing process is equally "violatable." And I think that's partly a carry over from the way I deal with structures to the way that I deal with photography. That kind of rigid, very academic, literary convention about photography, which doesn't interest me. Oh, it's not that it really doesn't interest me. It's that I find that for what I do, it's necessary to break away from it.
>
> — Gordon Matta-Clark, *Gordon Matta-Clark: Works and Collected Writings*

Gordon Matta-Clark's work bridges the division between installations or sited works preoccupied with the viewer's bodily experience and installations that can be photographed. Matta-Clark's work can be considered a study of frames in installation art and in photography. Commentators, such as artist Joseph Kosuth, regarded Matta-Clark's photographs as extraneous to his larger body of work, but Matta-Clark himself was aware that site-specific installation is bound to the photographic medium. Photographs, like Matta-Clark's building cuts, engage the issues of the representation of space, the passage of time, and the production of history. This was an important aspect of Matta-Clark's work, and he seemed fascinated by different ways one can explore a space: by a moving perceiving body and with the eyes alone in photographs. The photo collages that he published in his artist's book *Splitting* go beyond the *Rooms* catalog in exploring the differences between space explored by the embodied eye and space explored by the camera. Matta-Clark's photographs also reflect an interest in time and rates of transformation, experienced by the body and the environment.

In a general sense, Matta-Clark's work outlines some of the primary concerns of site-specific installation art. Not only do his building cuts seek to grasp the exhibition space as a comprehensive object or situation, but they also make the viewer sensitive to the alterations in that space. Installation brings the structure of the exhibition space in as one of the elements in the work, but even more, it positions the viewer as an active perceiving agent.

Recognizing the importance of documentation in his work, he tried various photographic solutions to the problem — from deadpan black-and-white snapshot documentation to large-scale Cibachromes that served as visual interpretations of the bodily experience of his spaces.[32] He was interested in photography both as a self-sustaining process generated by a reaction to light and as something that recorded his ephemeral site-specific work. These interests are present in his work from its beginning.

Matta-Clark graduated from Cornell University with a degree in architecture in 1968 but stayed on in Ithaca, New York, before moving back to New York City. His first photo-documented site-specific piece was *Rope Bridge* of 1968, where he strung ropes woven like a cat's cradle over a dramatically deep gorge in Ithaca. In the photograph, the thin tracery of rope is drawn like a delicate line across the surface of the image as a snowbound and icy waterfall cascades in the background. Shortly after he made this piece, he helped with the *Earth Art* exhibition organized by Willoughby Sharp that included the work of artists such as Dennis Oppenheim and Robert Smithson. As has been remarked by Pamela Lee and others, Robert Smithson's work was an important influence on Matta-Clark's work. For the exhibition, Smithson made works that compared mirrors to photographs, by placing large, square mirrors and photos in the landscape around Ithaca and then re-photographing them. These pieces, related to Smithson's mirror displacements, connected photography directly to sited works. As Matta-Clark was embarking on his career as an artist, the question of the status of representations and documentation of site-specific work was very much in the air. Smithson's work, as Craig Owens would later write, broke with the conventions of modernist "presentness" by insisting that representation in the form of photographs and language be at the heart of his piece.

Matta-Clark, too, was interested in establishing a break with modernism in his own work. There is in Matta-Clark's opinions and work already a critique of the scientific and rational aspects of modernity as represented by his rejection of the modernist ideology and principles being taught by his professors at the School of Architecture at Cornell University. As the art historian Lee has demonstrated, his work was in dialog with but also rejected many conventions and values of modernist architecture, including its faith in modernist utopian ideas of progress. He was skeptical of the notion that life can be improved by following principles of rational design.[33] In reaction against these ideas, Matta-Clark was fascinated with natural and organic processes of growth and decay, and the possibility of an architecture based on reuse rather than the new.

Part of Matta-Clark's response to modernism was a critical examination of the function of frames: from the frame of the cultural institution to the frame of the image. O'Doherty and Matta-Clark share the opinion that the frame of the work of art is something that not only confines but also defines and reveals new information to the viewer. Matta-Clark's photographs explore the formal and conceptual complexity of framing. And his work bridges the literalness of the frame in modernism and the ideological dimensions of framing that would come to preoccupy postmodernist critique.

O'Doherty argues that the frame is more than a formal device and regards it as a metaphor for the confining formalism of 1960s modernism, which he connects to an almost puritanical denial of the viewer's body. In this disavowal of the body, a disembodied "eye" is elevated. O'Doherty argues against the hygienic cleanliness of the "white cube" in favor of something where time, dirt, and, most of all, the viewer's body as a body is allowed access. O'Doherty associates the sullying of the modernist art gallery with a collage aesthetic that can be traced to Surrealism and Kurt Schwitters's *Merzbau*. By inviting in processes of time, dirtying, and decay as part of his work, Matta-Clark's site-specific installation art broke with the conventions of modernism as well. The fascination with organic processes and decay was a break with modernist notions of simplicity, clarity, and visuality in architecture and painting. He objected to modernist architecture's emphasis on innovation by describing it as hygienic and antihistorical.

> I am experimenting with alternative uses of space that are most familiar. I like to think of these works as by-passing questions of imaginative design by suggesting ways of rethinking what is already there. I do not want to create a totally new supportive field of vision, of cognition. I want to reuse the old one, the existing framework of thought and sight. I am altering the existing units of perception normally employed to discern the wholeness of a thing. It is an organic response to what already has been well done. More than a call for preservation, this work reacts against a hygienic obsession in the name of redevelopment which sweeps away what little there is of an American past, to be cleansed by pavement and parking. What might have been a richly layered underground is being excavated for deeper new building foundations.[34]

Greenbergian modernism's elevation of vision as the supreme aesthetic sense has its roots in Western traditions in which vision is connected to reason and knowledge.[35] Single-point perspective assumes that light travels in straight lines and that vision is determined by specific geometric principles, namely, the visual pyramid or angle whose apex ends at the viewer's eye but that also sweeps out a view of a space that seems consistent and measurable. The image that renders an illusionistic three-dimensional space and can be mapped out appears to be a visual analog to the space in which the viewer stands.[36] In this type of visual space, the image directs where a viewer should stand in order to see it correctly. In such a space, too, the viewer can ignore the frame that encloses it, even as the frame is part of the geometric space that renders the image comprehensible and measurable. Many theorists have connected single-point perspective and the space it renders with certain kinds of Western ideologies, such as the notion of a centered, rational subject for whom the visual space is rendered an object of study and knowledge.[37] The space of vision rendered by the photograph is connected to this one-point perspective developed in painting space in early modern Europe but also differs from it as well. The photographic process is charged with authority because it imitates the way that vision works, where light traveling in straight lines falls on a photosensitive surface. And photographic images, like the process of vision, are produced in whole at once without the need for human intervention. According to the art historian David Summers, "Photography imitates vision as a physical process, on the assumption that it is a physical process, and the analogy inherent in this imitation implies that vision and photography are events of the same kind."[38] Photography is then connected to the discourses of knowledge based on vision and rationality in Western traditions.

Furthermore, the photograph suggests that any event can be framed, captured, and rendered part of a discourse of knowledge. When a frame encloses an image space that is organized according to single-point perspective, it produces a "viewer space" where the image is made in such a way that it acknowledges the viewer that looks at it.[39] The space shown within the frame continues beyond the frame, as in a landscape, but cannot be seen by the viewer because the frame provides a limit. What is enclosed by this space is arbitrary and is not dependent on architecture within the image. It is as if what is enclosed in this space is "cut from" a larger view.[40] The camera can be pointed in any direction to frame an arbitrary portion of the field of vision. Photography acknowledges contingency. What is taken is a fragment of the visual field that nevertheless always has a certain relationship to the viewer who is positioned upright and facing the image. Cameras are able to provide images of spaces that appear to be the type of space that the viewer can enter, a consistent three-dimensional space subject to the same forces as the viewer's space but that are in fact spaces the viewer can enter only with the eyes.

The camera and photographic image seem to render the world open and available, if not to the human body then at least to the eye of a body standing still, upright, and facing forward. However, it always falls short, as Amelia Jones notes. Matta-Clark acknowledged that a viewer's perception always exceeds that of a camera, and hence, the photograph was inadequate to record the experience of a body moving through a space.

> I started out with an attempt to use multiple images to try and capture the all-around experience of the piece. It is an approximation of this kind of ambulatory "getting to know" what the space is about. Basically it is a way of passing through the space. One passes through in a number of ways; one can pass through by just moving your head; or [by] simple eye movements which defy the camera. You know it's very easy to trick a camera, to outdo a camera. With the eye's peripheral field of vision, any slight movement of the head would give us more information than the camera ever had.[41]

To understand the dilemma that Matta-Clark faced in documenting his site-specific pieces and exhibiting the photographs in a gallery, it may be useful to consider Henri Bergson's ideas about the "vitality" of bodily perception and experience. In Bergson's epistemology described in his 1911 book *Creative Evolution*, a division occurs between the continuous and vital experience, and the fragmentary and dispersed images produced by modern science and technology. Bergson argues that continuity and flux characterize the natural world and our experience of it. Modern science, however, has difficulty grasping the complexity of the perpetual differentiation and vitality of "life" and tries to break it down into units. In Bergson's characterization, the scientific approach to perception is modeled on photography and film. Consciousness takes *snapshots* of the perpetual movement and, based on these frozen instants, establishes ideas about form, essence, and laws of change. A visual analogy for Bergson's description is Eadweard Muybridge's motion studies of the 1880s. These images of men, women, and animals moving through spaces or performing athletic maneuvers provide the scientist or artist with not only the opportunity to study the position and gestures of a body as it occupies space at any instant in time but also, with each successive image, a sense of that body as it moves in time.

These images of the natural world obtain the illusion of continuity by being linked, either placed side by side or, in film, run through a projector that gives the illusion of continuous movement. In Bergson's description of perception as described by science of the early twentieth century, one moment follows another, like the frames of a film.[42] Bergson writes, "We may therefore sum up what we have been saying . . . that the *mechanism of our ordinary knowledge is of a cinematographical kind*."[43] In Bergson's analogy, time and experience, vital and fluid, decay into spatialized units in scientific perception — something material, dispersed, and rationalized. Experience as captured by scientific, modern technology for Bergson is drained and empty. Photography and film provided him with the figures necessary to articulate the characteristics of the natural world as captured and measured by science. In this analogy, we already see photography being cast as a negation or a reduction of "vitality" or "life."

If the photograph can be considered an instrument of modernist discourses of knowledge, science, and rationalism, as Bergson suggests, it can also historically be considered part of the discourse of natural philosophy and alchemy. Matta-Clark was also interested in these ideas; he thought of photography in terms of growth, development, and decay. In 1969, he had moved to New York and began combining the chemical processes of cooking and photography when he made a series of pieces for an exhibition titled *Documentations* at the John Gibson Gallery in which he fried photographs in the gallery. At the end of the year, he sent out boxes with small, fried Polaroid snapshots coated in gold leaf that depicted a Christmas tree.[44] In drawing the Polaroid photograph into the realm of stovetop cooking, Matta-Clark's work recalls that photography began as amateur experiments that considered the process of capturing one of many natural processes that were being discovered and exploited in the nineteenth century. The result of the photographic experiment was an object that combined science and nature. Mary Warner Marien in her cultural history of photography notes two perceptions of photography in its early days that support or reinforce the notion of the photograph as a "fragment of nature."[45] The first is the nineteenth-century perception of the photograph as not the result of a mechanical technique but rather a natural process that has been captured by the apparatus of photography. She quotes Louis-Jacques Mandé Daguerre who asserted, "The Daguerreotype is not an instrument which serves to draw nature; but a chemical and physical process which gives her the power to reproduce herself."[46]

Marien notes that this perception of the photograph emphasized its spontaneity — the magical appearance of the image on the negative — and its accuracy. These traits gave the photograph the merit of natural genius, Marien argues. In other words, it is something that is not achieved through painstaking craft or an artifice but rather wells up out of the natural world itself. The photograph obtained its connotations of innocence, objectivity, and universality from these perceptions. At the same time, because it is produced by a sophisticated mechanical technique, the photograph was also perceived to be a scientific object. Matta-Clark's cooked Polaroids recall the earliest experiments in photography, which were as much a cooking experiment with exotic chemicals and natural processes as anything else. Nicéphore Niépce, who produced the first successful permanent photograph, experimented with bitumen of Judea, derived from oil, oil of lavender, silver chloride, and iodine. Daguerre developed and perfected the process that ended by developing the image with mercury fumes.

Matta-Clark's experiments with agar, a gelatinous, nutritious environment for laboratory bacteria, also suggest a fascination with substances that develop and decay when placed in the light. In 1969, Matta-Clark began a series of pieces made from agar, sperm oil, vegetable and animal substances, and other materials that were mixed up into metal pans and placed in the air to become cultures for bacteria and mold. The interaction of the microscopic organisms and natural substances soon produced exotic colors and shapes.[47] In some of these, he placed a drop of mercury, perhaps as a reference to those earlier photographic experiments. Matta-Clark included these pieces in a work titled *Museum* at the Bykert Gallery in New York in 1970. These unusual works of art and chemistry caught the attention of the gallerist Holly Solomon who bought some of the pieces and hung them up in her home where they continued to change. After a while they became fragile and began to deteriorate.[48]

Matta-Clark soon made another flammable version of the agar pieces in which he dried and then burned the substance. He called these pieces *Incendiary Wafers*, and they were dangerous objects to exhibit or even have around. But they too hearken back to the dangerous production of plastics in the early days. Substances, such as celluloid, used in filmmaking, involved cooking up the chemicals and running the plastic through machines to produce film in factories where water dripped from the ceilings in order to prevent the random fires that would spring up.[49]

In each of Matta-Clark's organic-chemical pieces, as in these photographic processes, organic and chemical elements are catalyzed by the application of light and heat. And although these pieces involve the process of development and growth, they also incorporate the process of decay, as does the photograph. The *Incendiary Wafers* are literally used up and destroyed as they fill out their lives as artworks. Within a few months, Matta-Clark would be observing the same process with the cherry tree that he planted in the dark basement of 112 Greene Street and kept alive for three months with artificial light. When it died, Matta-Clark commemorated the life and death of the tree by taking its remains and burying them under a slab of concrete in the basement.

In these pieces and in his later building works that involve photography, arcs of development, decay, and disappearance are mapped out at various scales, some quick, as in *Incendiary Wafers*, and some that have lasted centuries as in his building cuts in seventeenth-century townhouses in Paris, titled *Conical Intersect*. By setting up these processes or by doing the work of cutting through the walls of buildings that will soon be destroyed, Matta-Clark is placing a kind of narrative frame or developmental frame around a process that takes place within a certain space and time. These processes involved not only the establishment of a form, the growth of a material, but also its decline and rot, which Matta-Clark seemed to regard as essential to acknowledge in the artwork.[50]

Site-Specific Art and Frames

In Matta-Clark's treatment of his cut buildings, there is an acknowledgment of the object-like quality of the structure, its immediacy as a work and as an opportunity to examine bodily experience in the present moment.[51] However, the work always guides the viewer's attention to the development of the site and the artwork over time. In this way, there is a synchronic dimension to the work, in which the material and structural aspects of the *space* are highlighted and put forth for inspection. However, there is always a diachronic dimension that is highlighted in the work, an acknowledgment that processes of development and decay in *time* take place at many levels.[52] In this way, Matta-Clark's work resembles that of other site-specific artists, such as Robert Smithson. Smithson's work acknowledges that entropy will inevitably act on the site of the work. And Smithson conceived the documentation of the site and even language in the form of essays to be part of the original site-specific work.[53]

Matta-Clark's dynamic of site and photograph clarifies one aspect of his site-specific installation art: photographs of installations, as do installations themselves, acknowledge the dimensions of space and time — and time at many different scales. In his still photography, there is an acknowledgment of the same synchronic and diachronic dimensions. The photographs sweep out the visual space of the architectural intervention, but they are also part of the diachronic dimension of the work. The photographs acknowledge the duration of the process of making the work, as well as its destruction.

> The act of cutting through from one space to another produces a certain complexity involving depth perception. Aspects of stratification interest me more than the unexpected views which are generated by the removals — not the surface but the thin edge, the severed surface that reveals the autobiographical process of its making. There is a kind of complexity which comes from taking an otherwise completely normal, conventional, albeit anonymous situation and redefining it, retranslating it into overlapping and multiple readings, conditions of past and present.[54]

In the quotation above, Matta-Clark invites the viewer to think about the issue of framing, representation, and display. The wall, Matta-Clark argued, and the edge produced by the cut not only produced a shape but also revealed a process of making — both the making of the wall and the production of the cut. This suggests that Matta-Clark was thinking of his work in terms of labor — both the labor of those who erected those buildings and his own when they were cut. The photographs of *Splitting* as well as the film acknowledge this aspect of labor.

In describing his work as revealing the process of making, Matta-Clark implies that somehow this process of production has been hidden in the final product. His statement points to another way that the piece of wall is framed and that is in terms of "cutting." In Marx's description of industrial production, the product is a result of not a work process but rather specialized systems of work that are unified only in the commodity. In a similar fashion, in the commodity, the traces of labor time are erased or illegible.[55] In making the cut, what Matta-Clark revealed is a process of production and the effect of the passage of time in the static and permanent structure of the building. There are multiple time scales being exposed in Matta-Clark's work: the process of producing the structure, the effect of time and weather on the structure, and the process of making the cut. The final work and the photographs document the physical labor and time that was required to cut through the wall.

The Artist's Book *Splitting* as Time Frame and Archive

Matta-Clark's piece *Splitting* combined both the alteration of a single structure and a record of spatial transformation in terms of a series of photo collages based on pictures taken of the interior and exterior of the house. Matta-Clark obtained the building from Holly and Horace Solomon, who owned the land in Englewood, New Jersey, on which the small house sat. Matta-Clark's idea for the work was simple enough: to cut the house down its center from the roof to the foundation and then to alter the foundation so the cut would be opened up like a crack down the center of the house.[56] The work was labor intensive, as testified by the film Matta-Clark produced to record the process of making the piece. In the end, it produced not only a space that was complex for a viewer who walked through it but also a work that was complex in terms of the way it marked and framed time and history.

Matta-Clark commented that he hoped the alterations in a simple structure like a suburban house would lead the viewer to pay attention to those aspects of the structure that had been taken for granted: "You see that light enters places it otherwise couldn't. Angles and depths can be perceived where they should have been hidden. Spaces are available to move through that were previously inaccessible. My hope is [that] the dynamism of the action can be seen as an alternative vocabulary with which to question the static inert building environment."[57]

In 1974, artist and critic Al Brunelle wrote about visiting *Splitting* in a gallery-sponsored bus trip out to the New Jersey site. He describes what it was like to be in the house. He, like many other writers, described how the light that entered through the cut was knife-like and surprising. The experience of walking through the house freshened his perceptions of such quotid-

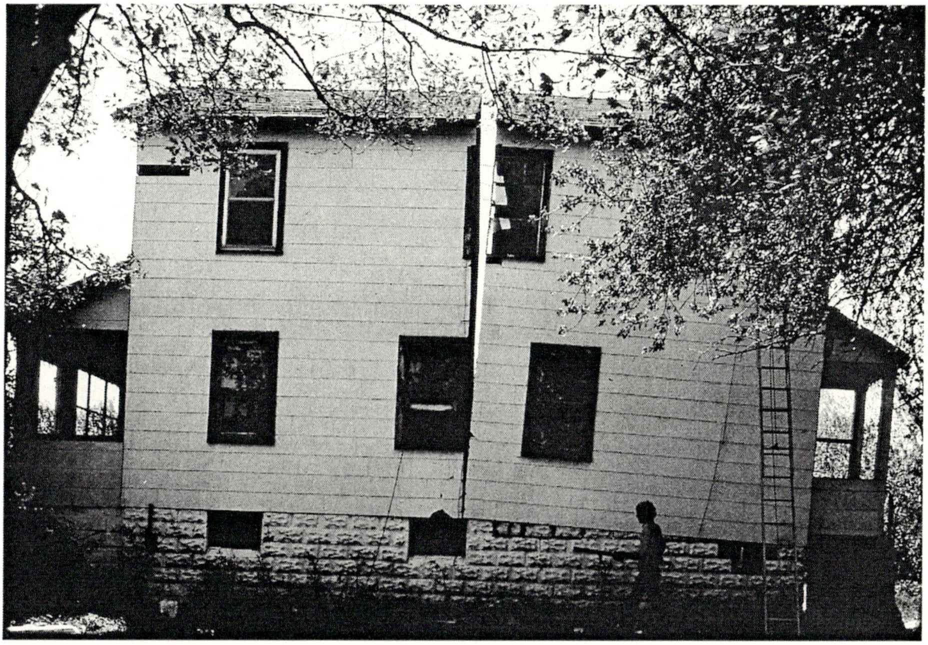

FIGURE 1.3 Gordon Matta-Clark, *Splitting*, documentation, 1974. *© 2011 Estate of Gordon Matta-Clark/Artists Rights Society (ARS), New York.*

ian architecture: "The entire web of meaning and associations generated by structures, and more particularly, houses, is left unburdened, freed from the weight of habitual assumptions."[58] The house seemed lighter in terms of both illumination and atmosphere.

Another commentator notes that it became more and more intimidating to cross the cut because, as one climbed the stairs, the gap between the two halves became wider and wider. The cut both joined inside and outside and made the interior a challenge to negotiate and to comprehend, even as it exposed the things that were hidden in a normal house: the basement and the attic. In the act of cutting open the house, privacy was evacuated from the house. It was a way of opening up an entire history and set of practices around domestic living that have become so habitual as to be invisible.

In looking at the small book *Splitting* that Matta-Clark produced after the project, it is clear that he wanted to emphasize not only the object-like quality of the small building when it was cut but also that this project was a small slice out of the longer history of the house. While turning the pages, the viewer gets a very clear sense that this was a project that had a beginning and an end that coincided with the demise of the old house itself. The book is small and cheaply produced with grainy black-and-white photographs. It is only thirty-four pages long and tells a story of the discovery of the house, its alteration, and final demise. With each page, the viewer moves not only through the house but also through time as the project goes forward.[59]

In the book, the photographs become the body of the house, and they define the space and limits of the house for the viewer. There are two kinds of images in the book: mug shots, which is a term that Anne Wagner uses, of the house, showing the façades and sides of the structure, and complex photo collages that show the alteration to the interior spaces of the house that took place when it was cut.[60] The mug shots also serve as a series of before and after images that demonstrate what happened to the house from the outside. They are comical because they show the house as a diminutive object that fits on a small book page. The exterior shots have been cut from larger photographs, freed of their backgrounds and printed as if the blank white of the page were the context for the house. In one image of the side of the house, bare tree branches stretch across the clapboard wall of the structure. In the book, the cut in the house is made by cutting a thin slice out of the photograph, and in this photograph, Matta-Clark is careful to keep the delicate paper branches of the tree intact.

Certain rules are adhered to in the construction of this photo world. The photo collages map the interior of the house for the viewer, and the span of the map is dictated by the expanse of the cut. Over the course of the thirty-four pages, the photo collages grow in complexity—from two photographs joined where the cut crosses the floor of a room to an entire half of the house that is composed of several different photographs joined together.

The photograph is at once a flat, thin surface and an illusionistic space. It points to the complex ways viewers read the frame of an image and what it frames. A frame is both a boundary and a signifier that directs the viewer's attention and renders what is within something "to be looked at," while designating what is outside it "something to be ignored." The manner in which viewers have regarded frames and the images and spaces they enclose/produce has developed over centuries, as Brian O'Doherty argued, and has been dictated by the cultural use to which images have been put. Matta-Clark's images

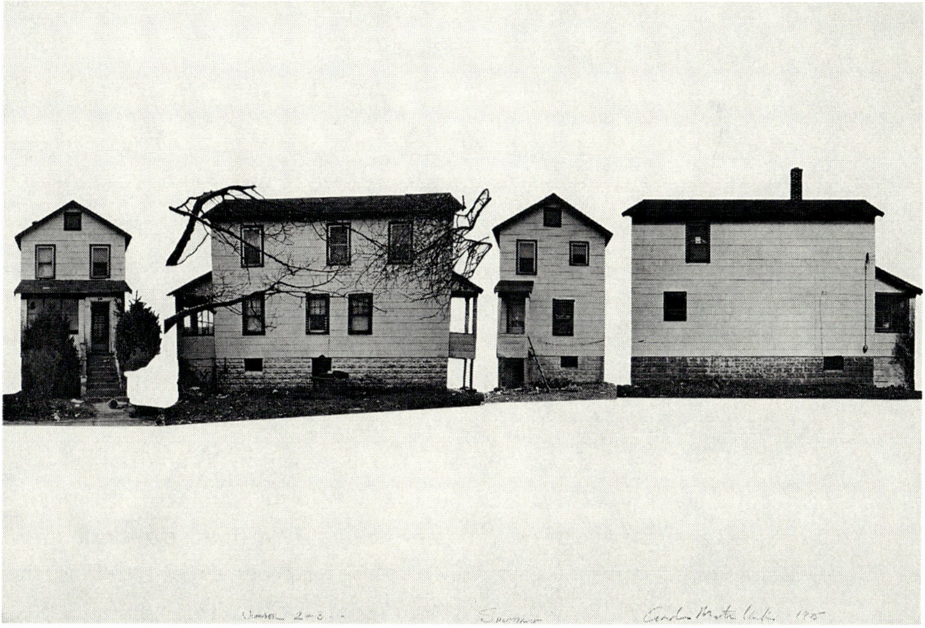

FIGURE 1.4 Gordon Matta-Clark, *Splitting*, collage, 1974. *© 2011 Estate of Gordon Matta-Clark/Artists Rights Society (ARS), New York.*

present us with three different ways of reading what we are presented with: an image that is read as a window; an image that is read as a surface; and a space presented as a unified object.

In an interview for the catalog for *Office Baroque*, which was made in Antwerp in 1977, Matta-Clark explained, "Why hang things on a wall when the wall itself is so much more a challenging medium? It is the rigid mentality that architects install the walls and artists decorate them that offends my sense of either profession. A simple cut or series of cuts acts as a powerful drawing device able to redefine spatial situations and structural components."[61] Matta-Clark is also talking about his photo-collage pieces in this paragraph and the way that these works break the conventional frame of the photograph and the single-point perspective in which the space of a photographic image is structured.

The book represents the movement of a seeing body that can walk on two legs, as it moves through the house. We begin in the basement where two snapshots show us a low-ceilinged room that is filled with old clothes and appliances. In one image, an old clothesline jags across the photograph as an old rumpled coat hangs from a wire hanger. It is unclear why these two images are joined where they are until we notice in the background a complete stairway that crosses the two images. It invites us to go upstairs.

When the cut has been made in house in the narrative of the book, we move through the house looking up staircases and across rooms to windows where the sunlight streams in to dusty bare spaces. The line of the cut that divides each room also dictates how the camera surveys each space. The sole coherent thing in the photo collages is the line of this cut, which jogs across stairs and streaks through the ceilings of rooms, while the rooms themselves tumble around its axis.

In the most dramatic example of this, the camera looks up from the bottom of the stairs over the second-floor hallway to the roof. In the lowest picture, the camera is placed on the stairs looking through the banister out the windows of a room on the first floor, as the cut slices across the stairs, the banister, and the ceiling of the first-floor room. The next two pictures, joined by the cut, look *up* the stairs and at the second floor banister from below, following the line of the cut through the ceiling and the banister. The next photograph frames the ceiling and an opening in the attic, showing us the cut as it opens to the sky and lets in sunlight. The cut opens the roof and then widens as it comes down the far wall (which would be on the other side of the camera and invisible).

However, the camera records as discontinuous a movement through a space that to the eyes is continuous. Because it conforms to the dictates of a flat surface rather than an illusionistic three-dimensional space, the photographic image distorts the way an embodied eye sees the space. Time has been infused into this image — the image portrays successive moments as if they were one moment and a space that cannot be grasped at one glance, as if it could be. The photographs try to acknowledge that a viewer turns and moves her head while staying in the same place. The collages are evocative of the way that Nick Kaye describes the viewer producing the space of a site-specific work by performing in it.

In these still images and static objects, Matta-Clark nearly captures a sense of *durée* — the word coined by Henri Bergson. Bergson describes how the process of perception is bound with memory. In memory, the immaterial past

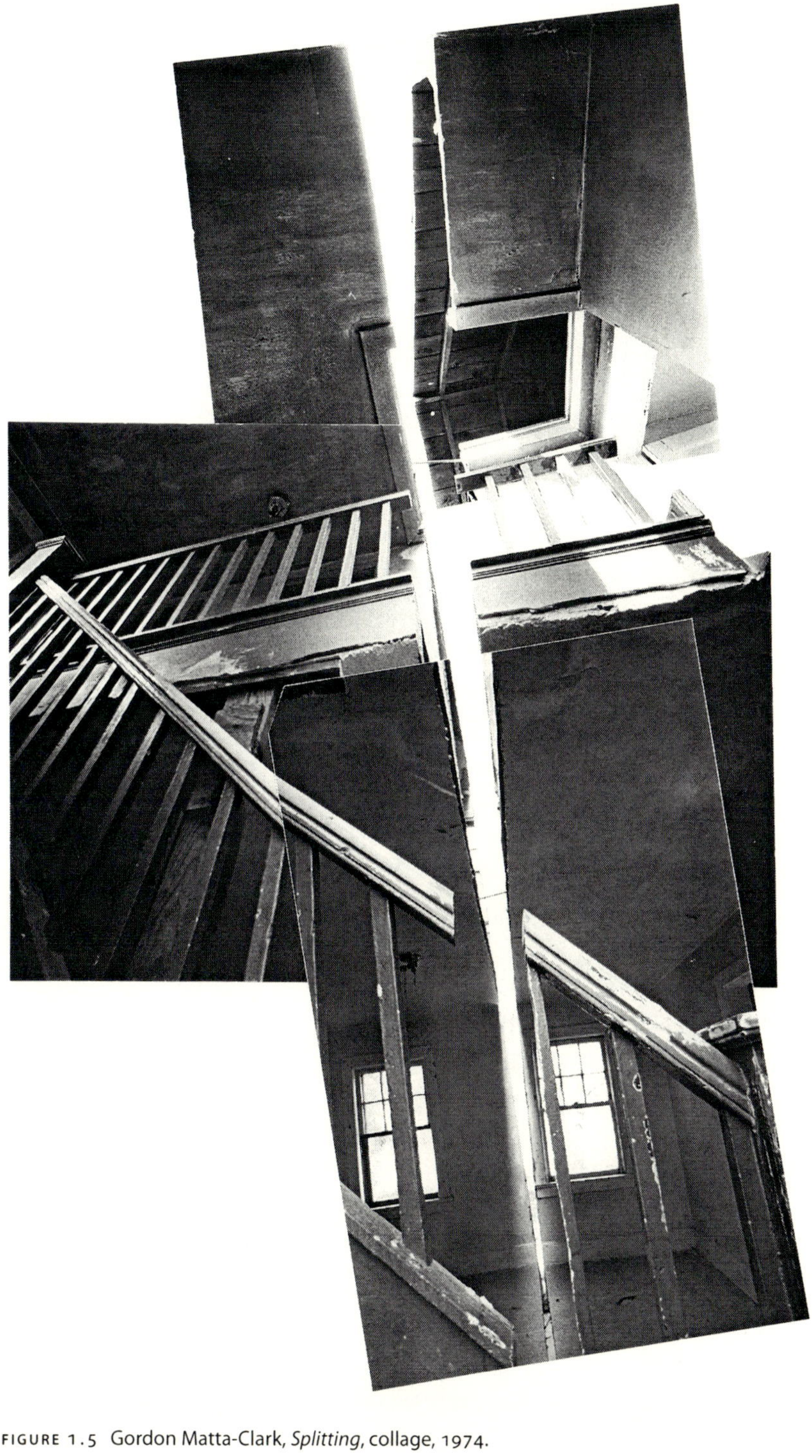

FIGURE 1.5 Gordon Matta-Clark, *Splitting*, collage, 1974.

expands into the present moment of somatic perception.[62] Instead of being a distinct instance of recollection, the process occurs continually. Each moment is divided between the past and the future. The virtual past moment contracts toward the future, and becomes material — a perception in the present. At the same time, the present dilates, is made virtual, and falls away into the past. *Duration* is the connection between these two moments, which are held together for a short while before they are differentiated. Memory, according to Gilles Deleuze, is duration. I say that Matta-Clark nearly captures the sense of duration because Bergson claims duration is more accurate than the "cinematographical" or scientific depiction of experience. We could say that the gap between Matta-Clark's snapshots, the flicker of the images, as in a film, points to the duration that we cannot experience as viewers of still photographs. And Matta-Clark arranged the text in the book as if it were a silent film.

Because of the nature of the photographs in *Splitting*, viewers of these images and objects are made aware of the simultaneity of time scales in the work. They are given a literal illustration via the collage technique of the difficulty of synthesizing many distinct perceptions into a meaningful whole. Bergson uses the mundane example of a person waiting for sugar to melt in a glass of water. Waiting bespeaks an expectation that time passes at a rate based on one's own duration, but it comes into direct conflict with the duration of sugar melting. In the impatience of waiting, the people who wait become aware both of their own duration and that of others.[63] In Matta-Clark's entire *Splitting* project, we become aware that there is the time scale of the house and its history, which as Anne Wagner notes, opens up the work to the social context of the site. But there is also the time scale of the cut and, finally, that of the photographs that form a flickering sequence. Bergson claims that one becomes aware of duration in the interaction of multiple rhythms. In Matta-Clark's work, the synchronic aspect of the work — the mapping of the space — is acknowledged. But so too is the diachronic in the movement of the body through the house and the making and eventual disappearance of the work in time. The photographs capture the sense of development and decay that fascinated Matta-Clark in organic processes.

The photographic documentation of Matta-Clark's work, like the catalog for the *Rooms* exhibition, is constructed as a narrative that tries to interject a sense of time and movement that the still photographs do not have. Narrative structures or sequences seem to be required to compensate for the stillness and silence of the photographs. This points to photography's connection to language.

The Act of Looking: ____________, *Louise Lawler, Adrian Piper and Cindy Sherman Have Agreed to Participate in an Exhibition Organized by Janelle Reiring at Artists Space, September 23 to October 28, 1978*

A year after Rosalind Krauss's second article titled "Notes on the Index" had appeared in *October*, a group of young artists invited by the gallerist Janelle Reiring participated in an exhibition titled ____________, *Louise Lawler, Adrian Piper and Cindy Sherman Have Agreed to Participate in an Exhibition Organized by Janelle Reiring at Artists Space, September 23 to October 28, 1978*, at the alternative space Artists Space in Manhattan. In this exhibition, photography replaced language as the device that presents questions about the frame. Each of the works uses language or refers to a narrative structure. Rather than engaging the viewer as a body, the works in this exhibition ask the viewer to interpret texts and to evaluate positions in the art world. The artists' works in the exhibition differed starkly from each other, underscoring the conceptual dimension of the theme of the exhibition, which emphasized the way that viewers see and "read" works in an exhibition space.

Artists Space opened in 1972 under the direction of Trudie Grace and Irving Sandler as a space that was devoted to showing the work of young artists that had been chosen by other artists.[64] The gallery was opened at the intersection of Wooster and Houston Street. In 1975, Helene Winer became the director of Artists Space and moved the gallery to 105 Hudson Street. When Winer became director of Artists Space, it marked a change in the direction of the gallery. Winer and the others at Artists Space wanted to give the gallery a clear identity. In an interview with Cindy Sherman, Valerie Smith, and Matt Mullican, Winer said, "I just wanted to set up a situation that would introduce a lot of challenging work. Artists Space took on an identity that a lot of artists wanted to be associated with. Also it was a different time in the art world. It was the beginning of this notion that art could be both visually seductive and conceptually serious."[65]

The exhibition initiated by Janelle Reiring the following year represented a careful look at the exhibition space as a political and social frame by using various strategies. Winer asked Reiring to organize a show at Artists Space, and Reiring had the idea of an exhibition of artists' work that "addresses the issue of how art is presented and, in turn, how it is seen."[66] At the time, Reiring was working for Leo Castelli Gallery, but she insists that the idea for the show did not come from her experience working at a gallery but rather from the work of the artists who were in the show.

At Castelli, she had met and become friends with Louise Lawler, and through that friendship met Christopher D'Arcangelo. Reiring describes the contemporary art scene in New York at the time as small and close knit.[67] The third participant in the exhibition was Cindy Sherman, who happened to be working at Artists Space at the time. According to Reiring, Sherman would arrive at her job as receptionist without fanfare, dressed in various outfits and disguises. Based on these spontaneous performances, Reiring thought her work would fit in well to the exhibition. The last participant was the best-known artist, but she was no longer participating in the New York art scene. After making important contributions in conceptual art, Adrian Piper had gone on to Harvard University to study for a PhD in philosophy. Piper had already exhibited in 1974 at Artists Space with a performance and series of photographs with text bubbles titled "Talking to Myself, the Ongoing Autobiography of an Art Object."[68] Reiring had seen Piper's work when she had first come to New York in the early 1970s and liked it. So, she wrote to Piper and asked her to participate in the show.

Between Viewer and Artwork

Louise Lawler and Christopher D'Arcangelo shared a large room at 105 Hudson Street; the room had a set of windows that looked out on the façade of the Citibank building across the street. Another set of windows looked into an interior space. Louise Lawler's untitled piece consisted of a painting that she had borrowed from the New York Racing Association's Aqueduct Race Track. The painting *Black Race Horse* depicted a horse in profile and was painted in 1863 by painter Henry Stull.[69] Lawler hung the painting so that it partially obscured some of the interior windows in the exhibition space. Above the painting she installed a bright theater light so that it shone directly at any viewer who tried to look at the painting.[70] She installed another so that it shone out the windows of Artists Space on Hudson Street onto the façade of the Citibank building across the way.

In turning the spotlight around on the viewer and on the street, Lawler made the viewer aware that the act of viewing, who was looking and who was not looking, was as much a part of the art as the arrangement itself. Lawler explained her choice this way in the Artists Space anniversary catalog: "In a very corny way, part of the point was to signal that something was going on at Artists Space. I felt it was a very distinct audience of young artists looking at each other's work; and being on the second floor, nobody in the neighborhood, in what wasn't yet called TriBeCa, was too aware of Artists Space."[71] Artists Space catered to the community of young avant-garde artists who knew enough to see the show and would never step foot in the gallery of paintings at the Aqueduct Race Track. Lawler planned to highlight the difference between a certain type of art (i.e., traditional naturalistic painting) and the new art being produced at the time. While squinting in the bright light, viewers were made aware that they wanted to see the painting and that, in a certain sense, they were being put on stage and looked at while they were trying to look at the painting. In this way, Lawler sought to raise the self-awareness of her viewers at Artists Space and underlined the social divisions between the audiences of the two exhibition spaces.

Christopher D'Arcangelo performed several procedures that provided an anonymous comment on the exhibition and the exhibition space itself. D'Arcangelo removed his name from the show and any announcement about the show. In an interesting way, D'Arcangelo's act of pulling his name from the promotion of the show means that his work has been ignored in popular memory of this exhibition, which points to the significance of the photographs and catalog in constructing our understanding of these exhibitions of installation art.

In his piece, four separate sheets of paper were pasted to a small wall that jutted out into the space that held Lawler's work. In looking at the painting hung on the wall after looking out the windows, the viewer would discover D'Arcangelo's work. The Artists Space archives have only a few slides showing the text on the wall. The text, however, appears in the anniversary catalog *5000 Artists Return to Artists Space*, and it demonstrates, as Lawler attests, that she and D'Arcangelo had been talking about their contribution to the exhibition. D'Arcangelo's text is divided into four parts: (1) Artists Space: Where Are You and What's in a Name? (2) Design, Name, Propaganda; (3) Propaganda/Context; and (4) Being in a Public Space. The texts comment

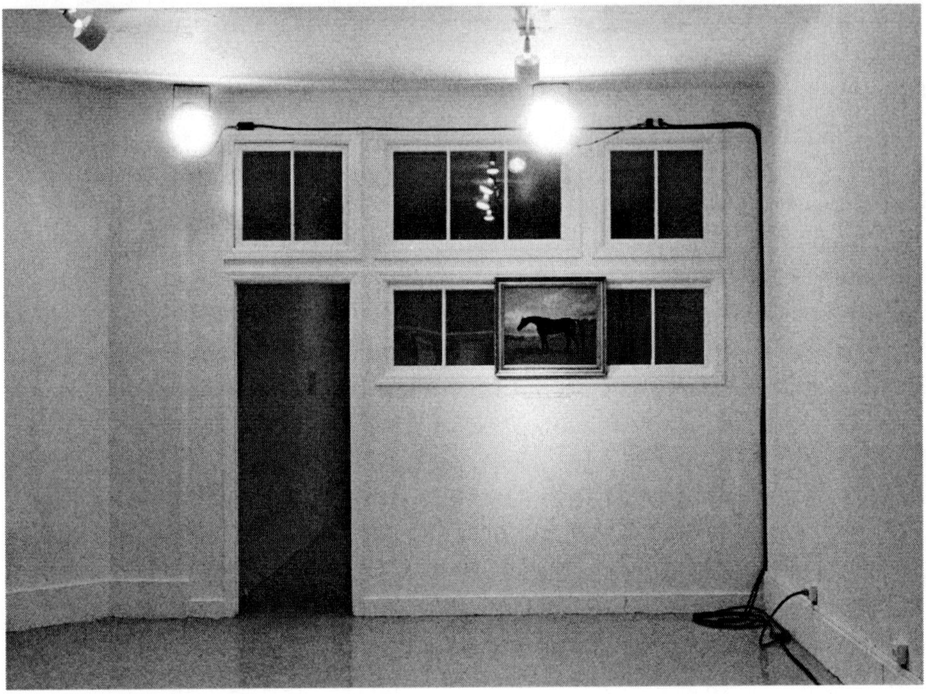

FIGURE 1.6 Louise Lawler, untitled, 1978. *Courtesy of Louise Lawler.*

on the significance of Artists Space and its relationship to the viewer but also the exhibition space's less visible connection to a system of money and "propaganda," to use the artist's term, incorporating larger social institutions and finally the capitalist system.

The texts appeared on different walls of the space as one walked through the exhibition. Louise Lawler has said that D'Arcangelo's work was to be included in every room of the space.[72] Addressing the viewer, they functioned like a narrator to the viewer's experience of the show. And they encompassed the space as a whole without interfering with the other artists' work. Like Lawler's arrangement, which, however, operates more on the level of the viewer's expectations of visual art, D'Arcangelo's text invites the reader to think about what the space is and how it functions:

> At this time you are in a divided space, Artists Space. Your reason for being here can be one of many, but your being here subjects you to the limitations

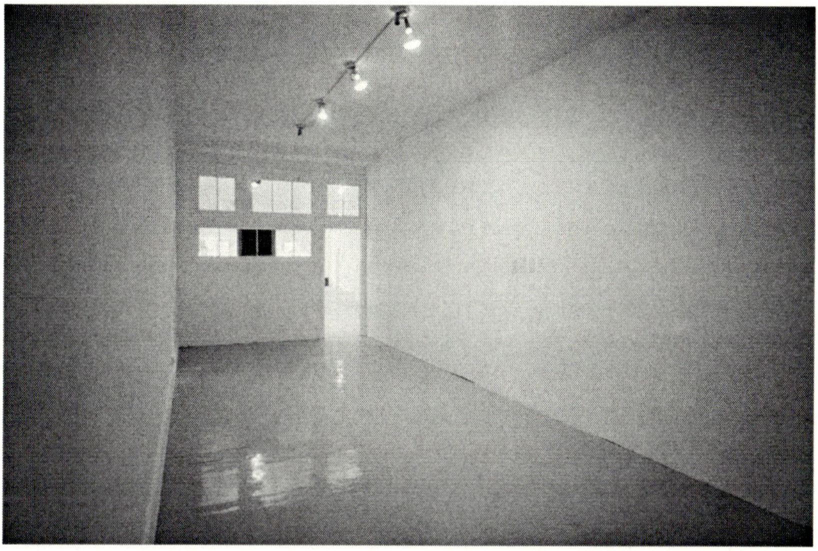

FIGURE 1.7 Christopher D'Arcangelo, untitled, 1978. *Courtesy of Louise Lawler.*

> imposed by design and based on the function of the space. How can you see its function? How can you know its limitations? . . . One could say that the austere design of this place helps to obscure its function. At this point one must be careful, for all this austerity can show the function of the space when it is connected with the idea that an object alone is more visible than an object in a group. Thus the design of Artists Space shows us one aspect of its function: to help us see (better) the objects placed in the space.[73]

This is an excerpt from D'Arcangelo's first section of text, but by the third the anonymous interlocutor has argued that in fact one of the functions of Artists Space is to obscure its connections to broader networks of government and corporate funding. Thus, the purpose of Artists Space, the anonymous text tells the viewer, is to highlight some aspects of Artists Space and distract attention from others in a conceptual act of spotlighting that parallels Lawler's own.

The final block of text brings the specificity of the work in time and place to the viewer's attention. It questions the art content of the text blocks themselves and then goes on to explain how the work was made: "The process used to install this work on the wall was the same process as that used to make the printing plate for the announcement and catalog for this exhibition. . . . Three copies of this work were made. The typeset and negative were destroyed at the time that the work was exposed." In this way, the text points to not only its own production but also its circumscription and destruction, as a site-specific installation.

Adrian Piper installed a piece in a small alcove at Artists Space that combined sound and images. The work was located in a room separated from the other pieces that a viewer was required to enter. Upon turning a corner, the viewer was greeted by an image depicting black South Africans descending a staircase. The photograph was printed at 30 by 30 inches and positioned so that viewers felt as if they were located in a space lower than the figures in the photograph. The artist intended the encounter to be confrontational or at least puzzling. The taped voice begins by telling viewers what they (the viewers) want: "It doesn't matter who these people are. They're parts of a piece of art, which is part of an art exhibit, in an art gallery, in Soho, in New York City. This gallery is one of the best: progressive, daring, shows some of the most interesting and aesthetically innovative work around. You expect, and hope, that when you leave this gallery, your conception of what art can be will be altered, maybe even expanded, if only by the smallest fraction."[74] Later, the voice goes on to say,

> In looking at this picture, you carefully monitor any subliminal or undisciplined reactions you have to this image of assertive aggressive, angry-looking blacks; they might be a part of the piece. In fact, all your reactions, all your thoughts about what you're now experiencing might be part of this piece. In this space, in this gallery, in front of this picture, you don't want to let your politics interfere with or deaden your aesthetic perceptions, but rather contribute to them: your political reactions are part of the art experience you are trying to have.

Like Lawler and D'Arcangelo's works, Piper makes the viewer aware of her act of looking, her attempt to read the image. And like Lawler's work, this self-awareness comes about in part because of the way the artist has arranged the material in the space and her use of language as a framing device. A photograph does not have intrinsic meaning. Allan Sekula describes the photograph as something that is always snatched up by a motivated discourse. The process of critique proceeds by discovering the historical discourse by which the photograph was snatched and analyzing its politics and their manifestation in readings of the image.

Piper's piece responds to other images of people of color. In an analysis of nineteenth-century anthropological photographs taken of people in Africa, anthropologist Gwyn Prins points to the way photographs are read differently by various audiences. Although a photograph may depict individuals in a way that within their own culture signifies dignity, in Western cultural contexts of the nineteenth and twentieth centuries the image will be read in a different way.[75] For instance, the scientific discourse steers viewers' readings of an image. They describe one photograph in which the individual does not look at the camera, which has been placed on a stand. The viewers see a profile of the individual, evincing a sense of distance between the viewer and the object of the camera gaze. The surveying position of the camera amplifies subjects' lack of engagement with the photographer. Circulating in a Western scientific context, the photograph might be read as a type or "a specimen," according to Prins.

As work from the 1970s on documentary photography argued, the documentary photograph underwrites and supports whatever reading is given to it by the discourse into which it is incorporated.[76] The photograph, in general, because of its portable, fragmentary nature, objectifies the subject depicted. The photograph is considered "evidence" because it is assumed to be objective, transparent, and an index. The invisibility of the photographer, the camera, and the viewer underscores that the viewer should read the photograph as objective.

Piper's work puts viewers in the position to question the way they read the image in her piece by using language to address the viewers. Piper has described her approach elsewhere as "the indexical present," which is an attempt to provoke the viewer's defensive reactions to images and then draw the viewer's attention to that defensive reaction or discomfort. In reflecting on this discomfort and transforming it into language, the artist hopes, viewers become aware of the rigid, stereotypical categories that they use to process encounters such as this.

Piper's work draws attention, as Roland Barthes argues that a critical reading of photographs should, to the ways in which viewers' cultural lexica condition their reading of photographic images in particular. By making it difficult to look at without thinking, Piper's piece defies the expectations that one carries to a traditional gallery space. Piper chose an image in which the subject looks directly at the camera, and she made it large enough that the figures depicted look down from a height at viewers. She then supplies an authoritative voice that insists that viewers pay attention to their responses to the image. Rather than offering up images of these black men to the viewer's gaze, the encounter borders on a confrontation that the viewer must contemplate.

Janelle Reiring had invited Sherman to exhibit because of her performance on the job at Artists Space, but Sherman instead exhibited her film stills for the first time. The film stills also drew on the ability of viewers to read cultural codes but challenged the viewer more obliquely. The Sherman images were hung along a corridor. As recorded in one of the images in the Artists Space archives, the film stills that Sherman showed have become well known. These included the image of the starlet with a dark, beehive hairdo and sunglasses, leaning out a sun-drenched patio door in a drunken manner ("Untitled Film Still #7") and the model, lying on a bed, robe thrown open to show her dressed in a bra and panties ("Untitled Film Still #6"). These prints were hung on the wall in a traditional manner: one after the other. They were large and tacked unframed to the wall of the gallery. Some commentators have noted that it is necessary to see Sherman's pieces one after another, in order to understand her work of dress up and play act, by comparing one image to the next. The images are traps that catch viewers in the act of looking and categorizing, by coaxing viewers to draw on their knowledge of visual codes acquired via the mass media. In the process, viewers realize that the figure in the photograph has become an object of the gaze and the subject of a sexist cultural discourse.

Reiring noted that the responses to the show were varied but that Sherman's pieces were an immediate hit. People, however, were more puzzled by the other artists' work. Lawler has indicated that the audience for the show was the usual art audience with a lot of young artists interested in looking at other young artists' work.[77] Although the artists knew the audience that was going to see the work, the intention of the work did not always convey clearly to viewers.[78] An example of this is April Kingsley's review of the show for the *Village Voice*. Adrian Piper is the only artist who stands out in the show, according to the review. Kingsley complains that artists' works spill into each other's spaces, and that, combined with the anonymity of some of the artists, makes it difficult to determine the limits and authorship of each piece. She cites the influences of artists, such as Hans Haacke, Joseph Kosuth, Rafael Ferrer, Michael Asher, and even Marcel Duchamp. She goes further in complaining about the lack of clear authorial integrity by asserting that "one of the artists seems embarrassingly derivative of the early work of another."[79] What the Kingsley review seems to miss is the site-specific aspect of the exhibition and the work in it. As such, the context and content of the work derives not so much from the careers and oeuvres of the individual artists but rather from the encounter with these works of art *in this particular space.*

One of the interesting aspects of the exhibition is that it was so spare. There was very little for the viewer to look at but the blank walls of the exhibition space. If we think about this in terms of framing the exhibition space and compare, for instance, Louise Lawler's work to Christopher D'Arcangelo's, it is easy to see that the significance of Lawler's maneuvers was more ambiguous — D'Arcangelo's less so because he used text.

And it is the textual aspect of the work that returns us to Krauss's comments about the function of the frame in the photograph. In her essay "Notes on the Index," Krauss argues that the framing that takes place in the photograph — or, I would add, the installation — brings the presence of the building to the viewer's attention and renders that framed portion significant but ambiguous. A supplementary text is required, a caption of some sort. And, rather than photographs, the materials that provide the most information about this exhibition thirty years on are the texts and narratives about the exhibition.

The Catalog

The catalog for the show is equally spare; the photographs are few, and there are no installation shots. Instead, language replaces the photographs. The catalog has twenty pages with a black paper cover sized 9.5 by 8 inches and a logo designed by Lawler of a white *A*, with "Artists Space" printed on the cross-bar, placed within a circle. The pages were shared out to the organizer and artists. Reiring contributed a text explaining the genesis of the exhibition. D'Arcangelo's section consists of blank pages, and Lawler's points to the cover as her design. Piper's pages begin with the question "What is the aesthetic content of this work?" Then it shows a detail of the photograph and gives its origin as *National Geographic* magazine. The next two pages give the complete text of the audio component of the piece. The catalog concludes with four reproductions of Sherman's photographs. The catalog gives no clue as to the layout of the space, as the *Rooms* catalog did, and even more it leaves Lawler's and D'Arcangelo's works a mystery.

The spare catalog suggests a few things. First, it is clear that Artists Space's budget was not lavish and the catalog designers and artists did what they could to adapt to these circumstances. Second, the engagement of the viewer's body is downplayed in the exhibition. Lawler says that she produced black-and-white press photographs of her work and that each was a detail of the work, underlining the sense that the work included not just the actual arrangement by Lawler but also the social context of the work.[80] The specific, material qualities of the space matter less than its position within a field of exhibition spaces and the social context of the art world. Language is what directs the viewer's attention to these aspects of the exhibition and the work of the artists who participated.

We have at least two examples in which dialog between the work (or the artist) and the viewer was established: Adrian Piper's sound installation and D'Arcangelo's text. In Lawler's, the pull of language is more subtle. Her piece performs the basic procedure of a system of meaning: it demonstrates difference. In other words, Lawler presents us with the opportunity to compare the difference between the painting and the space in which it has been hung. Furthermore, the difference between the commonplace conventions of the traditional or modernist gallery space and the exhibition situation presented at Artists Space is revealed by viewers' frustrated desire to see the painting obscured by the spotlight shining in their eyes.

Cindy Sherman's work, of course, points to a narrative structure of which each individual image is a part. Douglas Crimp presented this reading of Sherman's work in the essay written about an exhibition he organized at Artists Space the year previous. Sherman did not participate in this exhibition, titled *Pictures*, which took place in the fall of 1977, but she is forever associated with it because of the revised version of Crimp's essay, which later appeared in *October*, included an image and discussion of Sherman's work absent in the original text.[81] The show actually included work by Robert Longo, Sherrie Levine, Jack Goldstein, Troy Brauntuch, and Philip Smith.

Pictures was an exhibition in which the artists and the curator had absorbed ideas about the nature of photography presented in Walter Benjamin's writings. Echoing the end of Rosalind Krauss's second "Notes on the Index" essay, which draws from Benjamin and Barthes, Crimp argues that the films and photographs in the show were fragments of a narrative. Crimp's essay argued for the emergence of a new kind of art that played with the ambivalent nature of the photograph. The photograph is a kind of presence while at the same time being the physical manifestation of the absence of the thing it depicts. In Krauss's argument the direct presentation of a photographic image, the body of an old school building, or the cut-out section of an old tenement floor, begs for a supplementary text. This insight derives from Walter Benjamin's assertion that a photograph requires a caption in order to be read. Derrida argues something similar with reference to the *parergon*, the frame: "What constitutes them as *parerga* is not simply their exteriority as a surplus, it is the internal structural link which rivets them to the lack in the interior of the *ergon*. And this lack would be constitutive of the very unity of the *ergon*."[82] Both photography and language serve to frame site-specific installation in the 1970s. It is installation that draws the viewer's attention to the frame of the work in the form of the exhibition space and in the form of the procedures of the art institution that render the work a legitimate aspect of art practice.

Within the examples of installation art I have discussed, there seems to be a group of works that can be effectively photographed and another group that cannot be photographed. Those works that cannot be effectively photographed emphasize the viewer's experience and sense in real time. These works point back to the viewer and focus on the individual internal experience. Those works amenable to photography and that use language point outward, focusing on context and, as a result, often critique art world ideology. As such, the work in the Artists Space exhibition refuses to be autonomous and remains dependent on its particular place and time; this work draws on photography and language as a tool to critique the art practice in a particular site. Hence, even in this exhibition, a couple of years after the *Rooms* exhibition, site-specificity has been revealed to have another dimension.

The Frames of Installations

In the examples of installation art discussed in this chapter, the notion of the relationship between the work and the frame — *ergon* and *parergon* — the documentary photograph, and the installation has proved quite variable.

Rooms showed the variety of ways artists used the old school space as a kind of frame for their installations. In comparing the variety of ways that artists interpreted the relationship between their works and the spaces they were in, it is possible to see that the installations ranged from those in which the building surfaces or disappears in relation to the work to those in which the building surface is part of the work. It might be well at this point to return to another passage from Derrida's *The Truth in Painting*: "*Parerga* have a thickness, a surface which separates them not only (as Kant would have it) from the integral side, from the body proper of the *ergon*, but also from the outside, from the wall on which the painting is hung, from the space in which statue or column is erected."[83]

Brian O'Doherty noted that the flat surface of abstract, modernist painting had placed pressure on the frame and in turn brought the wall on which it was hung into play as part of the art. I argue that the *Rooms* exhibition demonstrates how flexibly the exhibition space functions as a frame for the work. In more site-specific pieces, such as Richard Serra's trench in the attic or in Gordon Matta-Clark's work, the wall was thinned until it folded into the material of the work itself. But the wall could also be thickened, as in Dennis Oppenheim's work, until it disappears altogether from the viewer's field of attention and becomes just support for a work, which functions more like a traditional naturalistic painting in relation to its frame.

In Gordon Matta-Clark's cuts, the cut itself is a kind of frame that not only points to the immediate object-quality of the house, room, or warehouse but also sets off the durational aspect of the site itself, highlighting the way the structure has changed over time and pointing inward to the temporary quality of Matta-Clark's own short-lived interventions. These arcs of development and decay are made concrete in Matta-Clark's photographs and books, which are presented as sequences.

The work at Artists Space differs from the previous examples. As in *Rooms* and Matta-Clark's works, the works in the exhibition point to the immediate conditions of the space. However, these artists are focusing on not the work's relationship to the exhibition space as a material limit to the work but rather the significance of the space as an institution in the art scene of the time. And as Janelle Reiring points out, the gesture, except for Cindy Sherman's work, was confusing to viewers. In contrast to the *Rooms* exhibition, they didn't quite know what to make of it. And perhaps this lack of communication has to do with the fact that viewers, such as Nancy Foote, were able to fit the work in the *Room* exhibition into the familiar language of postminimal, conceptual, and performance art. The Artists Space exhibition represented something new. In pointing to the wall of the exhibition space, the artists in the Artists Space exhibition were also pointing beyond to the *immediate* supporting systems of the art market, museum, mass media, and art history of the late 1970s, which is regarded by viewers as exterior to the progressive and uncompromised alternative art space. "*Parerga* have a thickness, a surface which separates them not only (as Kant would have it) from the integral side, from the body proper of the *ergon*, but also from the outside, from the wall on which the painting is hung, from the space in which statue or column is erected, *then, step by step, from the whole field of historical, economic, political inscription in which the drive to signature is produced*" (emphasis mine).[84]

One of the aspects of the Artists Space exhibition that distinguishes it from the *Rooms* exhibition at PS1 is how dispersed the elements of the show were. The artists pointed always to systems and media beyond the exhibition space itself. Christopher D'Arcangelo did so by removing any advertisement of his work or name beyond the confines of the gallery space. Lawler, on the other hand, created a succinct but ambiguous logo that was printed on 8½ by 11 inch paper and posted in various locations in Lower Manhattan. Piper and Sherman's work points to social practices in looking as well as the social conventions that condition understandings of race and gender that pervade the exhibition space and the world outside. In this way, we can say that the works in the Artists Space show function like photographs in their specificity in relation to time (in history) and place (material and social context), as well as their need for supplementary texts. Unlike in the *Rooms* exhibition or in Matta-Clark's *Splitting*, these artists relied on not photographs to frame their work within the context of the art world but rather language.

The Historical Impact of Catalogs as Photographic Archives

The catalogs, photographs, and texts are supplements that frame these works and exhibitions. We can consider them archives of a sort, and their rules guide how we read and understand and remember these exhibitions. The *Rooms* catalog substitutes for the pieces in the exhibition and they were removed and, in some cases, destroyed when the exhibition was over. The catalog systematically mapped the show via photographs, floor plans, and viewers' personal experiences. The photographs in the publication are treated as simple documentary images that have been arranged in book format in the same order that one might walk through the exhibition, providing a persuasive substitute for the experience itself.

The text that seems to have defined the exhibition the most in the context of art history, however, is Krauss's "Notes on the Index, Part 2," which focuses on only a few site-specific pieces in the show in order to make the claim that art of the 1970s differs from that of the 1960s. For instance, Krauss chose an earlier piece by Dennis Oppenheim titled *Identity Stretch* that was site specific and depended on photographic documentation. She included this piece rather than the more figurative and theatrical piece he made for the *Rooms* exhibition titled *Broken Record Blues*. As a result of Krauss's choices, the great variety of ways that artists in this show interpreted the installation format and context of the old school building as a frame has been overlooked in art history.

Matta-Clark's photographs shape how we understand his work and substitute for the now-lost buildings and cuts. The photographs bridge the lack that has been produced by the passage of time, serving as rough outlines for something one can no longer experience. They approximate the bodily experience of his altered spaces while remaining in themselves complex studies of the way that the frame of the photograph shapes visual spaces. In their partiality and insufficiency, the photographs serve as markers for the passage of time, marking the distance between the current viewer and the disappeared work.

The works in the Artists Space show differ once again from the two previous examples in that the photographic documentation is quite minimal and little published. The catalog includes very few images but at least two texts. The same is true of the archival material at Artists Space that has remained from the show. Christopher D'Arcangelo refused to have his name circulate outside the exhibition space in press releases or the catalog. For this reason and because of his unfortunate early death, he tends to be forgotten in this exhibition. Lawler, Piper, and especially Cindy Sherman are remembered in this exhibition because their works either outlasted the show (in the case of Piper and Sherman) or were documented by photographs. The works focused viewers' attention on their participation in or exclusion from broader structures and social practices in the art world. The artists chose to draw viewers' attention to the specificity of their placement in a social context at a particular time (this dimension of site-specificity) primarily via language.

Especially because it is a ubiquitous art practice, it is important to pay attention to the way works of installation art manipulate the notion of the frame. Like a photograph, installation always calls for a supplement, some kind of frame within the context of the art world, even as it may deny its need for a frame. This need for a supplement, as Derrida would say, points to a lack of a secure identity. Installation art can have an ever-expanding set of frames, ranging from the literal space and time in which it has been made to the less immediate ideological structures that lend it meaning. Much of the writing on installation art has noted this aspect of it. However, these ideological and discursive structures can include not only the literal exhibition space but also the photographs and texts that populate exhibition catalogs of installation art: the archives of these works. These images and documents, even if they are considered supplementary to the work, continue to condition our understanding of the work in important ways.

The next chapter describes the work of Renée Green whose pieces focus on the issue of framing and the archive and asks the viewer to question how the way photographs are hung, arranged, and framed affects our understanding of history and memory. Green's work takes the historical photographic archive and renders it something that we must read and criticize.

TWO

the politics of representation

ARCHIVE AND MEMORY IN THE WORK OF RENÉE GREEN

Photography in Site-Specific Installation Art

Fragments and ephemera from the past are gathered in an installation. Small pieces of crumbly concrete are arranged under a glass vitrine that is set on a simple white table along with a map and some paperback books. Music of the 1970s plays on a boom box, and black-and-white photographs of 1970s protesters are hung on the walls (figure 2.1).[1] Videotapes play on monitors alongside a collection of vinyl albums and a turntable. The narrator of one video relates the following event:

> The girl watched the news and waited anxiously, often. That's part of what she recollects of childhood. Waiting. Seeing the running text of news reporting students shot at Kent State moving across the bottom of the TV screen. TV programs were interrupted and her mother was late returning home from there. Across the street, kids played *Jackson 5* 45s and *Sly Stone*. The girl smoothed her bedspread and checked for order. Finally her mother did arrive, but she can't remember now what either said. It was May 4th, 1970. (Video transcript, *Partially Buried*)

The girl's memory recounted in the film *Partially Buried* is the artist's memory, which is then dispersed into the broader collection of objects and recordings that constitute the installation *Partially Buried in Three Parts* produced in 1996–1997. These vestiges of the 1970s are all connected with Robert Smithson's site-specific earthwork *Partially Buried Woodshed* and the shooting of student protesters at Kent State University in 1970. In this piece, Green examines the connections between personal memory, photographs, documents, and artifacts. This is a work of installation art that takes as part of its subject matter the documentation of a previous work of site-specific art and the historical context of which it is a part. *Partially Buried in Three Parts* asks questions about documentation and its relationship to memory and history.

This chapter argues that, in many of Renée Green's pieces, she uses the arrangement and examination of photographs and photographic media as a way of addressing issues of history and memory through the format of the archive. Green's work connects to conceptual art in the 1960s and 1970s, which utilized serial structures and was interested in scrutinizing systems of representation and language. It is already well established that Robert Smithson's work is a precedent for site-specific installation art such as Green's, but one could include as well Marcel Broodthaers's and John Baldessari's work as well. The artists who were included in the Artists Space exhibition, such as Adrian Piper, Christopher D'Arcangelo, and Louise Lawler, are also precedents for this type of work in installation art in that they ask the viewer to be active readers of the work and its situation.

Green's archival practice brings together issues of photography and site-specificity.[2] Analog photographs bear the touch of light and shadow available at a particular time and in a particular place. Photography has a specificity to it that, as we have seen, connects it to those site-specific installations built in place in spaces and structures, such as PS1 or Gordon Matta-Clark's old house. Like these works, the photograph is an index. In the writings of Roland Barthes, Allan Sekula, and Martha Rosler, the photograph is revealed, however, to be not just a simple document or index but also a complex of cultural codes and beliefs. Roland Barthes helped develop this more nuanced understanding of photography by considering the image from the perspective of the person who looked at it. Barthes tried to determine how the viewer would go about understanding the image. In his chapter "Rhetoric of the Image," Barthes teased out the various messages in a photograph and argued that viewers of photographs are in fact readers of images.

Hal Foster linked works interested in "site" beginning in the 1960s with Minimalism:

> These developments constitute a sequence of investigations: first of the material constituents of the art medium, then of the spatial conditions of perception, and then of the corporeal bases of this perception — shifts marked

> in Minimalist art in the early 1960s through conceptual, performance, body, and site-specific art in the early 1970s. Soon the institution of art could no longer be described only in spatial terms . . . it was also a discursive network of different practices and institutions, other subjectivities and communities.[3]

As with the understanding of the photograph, the definition of site-specificity has become more complicated. In the last twenty years, as I noted in the introduction, art historians such as Miwon Kwon and James Meyer have argued that sites are not simply material configurations but can be embedded in language or woven out of the relationships established among people, objects, places, and disciplines. Green has been seen as one of a generation of artists who helped to redefine site. Her installations are not site specific in the sense of being built at their place of exhibition and then dismantled once the exhibition is over. Their relation to a site, according to critics such as Kwon and Meyer, occurs as content.

While the writing on site-specific art has considered the structure of individual works and the social ramifications of the pieces, the viewer's relationship to these complex pieces has not been carefully considered. To simplify an argument made by Krauss, medium is defined in terms of the relationship between the viewer and the object.[4] This chapter argues that viewers engage with these site-specific works of installation art by reading them. The work gets viewers interested in the way they read and the way they make sense of the material world, asking them to pay attention to syntax, as in a photographic sequence, and to reflect on the way meaning is produced by the way things are framed and arranged. These arrangements have social and political ramifications. Green's work is an example of installation art that positions the viewer as a critical reader who must decode the meaning of images and objects within their context.

The memory showcased in the installation art of this sort is a materialized form of memory, bound to objects, documents, and photographic images. The installations are designed and the images arranged to engage the viewer in this critical reflection on photography, history, and memory. Green's works might be seen as engaging in the politics of representation, or perhaps the representation of a certain kind of politics. In her work, photographic practices and their ways of framing the world and producing orders of meaning form the underlying structure of the installations and the films.

Green's works tend to persist in various forms after their initial exhibition, and hence, there is less emphasis on the importance of the documentation of her work. Instead, *Partially Buried in Three Parts* begins with questions about the documentation of a site-specific work: Robert Smithson's *Partially Buried.* As the narrator says in the videotape *Partially Buried Continued,* "She wanted to probe the force of photographs and the ways they were bound to the specificity of time, light, and materiality, yet were more than that." This means too that, rather than being positioned outside the installation in a photographic archive that documents the installation, Green's work contains a photographic archive.

The art historian Benjamin Buchloh has examined photographic archives, comparing pre–World War II examples of artistic photographic archives to those that were made after the war. Using the examples of Aby Warburg and Dada artists, and those associated with the Russian avant-garde, he claims that these prewar examples were based on the avant-garde principle of collage, montage, and shock. The juxtaposition of images from different contexts produces an estranging effect for viewers, causing them to see the images in a new way. Postwar photographic practice, by contrast, is based on an archival and serial structure. This format has its origins in a counter-model that developed in the 1920s in Europe. "It was photography's ability to record serially and to present contextual and contingent information. In other words, photography could not only reproduce an almost unlimited number of individuals and objects, but, in addition, could convey an infinite number of different aspects of the same subject."[5] The archive format represented a belief in the truth of the photographic image that the collage format had, by contrast, invited the viewer to question.

The postwar format was a response to consumer culture and had a tendency toward anti-aestheticism. Buchloh uses as his examples Marcel Broodthaers, Gerhard Richter, and especially, Bernd and Hilla Becher. Each artist's work as archive reveals something different. For Richter, it is the rise of consumer culture in conjunction with the proliferation of photographs produced by both professionals and amateurs. In the Bechers' work, it is the sense of melancholy attached to the decline of industrialization, which at the same time suppresses the connection between industry and the Holocaust, the bomb, and other historical traumas. For Broodthaers's archives, it is the memory of myths and the revival of a kind of historical consciousness.[6] Based on a serial structure, these collections are uninflected, straightforward presentations of material—seemingly offering no clear opinions or referring in any way back to the subjectivity of the artist. Buchloh's argument suggests that these postwar archival practices result in both collective memory and forgetting.

In "An Archival Impulse," Hal Foster argues that a different set of motivations can be found in the work of contemporary artists who use installation as the format of their archives. Foster describes the works of Thomas Hirschhorn, Sam Durant, and Tacita Dean as archival.[7] However, he notes, rather than following a careful and systematic approach to their archival practice as we can see in the postwar work described by Buchloh, these artists are "idiosyncratic" and are drawn to unusual moments and failures in history. Or the works can celebrate without irony various unlikely heroes and heroines. These artists, Foster argues, seek to make history "physically present." He also distinguishes these artists from the artists-as-curators and from those who work to critique a totalizing system or even artists who conceive of the archive as a kind of database. Instead, these artists seek to build something new from ruins. Foster distinguishes these artists from those that Buchloh discusses by noting that these artists utilize a sense of affect and involve themselves personally in the narratives that their works address. The artists who do this kind of work are making small alternative archives.

Green, too, is building something from a ruin in *Partially Buried in Three Parts*. Green's work contradicts the historical order that Buchloh proposes in his chapter because the works that she produces utilize both a collage strategy and a serial strategy. Photographs, photographic series, photo archives, films, and digital databases constitute these installations. But Green's works break down the hierarchy of these systems of order. Her installations and online works allow us to see that each photograph and the object are at the meeting place of multiple connections. These objects fall into many categories at once, and it is the viewer's work to discover these categories and connections.

In Green's installations, the viewer is invited to explore the way the meanings of images and objects shift in the context of filmic and photographic sequences and arrangements. The installations are sometimes centered on the individual experience of Renée Green, the African American artist who has a specific identity and history, but they are also simply collections of information. Her memories and experiences are organized indifferently as lists and indexes, but they can also have a narrative structure that guides the viewer's interactions with the materials the artist has gathered. She manages to produce an archive that includes, or at least can be read, as expressing an artistic subjectivity. In this way, her work resembles more that of the artists discussed by Hal Foster, and in fact, both Sam Durant and Tacita Dean, like Green, have made works about the legacy of Robert Smithson. Green's work too can be seen as a kind alternative archive, pointing up a series of connections between people, places, and events that have not been recorded in the history books.

However, Green's work is closer to a database structure — something Foster excludes in his analysis of the archival impulse. New media theorist Lev Manovich has focused on the user interface in his discussion of digital databases, and it provides a way to describe how the viewer interacts with Green's work. The interface between a computer user and the information that the computer contains takes two forms: as a database — a digital archive — and a three-dimensional space that a computer user must navigate.[8] The process of negotiating this space is a linear, potentially narrative structure.

Green's work also operates as both narrative and database. In Green's pieces, syntax is connected to narrative, which becomes the means for exploring complicated collections of information and is the means by which she asks her viewers to be critical readers. Green applies this strategy in the context of her videotapes, which, like her installations, are collections of information, artifacts, and materials as well as stories like the one related at the beginning of this chapter.

Green's work is distinct among archival installations in the way it is concerned with the involvement of the viewer in the process of reading and in the process of research in the piece.

Archives

Renée Green is interested in how information is organized and evaluated in the context of systems of knowledge and memory. This may be because of her background and training: She did not receive a degree in fine arts but rather one in liberal arts and was then trained in the publishing industry. Green attended the School of the Visual Arts in New York but graduated from

Wesleyan University in 1981 and trained as a publishing intern under the auspices of the Radcliffe Institute at Harvard. She then attended the Whitney Independent Study Program in 1989–1990.[9]

Green's work in the 1990s consisted of projects in which she exhibited the research materials she gathered in her travels and work. Green's practice of including reflection on her travels as an artist connects her to other traveling artists who chronicled their trips in various ways, such as Robert Smithson.[10] Green's series and sequences of photographs and slides in her installations and films suggest Robert Smithson's *Incidents of Mirror Travel in the Yucatan.* Smithson traveled to the Yucatan Peninsula in Mexico to several different sites where he placed mirrors in the earth, in sand, and on the trunks of vine-covered trees; took photographs of these pieces; and then dismantled them. We learn of these mirror displacements through a travelogue he wrote to accompany the photographs. These nonsites, as Smithson called them, are able to circulate through art magazines, exhibitions, and catalogs while the site is submerged in the Mexican landscape. Combined with Smithson's text, the photographs point back to something that no longer exists. The text and photographs serve as both an erratic archive and a narrative of the travel. Green's work is similar to this piece in many ways.

Green's *Partially Buried in Three Parts* (1996–1997) explores the way history and memory are constructed in the archival structure in a work that seeks to piece together a vanished period of time, the year 1970. When Robert Smithson had made his site-specific piece *Partially Buried Woodshed* at Kent State University that year, Green's mother began attending a workshop in experimental music at the university. Intrigued by this personal connection to Smithson, the adult Green went back to Kent State to find the remains of the woodshed and to discover any other connections she may have forgotten. Her access to this time period comes in the form of materials — images, books, stories, objects, and films. These are the materials presented in her installation.

Partially Buried in Three Parts as it appeared at the Fundació Antoni Tàpies in 2000 took up three rooms. The first included Green's photographs and those from the nonfiction book *Kent State* by James Michener, which Green had re-photographed, framed, and hung on the walls. A trio of three lithographs of the philosopher and political activist Angela Davis hung on a third wall, while a poster referring to the work's original exhibition at Pat Hearn

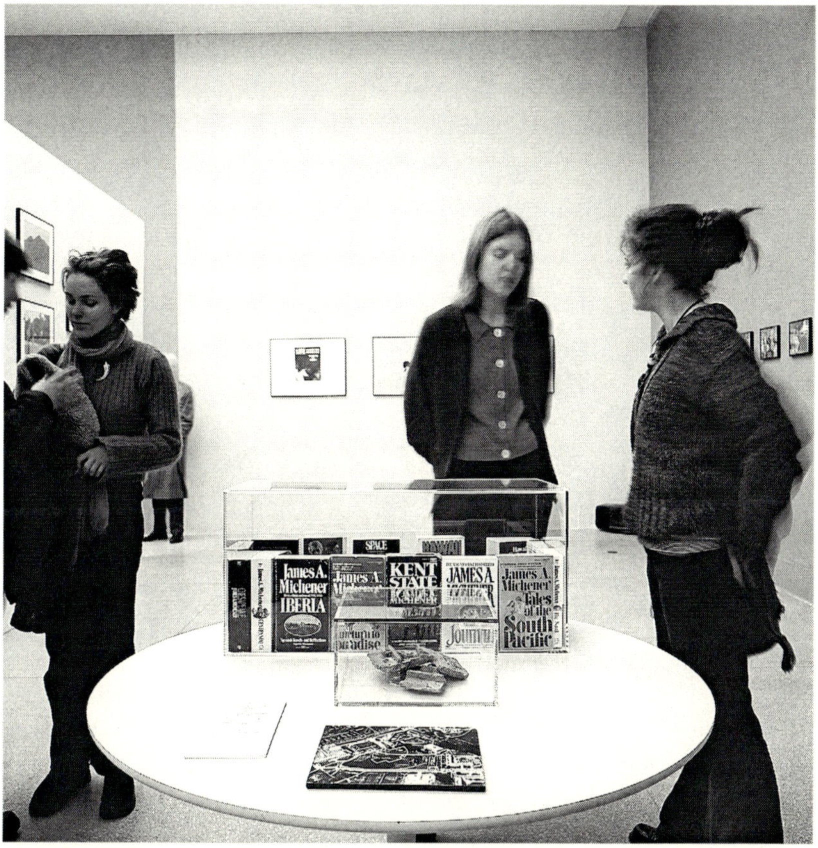

FIGURE 2.1 Renée Green, *Partially Buried in Three Parts*, 1996–1997. Secession, Vienna. Photograph by Matthias Herrmann. *Courtesy of the artist and Free Agent Media.*

Gallery in New York was hung on another. A boom box played music from the 1970s. At the entrance, Green set a table displaying Michener's other fiction books, debris from the woodshed, and an aerial map.

In the second room, Green conjured the atmosphere of the 1970s in the form of a comfortable and fashionable lounging area. The room included a mock-up of the set of the documentary *Underground*, the 1975 film produced by Haskell Wexler, Mary Lampson, and Emile de Antonio about the then fugitive political radicals the Weathermen. An afghan blanket decorated with the phrase "The Future Will Be What the People Struggle to Make It" hung on the wall above a mirror and behind a semicircular, brown velveteen chair. The room also featured period-style, mass-produced, metal tubular chairs and tables, a macramé wall hanging, single-channel video monitors, and a listening station with a record player and a collection of albums from the 1970s.

The order and sequence of objects and images in the installation was significant. The placement of photographs next to one another or books near other objects determined how one read the images and objects. And, as a result, the viewer came to question the order and status of photographs and objects in Green's installations. In the first room of Green's *Partially Buried in Three Parts*, photographs from Michener's book *Kent State* and Green's color images confronted each other on opposite walls. They were an abbreviated version of a photographic archive. Hung in a straight line, the Kent State images were press photographs that appeared in various publications at the time. The straight line suggested a chronological ordering, but Green disrupted the chronological sequence found in the book and changed their order at different exhibition sites. Green's photographs, hung in staggered rows, were all saturated Cibachromes and depicted her at various sites around the campus of Kent State looking for the remains of the woodshed. The pictures were framed elegantly with mats, as fine art prints, in contrast to the unmatted Kent State photographs whose frames cropped the images.

The differences between the photographs seem to point to the difference between their respective time periods and initial functions. Green's prints have the look, hanging, and framing of contemporary fine art images. Intended to be aesthetically appealing, they play the role of "art photographs." The press photographs—gray, grainy, and lacking mats—signal "neutral" documents with all the weight of natural fact and would seem to belong in an archive. The photograph as index is seen to be a product of culture that eludes the distorting effects of the rhetorical intentions of language or art. As Allan Sekula describes it, this perception of the photograph gives it "a primitive core of meaning, devoid of all cultural determination."[11]

Photograph as Fragment in a Series

In *The Archaeology of Knowledge*, Michel Foucault describes the relationship between "document" and "monument." History that is "memory" seeks to be

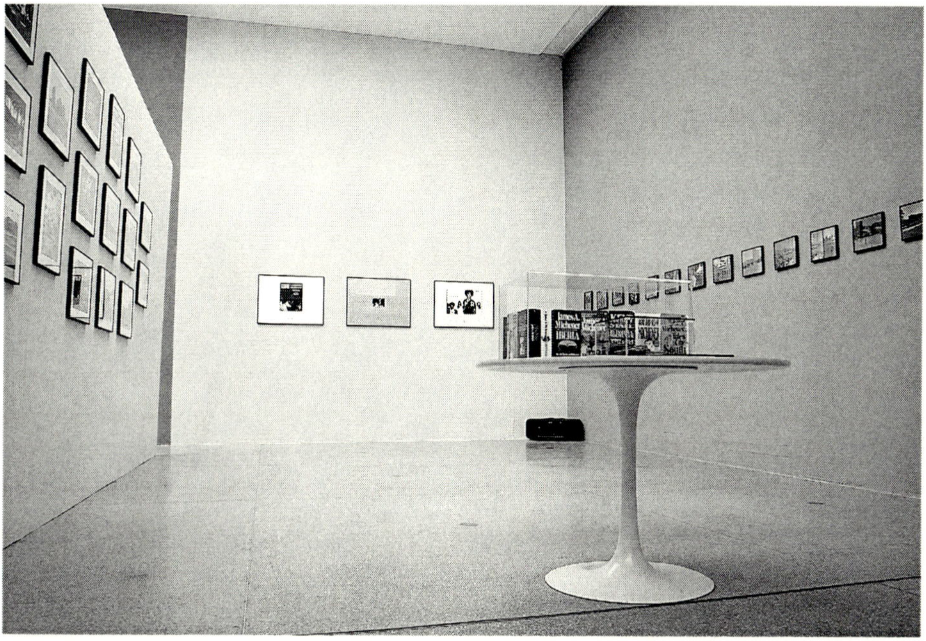

FIGURE 2.2 Renée Green, *Partially Buried in Three Parts*, 1996–1997. Secession, Vienna. Photograph by Matthias Herrmann. *Courtesy of the artist and Free Agent Media.*

straightforward and truthful and to establish continuity from one point in history to the next. This history "undertook to 'memorize' the monuments of the past, transform them into documents, and lend speech to those traces which, in themselves, are often not verbal."[12] In other words, history as memory attempted to connect monuments and artifacts into clear, continuous narratives. Therefore, Foucault implies, in memory, the monuments of the past, which have no moral meaning or educational function in themselves, are enlisted in support of these functions. Archaeology, on the other hand, as a discipline, is able to describe monuments but without placing the objects within a historical narrative or totality. The "document," in this sense, is something that is analyzed, articulated, and dispersed among various categories. Foucault's first definition treats the document as a trace that must be revivified by the historian and then enlisted for the sake of a moral cause or historical account.[13] The second, aligned with archaeology, treats the document as an already dispersed object, analyzed and divided into many different categories.

The photograph can participate in both kinds of historical production in an archive. Green's photographic arrangement can be considered in terms of this relationship between document and memory.

The proliferation of institutions to collect, document, catalog, and preserve objects and information in the nineteenth and twentieth centuries distinguish modern culture from traditional cultures.[14] The photograph was another way to collect information. It served multiple purposes and eluded strict categorization from its earliest days. In early assessments of photography, enthusiasts of the period, such as Oliver Wendell Holmes, exult in the camera's ability to go to places that the viewer may never see in person and to discover images invisible to the naked eye "in the compressed or expanded reaches of clock-time," as the filmmaker and critic Hollis Frampton puts it. One could explore a moment of time as one would explore a space. Photographer-explorers of time such as Eadweard Muybridge took the moment as their field of study. Frampton notes, "In much of its early history still photography might be seen as art trying to purge itself of temporality. The snapshot is an ideal, infinitely thin, wholly static cross section through a four-dimensional solid or tesseract of unimaginable intricacy."[15]

The moment, caught on the surface of a photograph, can be examined like a slide under a microscope. Because of its stilling effect, the photograph is an effective means to explore the complexity of the visual and temporal world. The stillness of the photograph suggests that it is also an agent of death, as Roland Barthes claims in *Camera Lucida*. In this book, Barthes returns to early notions of the photograph where the image is seen almost as a natural deposit that holds a frozen moment of time. Photographs record the closing of each instant, the movement of time. Each photograph, as a "that has been," maps and confirms the structure of time as a series of discrete moments. The photograph represents the modern understanding of time as rational and irreversible.

Photography also presented the possibility of a complete visual record. In the nineteenth century, Oliver Wendell Holmes, bewitched by the power of photography to document, wrote, "There is only one Coliseum or Pantheon . . . but how many millions of potential negatives have they shed — representatives of billions of pictures. . . . Give us a few negatives of a thing worth seeing, taken from different points of view, and that is all we want of it. Pull it down or burn it up, if you please."[16]

Photographs replace the actual site in Holmes's dream. It suggests a possibility of a totalizing structure that can capture every aspect of an object. Photography introduced the possibility of creating world-spanning archives of photographic images that have the same status as other scientific collections. These collections of images, such as photographs of works of art, were to democratize education, its advocates argued, and increase knowledge. They also risked the possibility of producing a collection of meaningless historical details. The development of these technologies of recording and preserving also prompted anxiety—a sense that the materials being saved would be beyond the scope of meaningful memory.[17] The proliferation of photographs in the nineteenth and twentieth centuries demanded a kind of order, which was provided by the archive.

Daguerre's contemporaries grasped photography's potential to aid in the preservation and study of historic monuments. In his report to the Commission of the Chamber of Deputies in 1839, Dominique François Arago spoke of how useful photography would have been during the expedition to Egypt thirty years previously. In Arago's report, it is evident that, even before it was disseminated, photography was a tool in the colonization and study of non-European cultures. In this way, the photograph became another artifact collected in the anthropological, historical, and scientific expeditions of the nineteenth century. Because of their multiple uses, photographs are objects that seem to be already analyzed, articulated, and dispersed among many categories.

The photograph is therefore tied to the archive and the museum collection. It is one of the objects, along with paintings, sculptures, ethnographic materials, books, and buildings, preserved in large-scale projects of the nineteenth century in an effort to guard against the loss of "tradition" and history. During this period of wrenching social and technological change, historical and preservation societies, such as England's National Trust, established in 1895, sprang up in Europe and the United States. Aided by the new recording technology available in the phonograph, the camera, and the movie camera, these societies undertook projects to record and preserve endangered wild places and historical sites, such as those of rapidly transforming Paris.[18] Secondary archival and memory mechanisms of the sociological disciplines and the museum took over the work of individual memory, storytelling, and traditional practices. The photograph was part of a project inspired by a sense of urgency in the face of rapid irreversible changes in this century of increasing "time consciousness."

From the beginning, photography was touted as a type of mnemonic device that produced artifacts. Portrait photography was perceived to be materialized memory.[19] Louis-Jacques Mandé Daguerre, himself, was quite excited by the possibilities of photographs as indestructible and *collectible* fragments of nature: "Everyone, with the aid of the Daguerreotype, will make a view of his castle or country-house: people will form collections of all kinds, which will be the more precious because art cannot imitate their accuracy and perfection of detail; besides, they are unalterable by light."[20] When the photograph is viewed as evidence, as something replete, it gathers all the old connotations of "natural wonder," magic, truth, and fetish, directing attention away from its fundamental lack of what is temporally and spatially beyond the frame. Early on, the photograph was associated with the idea of the fetish as a magical object.[21] This fetishistic quality accords with Benjamin's description of the daguerreotype as a relic. The photographic portrait becomes a fetish because it is perceived as the image of a now-lost person that has been detached and preserved in material form. The photograph stands for an absent presence.

At the same time, artifacts and photographs are always fragments.[22] The photograph and the artifact correspond in the sense that they are both fragments of the milieu from which they have been taken. Barbara Kirshenblatt-Gimblett describes the process of collecting artifacts as one of "defining, segmenting, and detaching" an object from its context. She describes the relationship between artifact and culture as the relationship of part to whole. There is a tangible connection to the culture the artifact comes to represent in the museum collection or display. Both artifacts and photographs, like documents, were collected in archives with ambitions of being totalizing displays of knowledge.

However, the photograph is an object that suppresses its inherent lack. Not only is it an isolated object that fits into your hand, the snapshot, "like death, is an instantaneous abduction of the object out of the world into another world, into another kind of time."[23] Christian Metz goes on to identify this spectral aspect of the photograph with the fetish. The off-frame space is one of "terrifying absence." It is terrifying because it is unframed, uncategorized, and unincorporated into a discourse of knowledge. In anthropological or ethnographic photographs and collections of artifacts, the photographic series is employed for comparison purposes. The series is also employed for the development of a narrative sequence, without which no basis for comparison of the details presents itself to the viewer or any means to establish categories and classifications. In the process of looking at these images, viewers become aware of themselves looking, as the process becomes the conscious effort to construct meaning.

Photography Exhibitions

One of the lessons we have learned about photography is that the arrangement of the images in an exhibition context guides our reading of the images.[24] As an element in a certain discourse, as Allan Sekula has argued in his essay "The Body and the Archive," the image yields the type of information demanded by the logic of the archive or display itself. In Green's simple hanging of photographs of the Kent State shootings in *Partially Buried in Three Parts*, there is an allusion to this history of the way photographs have been used and displayed. The hanging of the black-and-white press photographs of May 4 suggests that the photographs be regarded as evidence—evidence that can be used for creating categories and classifications in the context of a photographic archive. The photographs in Michener's book that hang on the wall in *Partially Buried* function to support Michener's narrative as something that tells the truth.

There has been debate in fine art museums about how photographs should be exhibited. Should these collections of photographs be exhibited as works of fine art or as evidence? In the twentieth century, the Museum of Modern Art in New York has been involved in these battles. One exemplary photography exhibition that uses its images as if they were evidence that tells a story is *The Family of Man*, one in a series of photography exhibitions organized beginning in the 1940s and 1950s by photographer Edward Steichen at the Museum of Modern Art in New York. Steichen's shows treated each print not as an individual artistic object but rather as part of an overall argument or story. For the show, the exhibition designer Paul Rudolph chose to hang large, unframed prints one in front of the other. Sometimes prints were allowed to overlap one another or were hung cheek by jowl, guiding the way viewers read the images. He clustered photographs with similar themes on the walls and even designed a short cone-shaped stand on which photographs were positioned. Mary Ann Staniszewski has even suggested that the hanging was cinematic. The exhibition design was dynamic, guiding viewers into small intimate spaces and inviting them to look at prints on ceilings and near the floor.[25] At the same time, the background colors were muted and neutral, as is typical of modernist exhibition design. *The Family of Man* exhibition format invited viewers not to contemplate each image but rather to scan several images at once and determine the connection between them.

And as conveyed by the exhibition's critics, the theme was the fundamental unity of "mankind" across differences of class, race, and ethnicity, which was reinforced by a narrative structure and even mimicked the design of the illustrated weekly magazines such as *Life*, which were popular in the 1930s and 1940s. As viewers walked through the exhibition, they followed a dramatized story of love, birth, family, work, and death in which conflicts and differences are resolved. Composed of photographs made by not only fine art photographers but also photojournalists and others, the exhibition was based on the notion that photographs tell the truth, as expressed in Steichen's essay at the beginning of the exhibition catalog, in which he describes the exhibition as a kind of mirror "of the essential oneness of mankind throughout the world."[26]

What the viewer is able to read in a photograph is conditioned by culture and history.[27] In his discussion of photographic connotation, Barthes suggests that photographs are evocative because of the way they produce meaning. The frame is an essential part of the production of meaning. Objects depicted in photographs induce the associations but do not signify much in isolation. These rootless fragments can stand for anything. In trying to secure their significance, the viewer seeks connections between the images, moving across the rows of photographs, linking together the fragments. Her instinct is to develop a larger and larger field of comparison, a context, in order to limit the possible field of meanings in the group of photographs. But even at this level, the significance of these fragments is uncertain — and the process of seeing becomes a conscious one of studying and puzzle solving. In the photographs from the Michener novel in *Partially Buried in Three Parts*, the viewer tries to discern the narrative of the events of May 4, 1970.

Green's fine art Cibachromes on the facing wall are part of a different kind of discourse: the photograph as fine art. These images are hung in a traditional museum style so that they can be evaluated in terms of aesthetic criteria. Museum discourse applies various frames to objects in order to abstract them from their original contexts. According to Svetlana Alpers, "The taste for isolating, this kind of attentive looking at crafted objects, is as peculiar to our culture as is the museum as a space or institution where the activity takes place."[28] The isolation of the object parallels the photographic frame. In Alpers's statement, it is the frame of "visual interest." This is part of the "ideology of seeing," to quote Jennifer González, and, unexamined, remains embedded in the communications and workings of the museum.[29]

The treatment of the photograph as an object of fine art was epitomized by many of the photography exhibitions at the Museum of Modern Art by the curator John Szarkowski in the 1960s. Derived from Alexander Dorner's spare, modern installation designs at the Hanover Landesmuseum in the 1920s, Szarkowski's installation design for his exhibitions imparted his opinion about the fine art status of photography.[30] In these exhibitions, the prints were matted, framed, and hung in rows with a liberal amount of space around each. Even photographs that were not originally conceived as fine art, such as Timothy O'Sullivan's photographs from survey expeditions to the West, were hung in the same manner. The hanging invited viewers to attend to the aesthetic quality of each individual print. This was a design that was also typical for the painting galleries in the Museum of Modern Art for many decades.

In Green's hanging, two competing forms of the exhibition and display of photographs are presented: the aesthetic and the nonaesthetic.[31]

In the context of a newspaper or book, the viewer might not pay attention to how the images were framed and lit or to the photographer's choice of subject matter but rather look through them for information. However, as Walter Benjamin noted, every document of history holds a set of hidden social relations that it is necessary to expose. "Denaturalizing" and defetishizing the photograph begins by placing it within its historical context.[32] First, it is necessary to understand that a photograph does not have an intrinsic meaning. Allan Sekula describes the photograph as something that is always snatched up by a motivated discourse. The process of critique proceeds by discovering the historical discourse by which the photograph was snatched and analyzing *its* politics and their manifestation in readings of the image. As work from the 1970s on the problem of documentary photography argued, the documentary photograph underwrites and supports whatever reading is given to it by the discourse into which it is incorporated. The photograph can be analyzed to reveal the *conflicting* discourses that "inscribe" it. But this type of analysis can take place only after the truth value of the photograph has been called into question.

Green's hanging of photographs asks us to engage in this type of inquiry. It alludes to the way the notion of "document" has been complicated since the 1970s, and we can see a similar tendency in the use of photographs by other artists such as Mark Dion, Fred Wilson, and Matthew Buckingham. In Green's installation, it is obvious that the viewer is removed, by many layers of material, from the original event represented, as well as the original context of the recording. This naturally leads the viewer to question the story being told by this sequence of images of the events leading up to the Kent State shootings. This critical awareness is encouraged throughout the various elements of *Partially Buried in Three Parts*.

This form of inquiry about the past is made possible by the materialization of memory in the form of photographs and recordings. In *Partially Buried in Three Parts*, the framed photographs and fragments from Robert Smithson's woodshed allude to a history and culture of preservation and recording. The objects and images are materialized memory. All of the materials in the installation and the artist's memory are threaded through objects that have been mass produced or reproduced by these recording technologies. The representation of time has altered since those salvage projects were begun in the nineteenth century. Green's work perhaps helps to deal with the anxiety of a culture that tries to save so much of the past.

> The present epoch will perhaps be above all the epoch of space. We are in the epoch of simultaneity: we are in the epoch of juxtaposition, the epoch of near and far, of the side-by-side, of the dispersed. We are at a moment, I believe, when our experience of the world is less that of a long life developing through time than that of a network that connects points and intersects with its own skein.[33]

It is the twentieth-century version of these same recording technologies that have provided the materials for Green's installation but also connect to the childhood memory in the work. These images, incidents, and objects are part of a network. This quotation from Foucault is also suggestive in terms of Green's work on particular sites. The artist's assemblage of a material archive connects sites as disparate as Korea and Ohio in both time and space. These sites have been connected in a network through these objects, materials, and photographs. For instance, the music played by neighboring kids belongs to the general category of 1970s popular music. And each record in itself is only one of a vast collection of identical *Jackson 5* and *Sly Stone* vinyl records that have been produced. The music also refers to a genre of "American pop music," which has its own history and cultural connotations in the United States in the 1970s. The record is also connected to a vast marketing industry that promotes music from the 1970s as nostalgia. A single object, such as a vinyl LP, pressed in 1970, is a complex historical object located in a network of relationships.

Green has stated that her interest in recording devices was inspired by her father, who worked in electronic engineering and was also an avid photographer. As a young child, she began taking photographs with an Instamatic camera and recording sound with an Aiwa reel-to-reel tape recorder. These interests are reflected in the connection between the materials in *Partially Buried* and the personal memory that is related.[34] The TV news of the shootings at Kent State connects to newspaper and television accounts across the country of the events, which in turn informed James Michener's narrative in the book *Kent State*. These accounts have now become recordings, video and film tapes, and archival material. The broadcast images are now part of a series of images shot by camerapersons and photographers at Kent State. These snapshots belong to a series of identical reproductions in papers and books around the world.

In the video *Partially Buried Continued*, Green underlines the fact that these images have been reproduced in a variety of contexts by filming a slide as it is projected on the living-room wall. It also occurs in Green's filming of hands flipping through books with photographs or in the frequent panning over photographs. In this way, by using this collage structure, Green questions the authority of the original context and discourse in which the image was placed by showing that the image can be placed in several categories at once: representation, documentation, art, history, nostalgia, mass-media images, and personal memory.

Archival Art

Archival installations could be said to fall out of the photo conceptual practices of individuals such as Hollis Frampton and Sol LeWitt in the 1960s, as well as the work of Marcel Broodthaers, whose Musée d'art moderne de la ville is usually cited as an early example of archival work that questions the assumptions and precepts of the museum. These strategies have been particularly useful for artists who are interested in questioning how we understand memory and how history is produced. For artists of color or of ethnicities whose histories have been distorted, suppressed, or exploited, these are important practices, as Jennifer González has cogently demonstrated.[35]

Some works of this sort question categories and hierarchies produced in various disciplines—from anthropology to history. Fred Wilson's most critically discussed work *Mining the Museum* in 1992 at the Maryland Historical Society is the quintessential example. The work in that exhibition was to bring to the surface an African American history that was conspicuously absent in the museum prior to Wilson's arrival. At the Seattle Art Museum, for the exhibition *Mixed Metaphors*, he performed another kind of intervention in the Egyptian section of the museum. In a small, vertical wall-mounted display case, Wilson exhibited an arrangement of traditional African headrests. The arrangement conforms to the expected format of an ethnographic display where many examples are housed in a glass case for comparison.[36] Because the forms of the headrests are all very similar, Wilson was able to compose an arrangement based on repetition and variation within a square format. He surrounds a large, bright alabaster headrest with four dark, wooden ones. These shifting categories based on form create a unity of repetition and difference. The shapes form a unified, abstract composition. The stated purpose of the display is to demonstrate the mutual influence of styles of headrests in the continent of Africa, including the culture in Egypt of which the alabaster headrest is an example. The categories and meanings that are highlighted in Wilson's work raise questions about how institutions organize knowledge and objects.

Mark Dion's work is also an archival practice that is research based and focuses on specific sites, their histories, and their ecologies. In *New England Digs* (2001), Dion and a group of volunteers dug at three different sites near Brockton and New Bedford, Massachusetts, and Providence, Rhode Island. The resulting materials, ranging from buttons to antique marbles, were then displayed in wooden cases—according to not a scientific classification but other criteria instead, such as color or material. Like Wilson and Green, Dion encourages his viewers to question the systems of knowledge and ordering by which he or any other institution or authority might frame objects. He takes as his inspiration the cabinet of curiosity and the notion of the dilettante or amateur scientist. Karsten Bott's work *One of Each* (1993) comes from his *Archive of Contemporary History*—an ongoing project whereby he collects everyday objects, cataloging and storing them—and is another form of archival installation. This is a project that because of its overwhelming scale essentially renders the effort to collect, categorize, and classify meaningless. He brings out specific parts of the collection for exhibitions, organizing the objects in various ways. David Bunn makes pieces using the discarded card catalog of the Los Angeles Public Library. The work consists of found language and poetry, produced by arranging the cards to make sentences or bits of verse. In this work, sequence and syntax are literally the structure of the work because the material derives from a system of categorization.

The Center for Land Use Interpretation (CLUI) based in Los Angeles gathers and displays information about certain aspects of land use in the United States and other countries. Their project *Urban Crude: The Oil Fields of the Los Angeles Basin* is a tour of active oil fields in the city of Los Angeles. The project provides maps and photographs with captions that give information about these sites. The project currently has a website but also existed as an exhibit. The work of the CLUI is archival and based on the display of information, but the overall goal of the group is to interpret and give a historical context to the interventions in the land. The group's work epitomizes an archival installation practice.

The second type of installation practice I call photographic installation, and it often includes still photographs installed in an exhibition space in a manner that encourages reflection on how images and language acquire meaning. They use the strategies of position, juxtaposition, and shock, as in avant-garde collage. Like archival installations, these works are sometimes site specific or site focused, but unlike archival installations, which have a flexibility of form, photographic installations are sensitive to the manner in which they are hung and the sequence in which each individual image is seen. These works ultimately have their origin in the photo practices of artists such as John Baldessari with his work from the *Rooms* exhibition or of Hans Haacke with his work *Shapolsky et al*, which was to be displayed at the Guggenheim Museum in 1971. These installations of photographs focus on the series and sequence of photographic images and the ideological function of captions. They tend to use the conceptual practice of combining image and text, using the sequence of images to produce meaning.

This category could include the work of Adrian Piper, Louise Lawler, and even Cindy Sherman in the Artists Space exhibition in 1978. Piper and Lawler continue to make work that responds to the literal and figurative context of photographic display. Lawler has made subsequent works that responded to the context, asking the viewer to think about the meaning of the images and the objects displayed in the images. In 1982, at Metro Pictures, for instance, Lawler put together an exhibition of artists who were all part of Metro Pictures. She then titled the installation *Arranged by Louise Lawler*, making the installation her own work. In a doubling of the activity of the gallery, Lawler calls into question the gallery's choices and exclusions. Another different manifestation of this might be Barbara Kruger's room-sized installations of images and text at Mary Boone Gallery. In that installation, which took place in three different exhibitions between 1989 and the early 1990s, the walls were covered with text and images that the viewer was expected to read. Kruger's work in this project produced an installation that one could literally read but that also responded to a certain extent to the viewer's position in the room.

Another group includes works that place photographs and text in a narrative or linear sequence. Carrie Mae Weems's *From Here I Saw What Happened and I Cried* (1995–1996) is an installation of thirty-three archival photographs, tinted red, depicting men and women of African descent framed in black, round frames. Each image has a text commenting on the image or the experience of the individual in the photograph. Some are slaves or victims of lynching, and others are musicians and writers. The text and images respond to each other and must be read in a sequence. The rhetorical and emotional power of the work comes from the order in which the images are read. This piece works to undo the objectifying aspect of these pictures of people of African descent.

Douglas Blau's works comprise archives of reproductions of paintings, photographs, and other kinds of images. In these works, Blau knits together a story based on the categorization of a group of images. The images are small and hung cheek by jowl in a manner to get the viewer to read from one image to the next. His work is similar in many ways to both Green's installations and some of Fred Wilson's, such as a series developed from the photo archives of the American Jewish Joint Distribution Committee (JJDC) in New York in 1999 for the exhibition *To the Rescue: Eight Artists in an Archive*. The archive photographs of *H* RR *R and H* PE were taken to record the history of the JJDC in action around the world. Wilson chose a series of images and covered them with matte board, leaving only a small portion of them visible. In the remainder of the sixty images, Wilson denies the viewer the context of the fragment. The photographs are arranged on three walls in grids of 4 by 5 inch matted and framed images. Only small segments of each photograph are revealed in slits and squares. The structure of the project is an invitation to the viewer to make sense of a series of fragments. Photographic installations of this sort are about making sense of a group of visual fragments.

Matthew Buckingham's *The Six Grandfathers, Paha Sapa, in the Year 502,002* C.E. takes the form of a timeline focused on the Mt. Rushmore monument in South Dakota. The timeline extends into the prehistoric past and far into the future, when the famous presidential faces have eroded from the rock. Across the timeline, the viewer learns of the political deception played on the Native Americans and the social context of the monument. It ends with a "photograph" of the eroded monument five hundred thousand years in the future. The timeline raises questions about the history of the monument by framing it in a different way, especially in the context of Native American history. Each of these artists and collectives uses an archival strategy to raise questions about how information is produced, how history is written, and how subaltern identities are framed and positioned within contemporary culture.

The Serial and Syntactical Structure of Green's Work

In addition to the Kent State photos, the first room of *Partially Buried in Three Parts* included a trio of lithographs of the philosopher and political activist Angela Davis. The first lithograph is the cover of a 1970 *Life* magazine, which featured her involvement with the Black Panthers. The photograph catches her in a moment in court when her head is slightly bowed, and her eyes are cast downward, as if she is contrite. She sports her "natural" hairstyle, which indicates her commitment to black radical politics. The caption reads "The Making of a Fugitive: Wanted by the FBI — Angela Davis." The photograph and the caption seem to promise a girl-gone-wrong magazine story. But the next lithograph of the series juxtaposes an image of Davis in a classical-style portrait with the Marxist philosopher Theodor Adorno with whom she studied in Germany. Davis's image in this context connotes not "young regretful outlaw" but an intellectual whose political position is supported by a history of radical political philosophy. In the final lithograph, however, Davis's image has dropped out, and what remains is the hairstyle. It is a 1990s fashion advertisement with the words "Afro Power," which features young models with the same hairstyle. The notion of outlaw and radicalism is being used to sell clothing. The image has ossified into pure connotation. As critics such as Brian Wallis have noted, the lithographs seem to tell a story of decline. Roland Barthes demonstrated that cultural connotations and codes supplied by TV shows and the mass media colonize photographs so that the image becomes a collection of cultural signs. The specificity and urgency of the historical moment when the shutter clicked is replaced by something else.

In the context of Green's installation, however, as can be seen in Green's other arrangements of images, the trio of lithographs connected to Angela Davis need not be read in one direction as a narrative of tragic decline into hollow connotation. We can read the order in reverse, from the advertising image of the "natural" hairstyle to the original context for that connotation, which is the life and activism of Angela Davis. For, in fact, when read in this way, the connotation that accrues to the hairstyle in the 1990s ad, as hip, edgy, and defiant, spins the original reading of the *Life* magazine image of Davis as defeated and on the run. A sense of Davis as a historic heroine is reawakened. The piece suggests that neither the affective and associative aspects of these images — the historical — nor their structural relationships should take precedence in our consideration of them. The lithographs form a series that can be read in either direction, and the sequence allows us to see that the images that can fall into many categories at once.

The nonhierarchical and serial nature of Green's work recalls the structure of a Minimalist or conceptual work of art, based on a series of units, which Robert Morris describes in "Notes on Sculpture" as "sets, series, modules, and simple systems."[37] Donald Judd favored the compositional strategy of the repetition of identical units because it was a means of avoiding work based on subjective choices or the balance of separate parts. Green has also mentioned her interest in Sol LeWitt's method of producing works by objective logical systems. But unlike the Minimalist cube, Green's unit, the photograph

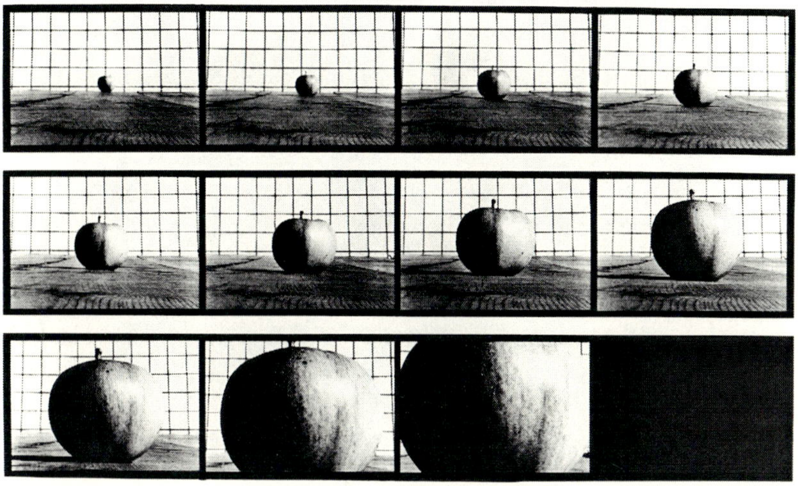

FIGURE 2.3 Marion Faller (1941–) and Hollis Frampton (1936–1984), *# 782 Apple Advancing [var. "Northern Spy"]*, from *Sixteen Studies from Vegetable Locomotion*, 1975. Gelatin silver print, 7⅛ in. x 12$^{7}/_{16}$ (18.1 cm x 31.59 cm). *Gift of Frank Stella (PA 1954). Black-and-white photograph © Marion Faller. Addison Gallery of American Art, Phillips Academy, Andover, Massachusetts, 1990.52.16.*

or the frame of film, has historical or narrative content and is shot through with associations. It is illusionistic, as Hollis Frampton would say.

Frampton's photographic practice also shares the basic structure of a Minimalist work of art. Frampton turned to photography and pop art in the 1960s in the midst of abstract, anti-illusionist art, because they "harbored illusionism, language, and explorations of visual syntax and humor."[38] Frampton made series of photographs employing a modular format in his Eadweard Muybridge–influenced photography. His series, however, such as *Sixteen Studies from Vegetable Locomotion* from 1975, with titles such as *Squashes Vacillating* or *Mature Radishes Bathing*, were actually funny.

A similar project from the early 1970s, *A Visitation of Insomnia* was a series of photographs taken of a nude woman arriving, performing exercises, and leaving. The series was divided into twenty-four sections, the same number of frames in one second of film. Frampton's image lightens the seriousness of these images, which in their nineteenth-century context demonstrated the triumph of rational constructions of time.

The serial structure and interest in numerical and alphabetical order recurs in Frampton's films. Frampton made the single image a unit in a structure whose order is established by the relationships between the images of his films and the structure of the film itself. Frampton was interested in producing a photographic/filmic project as extensive and encyclopedic as the world. His ambition is reminiscent of Oliver Wendell Holmes's dreams of a totalizing photographic archive. Frampton tried to realize his idea of an infinite cinema in his epic thirty-six-hour film *Magellan*. Nora Alter points to the fact that Green in her videos also seems to have the goal of producing a total cinema. Green quotes Frampton in several places in her work, and she showed his film *Nostalgia* in the film series she organized for the exhibition *Between and Including* in 1999 in Vienna.

Frampton the filmmaker conceived of his films as fragments or as a vocabulary of images organized, like Sol LeWitt's work, according to random sequences and series based on different categories. He also conceived of his films as archives of images but organized in playful and arbitrary orders. In Hollis Frampton's 1971 film *Nostalgia*, the camera focuses on a burner on which a photograph is placed and reduced to cinders. As the photograph burns, a voice describes a scene that the viewer cannot see, relating interesting anecdotes about it. As the film continues, the viewer realizes that the narrator is describing photographs — not the photograph that is burning but rather the next photograph in the series to be burned.[39] Important information and stories about the circumstances of the shot are being related before viewers can even see the image, prompting them, once they see the image, to scramble to remember what the narrator said about it as it disappears. These images are photographs taken by Hollis Frampton before he became a filmmaker. Frampton destroys his photographic archive to produce a filmic one, while at the same time pointing to the gap between experience and representation, and photograph and memory.

Journeys through Archives: *Some Chance Operations*

> She tries to remain calm in the face of the disorder of the project. Reading film encyclopedias and surviving film stills, she also reads about alphabets, as a memory device and order, A–Z over and over, 26 locations to store everything.
>
> — *Some Chance Operations*

Mary Ann Doane describes film as an archive. "In it," she writes, "images are stored, time itself is stored."[40] Considering Green's videos as a sort of filmic archive reveals a key connection between her installations and videos. Both involve identification with a protagonist and the practice of walking. The protagonist acts as the point of connection between the viewer and the complex archival structure of the film, represented in *Some Chance Operations* by the complexity of the city of Naples. In the video *Some Chance Operations*, the filmmaker seems to be searching for order in the midst of an ever-expanding cache of images and anecdotes. The pretext for the film was the artist's journey to Naples to uncover memories of the now-forgotten early twentieth-century Neapolitan silent filmmaker Elvira Notari. Green was interested in the ephemerality of film as an archival medium exemplified by the fact that the film scholar Giuliana Bruno was able to uncover only a single complete film by Notari, some scripts, and a few film stills.[41] In her videotape, Green explored the possibility that Neapolitans might remember Notari. *Some Chance Operations* is made of found footage; films shot in Super 8; texts from writers such as Walter Benjamin, Hollis Frampton, and Eduardo Cadava; and interview sequences that tell a story of looking for evidence of Elvira Notari. The film itself utilizes collage and serial structures.

Green creates a protagonist for the viewer to follow through Naples, a Neapolitan woman with red hair named Clara, who takes the place of the filmmaker herself and who navigates the complex space of Naples. Because Green shuns a single, coherent plot line, the viewer is forced to pay attention to the order and sequence of the images, texts, and other information in the film, prompting a desire to rewind the tape and retrace the threads that are lost to memory as the film proceeds. The intricate quality of Green's films rhymes the avant-garde films of other artists, of an older generation, such as Frampton, Chris Marker, and Yvonne Rainer.

Some Chance Operations has both structural elements and image sequences similar to Rainer's *Journeys from Berlin*. Both films were inspired by Walter Benjamin's meditations on memory, artistic production, and political action. *Journeys from Berlin* interweaves the dialogs of three different groups of people: a woman with her psychoanalyst, a couple at home discussing political activism, and an adolescent girl with her diary. The woman (Annette Michelson) with her psychoanalyst recalls her life in disjointed, disconnected phrases and images. At times, her difficult-to-follow recollections are quotations from political writings or poetry. Although the couple's conversation is easy to follow, we can only hear them making meals or drawing baths as they recall the history of radical political action in Europe. As they talk, the camera pans over a typical fireplace mantle of a middle-class home on which rest framed pictures, as well as piles of cold spaghetti, handguns, and pliers. We never see the teenage girl. Instead, she reads her diary entries as the camera films cities and ruins from the air. Each character's dialog is a collage of quotations that is adopted or inserted into a personal situation.[42]

Green's videotape is less fragmented and much shorter than Rainer's film, but both have silent sequences in which only quotations flash on the screen. They both use a variety of film stocks that help create a visual rhythm and collage structure in each film. Both have images of the ruins of Pompeii and interviews — psychoanalytic sessions in *Journeys* — where people are questioned about their experiences and memories, as well as shots of people walking through city streets.

Journeys from Berlin is built around and titled after a quotation in Walter Benjamin's chapter "Surrealism: The Last Snapshot of the European Intelligentsia," which Rainer surreptitiously inserts as part of one of the character's own memories in the film. "[Breton and Nadja are the lovers who convert] everything that we have experienced on mournful railway journeys (railways are beginning to age), on godforsaken Sunday afternoons in the proletarian quarters of great cities, in the first glance through a rain-blurred window of a new apartment, into revolutionary experience, if not action."[43]

The same sense of lonely journeying occurs in Green's *Partially Buried* and *Partially Buried Continued*. A body walks the streets of these cities. In sequences produced in neighborhoods in Cleveland and the streets of Seoul and Kwangju, the camera acts as an eye filming the streets, electric signs, and buildings. This body must read the space and make sense of it. In an opening sequence in the film *Some Chance Operations* (1999), the narrator speaking on behalf of "the filmmaker" explains,

> She'd read a book called *Streetwalking on a Ruined Map* about Elvira Notari and her city films. The title reminded her of her own walks and circuitous searches in different cities. The ruined map made her think of places she'd tried to visit where the map no longer coincided to the locations in the present. She'd spent time walking daily in a crumbling European seaside city

> searching for old maps of travel routes and for places reconfigured many times before she'd arrived. . . . Her voyage became symbolic, a quirky meditation among tourists. The distance between the times and locations always seemed in excess of her goals. The goals themselves seemed arbitrary, erratic. Based on chance.[44]

Although the film has a disconnected structure, the protagonist is the thread that wends its way through *Some Chance Operations*. As she walks through the streets of Naples, each of her encounters flashes on the screen in the form of images. In both *Journeys from Berlin* and *Some Chance Operations*, the viewer is invited to identify with a protagonist as a way of navigating through the proliferation of random images, quotations, and sounds. Green describes herself as an "avid pedestrian."[45] Walking forms a significant part of her research process, and its documentation in the form of photographs and videotapes appears in many of Green's installations. These range from *Import/Export Funk Office*, which includes a video of the streets of Manhattan at night, to the film *Some Chance Operations*. The documentation of Green's wandering in videos and photographs depicts the artist walking and sometimes filming the streets of cities in Europe and Asia from moving cars.

Green's videos, which trace journeys through various localities, recall another archival film: Soviet filmmaker Dziga Vertov's 1928 *Man with a Movie Camera*. In this film, the protagonist films various things while wandering in Odessa, Russia. According to Lev Manovich, "Its subject is the filmmaker's struggle to reveal (social) structure among the multitude of observed phenomena. Its project is a brave attempt at an empirical epistemology that has but one tool—perception."[46] Vertov gathered archival material of life in this city with his movie camera and assembled it to produce the film. This film is an archive, but it also tells the story of its own making, including sequences depicting Vertov's partner, Elizaveta Svilova, sorting and editing reels of film that will be used in the final cut. Manovich points to this as an example of a film that is at the intersection of the database and the narrative film.

Green's videos are similarly complex and self-reflexive. The filmmaker-artist is one of the protagonists with whom we, as viewers, are invited to identify as we watch the film. There are three characters in this film that guide the viewer. The visible character, the filmmaker's double, Clara, is the figure we follow through the streets. The camera assumes Clara's point of view, taking in random shots of street life in Naples: crowds, the marble *Galleria*, the port, and the fish market, as she/the camera moves through the city. We are also made aware of the filmmaker, who one assumes to be behind the camera and whose experiences conceiving and making the film a male narrator relates.

In Green's installation work, the viewer also encounters the installation by strolling and reading, and this relationship of viewer to installation is figured in her films by the wandering and searching of the protagonist. In Green's videos, it is the body moving through the streets that links the films to the installations. The movement of Clara's body through the streets also signifies the process of navigating through a collection of information. This is the same process that the artist performed in producing her archive-like installations. The protagonist in the film connects the filmmaker-artist and the viewer who moves her body around and reads in Green's archival installations.

The Examination of Document, Memory, and History in *Partially Buried Continued*

The final darkened room in *Partially Buried in Three Parts* held video projections of Green's videos *Partially Buried Continued* and *Slides of Korea*. These videos derive from Green's childhood experience of watching her father's slide show of photographs he took in Korea during the Korean War.[47] *Partially Buried Continued* opens with a familiar but now-outmoded private ritual. We hear the whir of a slide projector as the image of a bird flying in a blue sky comes into focus. The slides click and change while a narrator's voice explains the circumstances of this scene. This slide show consists of snapshots that the artist's father took during the Korean War. As a young girl, it was the artist's first encounter with Korea. She has now been invited decades later to make a site-specific work for a biennial there, in the city of Kwangju, and out of curiosity she revisits the images and her father's stories. Along with the familiar sounds of the slide projector, she has recorded her father's voice as he tells the story of his deployment to Korea. We see her father in swim trunks, arms outstretched on a Texas beach. We see the deck of a military ship at sea, streets in downtown Seoul, and the dusty, dry air force base where planes landed to refuel and where the artist's plane lands some forty-odd years later.

The videotape is a travelogue of sorts, composed as a montage, documenting the artist's trip and her encounters with evidence of the past. The video revolves around her father's slide show and a scene where the artist and a young Korean woman look at a book of photographs of a deadly 1980 protest in Kwangju. These sequences are interspersed with historical footage of 1960s protests in Berlin and Paris, still shots of Robert Smithson's and other artists' work in the 1970s, and various scenes of modern-day Kwangju. Throughout, an anonymous narrator tells us of the artist's thoughts about war, memory, and memorials. *Partially Buried in Three Parts* and *Partially Buried Continued* could be read as a way of connecting with public history via private memories. Both the installation and the videotape, as heterotopias, are built around correspondences between different times and places. And the video uses the strategies of collage and serial structure to raise questions about the relationship among these places and the memories of them.

The photograph plays a central role in this work as well. Green was interested in Smithson's *Partially Buried Woodshed* in part because it is a work known through photos.[48] As I suggested at the outset, Green's work is in part a response to questions about the documentation of an earlier site-specific work and its meaning. Later in the sequence of the videotape *Partially Buried Continued*, when the artist looks at the book of images taken during the 1980 protest in Kwangju, the narrator explains her interest in the photograph: "She wanted to probe the force of photographs and the ways they were bound to the specificity of time, light, and materiality, yet were more than that." Because the private ritual of the family slide show is now outmoded, it can be recontextualized within the broader scope of history. And because it was such a widespread format, the slide show can establish connections among different social groups and photographic practices. The slide show is also a kind of small-scale archive, and the way it is showcased in this film demonstrates the ways in which Green's work asks us to question archival structures.

The family slide show in *Partially Buried Continued* provides another example of Green's critical practice in relation to photography and is an example of the use of a serial structure in her work. Green also uses the pleasure of the family slide show to connect with her viewers and to engage them in a process of critical comparison that draws together the production of history, the limits of Green's site-specific art practice, and finally, the production of Green's own artistic subjectivity in her work. In this procedure of comparison, the strict divisions between historical document and personal memory, site and its representation, and autobiography and fiction are broken down.

The images in the slide show, like the other images in *Partially Buried*, belong in many categories at once.

Darsie Alexander notes that the slide show, consisting of individual images shown in sequence, bridges the gap between still photography and film.[49] Slide shows were attractive to artists in the late 1960s because, unlike film, the sequences could be edited at any time. In a slide show, there can always be one more slide. It brings to mind Hollis Frampton's description of the relationship between photographs and film. He writes, "There is nothing in the structural logic of the cinema filmstrip that precludes sequestering any single image. A still photograph is simply an isolated frame taken out of the infinite cinema."[50] At the same time, one could argue that the common format of the photograph connects images taken at any time and any place. The slide show in Green's videotape, then, is a nexus where different images and photographic practices intersect. As the format used in art history slide lectures and classrooms, the slide show is a conceptual "common space" by means of which it is possible to make comparisons.

Slide Show as Memory

At the same time, the family slide show generates a sense of familiarity and even identification among viewers who experienced this format, which is becoming a thing of the past as major photography companies shift to digital cameras and projectors. Kodak decided to cease the manufacture of slide projectors and bulbs in 2004. The slide show now marks a particular moment in history and has become a site charged with personal memory.

The narrator of *Partially Buried Continued* describes in vivid terms how the artist experienced her father's slide show as a child.

> When Korea was first presented to her, it was in the form of still slide colour projections. Her father would say that these were taken during the war. He would describe what was in the image. She would ask the who and where of the images and he would give her an answer. Consecutive still colour images clicked one after another, shining on the screen in a dark living room, her father's voice linking them together, the images, the distant location, the past and present.

As a child, the slide show was the means by which the artist experienced both a strange place and a distant past. The slide show fulfills some of the functions of photography laid out by Dominique François Arago in 1839, but it takes on in the twentieth century the added role of private memory practice. Green said she included the slide show in the videotape because it was so common in middle-class homes in the 1960s and 1970s.[51] This sequence in *Partially Buried Continued* undoubtedly evokes a warm feeling of recognition for many of Green's audience, as a large segment of middle-class families in the twentieth century had been persuaded by Kodak and other photography companies that it was important to preserve their memories in the form of still color slide projections.

When Mr. Green bought his Bosley B2 camera in the 1950s, Kodak was in the midst of a new effort to market color photography in the form of Kodachrome slide film.[52] The introduction of the slide film and the Kodaslide color transparency projector in the 1930s was intended to increase the sales of snapshot photography equipment. Although the equipment itself required little skill, after the war the company aggressively educated its consumers via television ads to photograph the best moments of life, such as exotic travels, hunting trips, personal milestones, and family time.

The luminous colors of the Kodachrome slide were an important part of its appeal. The color connected the images that one made at home to the movie screen, and advertisements where various color processes, such as the Technicolor process in film, had already been introduced. One slide manual from 1962 even holds up cinema as an example to its readers, advising them to make stories from their slide sequences, complete with title shots. The text reads, "Every Hollywood epic has titles and so should your slide stories."[53] In this way, the private experiences and stories of the family slide show were connected to other mass media, such as movies, magazines, and television advertisements, and idealized in the process. But also, the process of composing narratives or storytelling was part of the practice. In this way, the slide show fits in well with Green's other works, which have the same structure of narrative and archive.

Kodak's slide manuals were an important part of this process. The company published them to show customers how to produce good pictures using their products and how to organize a good show. Like the early advocates of photography, the representatives of Kodak felt it necessary to demonstrate the varied uses of the color slide. The manuals seem to provide the technical information for any possible subject that an individual would like to photograph. And the authors emphasize the unique and fresh picture. At the same time, however, these manuals recommend to their readers what is appropriate to photograph. This contributed to the familiar poses and subject matter that populate amateur photographs and prompted Pierre Bourdieu to observe that, to an outsider looking at such pictures, the images depict not uniqueness or individuality but merely social role.[54]

If the family slide show was a way of practicing memory, then it was an idealized form of family memory. The idealization of experience in the family snapshot connects it to nostalgia. The sociologist Fred Davis describes nostalgia as an emotion that "envelopes all that may have been painful or unattractive about the past in a kind of fuzzy, redeeming, benign aura."[55] The family slide show was one of the rituals of modern consumer culture that flourished in the nostalgia produced by the dislocations of modernization. In its marketing, amateur photography both encouraged and satisfied nostalgic longing. Based on the notion of an irretrievable but ideal past, according to Svetlana Boym, the pleasure of nostalgia arises in the sense of identification that it activates.[56] The power of the family snapshot to solidify this sense of connection was well understood by the Kodak Company early in the company's history. But the sense of longing that characterizes nostalgia did not enter into Kodak's advertising until the turn of the twentieth century, according to Nancy Martha West. In her book *Kodak and the Lens of Nostalgia*, West pinpoints a shift in the company's advertising between the 1880s and the First World War. Initially, West argues, Kodak advertised photography as a healthy leisure-time activity. However, after 1900, Kodak began advertising photography as a way to preserve the fleeting experiences of modern life.[57] This marketing approach emerged within the context of a new understanding that the pleasures of a carefree, middle-class childhood are soon over in modern capitalist culture. The photograph becomes the means by which to reconnect with these vanished pleasures. At the same time, according to West, any suggestion of death, such as the nineteenth-century practice of postmortem photography, was expunged from the photograph itself. Death is only implied in the framing of the motivation to photograph. In other words, life is fleeting; take pictures.

West characterizes this evacuation of conflict from the snapshot as an aestheticization of experience and connects it to modern consumer culture. This aspect of the snapshot seems to exclude it from the role of documentary photograph. Transforming memory into something pleasant and easily consumed, the snapshot as nostalgia takes its place instead alongside other consumer goods that were populating private life and leisure time in the twentieth century.

History as Representation

As a means of encountering history then, the family slide show seems problematic because the snapshot is an idealized version of experience conditioned by mass culture. Green's videotape suggests there is something further to discover than what is initially offered by these images and the words that guide our understanding of them. The artist asks herself, what lies between the words and the photos? The notion of the slide show as a "common space" where a dialog can take place is reinforced by the serial structure of the videotape in which times, places, and photographic practices are juxtaposed.

The common space created by Green's use of the slide show provides the critical distance from which to survey the marketing of the slide show itself. Despite the emphasis on variety, uniqueness, and difference, the images in slide manuals of the 1950s and 1960s are quite uniform. The individuals depicted are middle-class white people caught in joyful moments. They could be the inhabitants of any number of advertisements from those decades. And Mr. Green's snapshots look like any number of vacation photographs. He took pictures of Koreans and their houses and monuments, of his friends and associates, and of himself. But in the 1950s, an image of Mr. Green posing with white fellow soldiers, arms entwined, was not yet a marketable image. And as such, it remained in the private realm of the family slide show until it was released in the historical context provided by the younger Green's video. In this context, Mr. Green's private snapshots highlight the exclusions of the ideal images used in marketing amateur snapshot photography in the 1950s.

However, Mr. Green's slides are typical of slide manual photographs in other ways. The narrator in the videotape notes that from the artist's perspective the war seemed to have been incidental in Mr. Green's images. And there is little sense of trauma, violence, or conflict in any of them. Mr. Green recorded only leisure-time images and relatively happy moments — shots of the unit's Korean house boys playing soccer, of the air force base when it is still and empty, or rice paddies on a sunny afternoon. Because these images seem

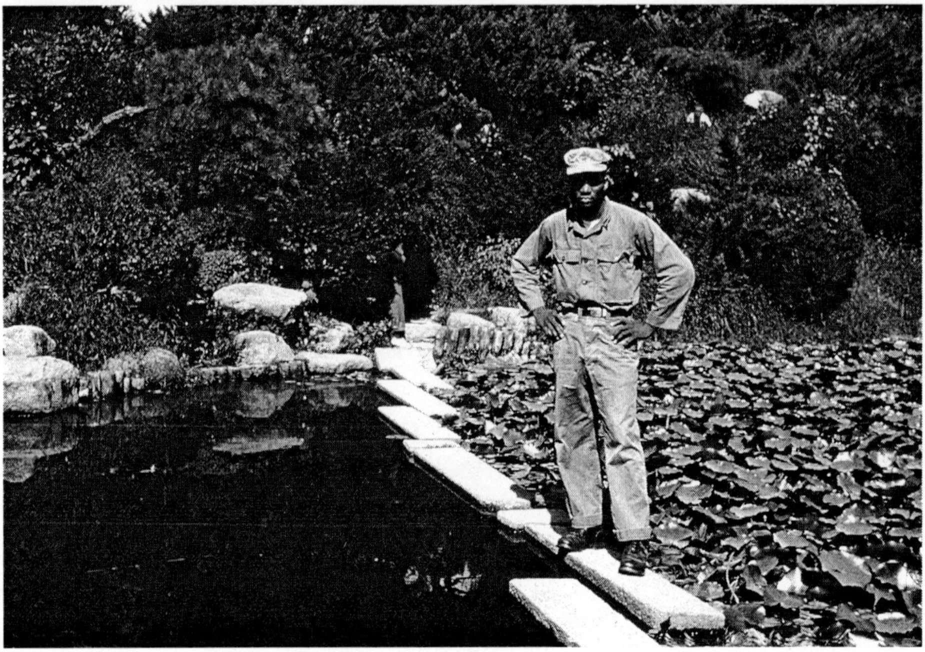

FIGURE 2.4 Renée Green, *Korea Slides*, 1997, still. *Courtesy of the artist and Free Agent Media.*

to be familiar vacation photographs, we even read the shots of bombed-out buildings and a woman squatting among ruins more as tourist photos than war images. The violence of the war seems quieted in Mr. Green's slides, rendering them material for nostalgia.

In the videotape, the family slide show scene mirrors another in which the young Korean woman Hae Sun Kim describes graphic images in a book about the deadly Kwangju protest in 1980. Green included Kim in the film because she remembered the Kwangju killings from childhood, but like the Kent State shootings for the artist, she only knew of the events through photographs. Kim was part of a collective of photographers that was documenting these killings by government soldiers in order to keep memory of the incident alive. In a dialog with the Kwangju documentary photographs via a collage structure, the suppressed historical and violent context of Mr. Green's nostalgic slides resurfaces, revealing their connections to a longer history of political conflict and oppression in Korea.

In describing her efforts to research the traumatic history of the May 18 protests, Kim says something interesting about memory: "The only people who really know what happened on May 18 were there at the time. Those who survived tend to be emotionally subjective rather than objective about what happened. Documenting what happened will take place after uncovering the truth about it." Kim articulates the suspicion that personal memory arouses. What is the status of personal memory in the practice of history? How does one negotiate the gap between memory and document? The same question can be asked of any documentary photograph.

Genealogy

When Renée Green was watching her father's slide show as a child, Robert Smithson also happened to be making his slide works. Darsie Alexander observes that slide projection did not enter art practice until the late 1960s when artists, such as Dan Graham, Marcel Broodthaers, and Robert Barry, began using it as a way of working through the differences among various media and as a tool in conceptual art strategies. Alexander suggests that the inspiration to use slide projection may have come from its use in other parts of an artist's life, such as Robert Smithson and Nancy Holt's salons where fellow artists showed and discussed their work.

Green included in *Partially Buried Continued* an image, a slide work, of Smithson setting up a mirror displacement in a compost heap in Düsseldorf, Germany, in 1969.[58] When asked about the connection between her father's slides and Smithson's slide works, Green said it was not direct. Her interest in Smithson and the history of avant-garde art, she said, is a critical interest. Slide projection, as a bridge between photography and film, allows artists to explore temporality, sequence, and duration. However, Green makes a reference to this practice as outmoded.

For Green in the 1990s, the slide show is the means by which to explore time in the form of history and memory, which crosses both the private and public realms. For this reason, we should regard the inclusion of Smithson's slide work in the videotape, then, not as a reference to Smithson as a privileged artistic precedent who employed the slide show format but rather as one example of many different photographic practices, including Green's father's own practice, that mark the period. The common format of the slide show allows a dialog to be established between the photographs of a white avant-garde artist in the 1960s and a middle-class black father and former soldier from Ohio.

As I noted in the introduction, Craig Owens argued that photography is at the center of Smithson's relationship of site to nonsite.[59] For *Incidents of Mirror Travel in the Yucatan*, Smithson travelled to Mexico in 1969 and placed mirrors in the earth and on the trunks of vine-covered trees, took photographs of these sited arrangements, and then dismantled them.[60] In one image, the mirrors, fixed in the earth, reflect the sky, a literal displacement of sky into earth. Like the mirrors, the photographs frame, crop, and flatten the visual information they hold. The photographs are the displacements of the actual sites. Combined with Smithson's text, the photographs point back to something that no longer exists. The site exists only as representation. In this sense, the connection with Mr. Green's slide show is clear.

The process of mediation is clarified in Smithson's *Hotel Palenque*, which is another set of slides taken with his Instamatic camera during his Mexico trip that he then exhibited as part of a lecture at the University of Utah in 1972. In the lecture, Smithson narrates his photos of a partially built but already decaying hotel. He guides his audience through the rooms of the hotel, marveling at hallways and abandoned swimming pools in the enthusiastic tones of the connoisseur, comparing tile floors and stairways to the work of Jasper Johns and Giovanni Battista Piranesi, and pointing to the incomplete walls and partial stairways as an example of "de-architecturization." In the process, he romanticizes what he describes as the "Mexican temperament."[61] While documenting the hotel, Smithson's lecture critiques art history or the power of any academic discourse to interpret the foreign object and the exotic site. At the same time, Smithson appropriates the Mexican hotel as his own work of North American avant-garde art.

In a certain sense, Mr. Green also treated his photographs as documents. He selected subjects in terms of the types of memories he wanted to preserve, choosing to photograph sites and incidents that, from his perspective as an American soldier in Korea, were unusual or interesting. His slide show also reveals his thorny position as a foreigner who interprets the Korean culture from his limited perspective. He expresses admiration for the history of Korea and the persistence of people in Seoul, but it is his description of the Koreans' reactions to his camera that reveals the complexity of his position as a foreigner or tourist. Sometimes, he notes, Koreans would obligingly pose for him, but other times they would turn their backs or hide because, Mr. Green tells his daughter, "They didn't want you to take pictures of them."

The common format of the slide show as travelogue becomes the means by which we can draw connections between Smithson's work in the late 1960s and Mr. Green's snapshots in the 1950s. Mr. Green's snapshots and his stories are conditioned by both his position as an outsider to Korean culture and the conventional format of the amateur photograph. We see Korea through the filters of personal memory and mass culture in the form of conventional poses and subject matter. In Smithson's slide show, we see the difficulty of documentation, interpretation, and authority exaggerated in his pose as a critic or historian. These connections between the slide shows draw us to the material context, which is Renée Green's videotape produced in the late 1990s. Green uses this format to make a point about her own position as an artist in relation to the site of Kwangju.

Green's videotape was made as part of an invitation to the Kwangju Biennial in 1997. As critics such as Miwon Kwon, James Meyer, and Hal Foster noted, the position of site-specific artists in a global art market is complicated. Asked to participate in exhibitions around the globe and often to produce work that addresses the culture and history of their sites, these artists are placed in the position of interpreters and historians for their art audiences. They are asked to produce knowledge. *Partially Buried Continued* is a response to these difficulties. The narrator alerts us to the artist's problem as foreigner in Korea, like her father's, by noting, "Her status was fragile, relative. She tried to tread softly."

Partially Buried Continued presents itself as documentation of the artist's trip to Korea. The photograph as document is read as a source of knowledge. Green is aware of the authority she assumes when she engages in this practice. However, the videotape uncovers many possible readings of its own material by emphasizing the ambiguity of the photograph in the context of the serial structure Green appropriates via the slide show and by the collage structure produced in her film. In Green's work, visual documents of a deadly protest in the 1980s and photo-conceptual practices of the 1960s are connected to the private memory practices of an African American family. The implicit juxtaposition of these photographic practices and their modes of presentation trouble the boundaries between memory and document. The way the photograph was dispersed among these many categories in the video *Partially Buried Continued* parallels the way they are treated in the installation of protest photographs in the first room of *Partially Buried*.

The tension between the document and the memory is heightened in the juxtaposition of the photographs of the deadly 1980 protest in Kwangju with Mr. Green's snapshots. Described by Hae Sun Kim, the images follow the conventions of photojournalism rather than those of the amateur snapshot. We see them as evidence of a violent event. Placed in a dialog with Mr. Green's Korea slides, it is clear how much is left out of his more nostalgic images. It is also clear that the individual memory and social perspective presented in amateur photography are conditioned by mass media conventions.

But while the subjectivity produced in the photographs is conditioned by the conventions of amateur photography, the stories that accompany them reveal overlooked aspects of these histories. It is Mr. Green's personal stories that illuminate the circumstances of each of the photographs and that draw their connections to an event that belongs to the realm of public history. In these photographs and stories, we as viewers become privy to the personal experience of this historical event. Where Smithson's narration of his *Hotel Palenque* slides emphasized the biased and partial interpretations of his experience of a foreign site, it is the very sort of biased and partial narration in Mr. Green's personal stories that reveal new perspectives in the history of the Korean War.

In this dialectical relationship, the photo document loosens the grip of the subjective identification of its interpreter. As representation in the form of photographs, slides, and stories, memory can be analyzed and critiqued. At the same time, the photograph in the context of the family slide show is permitted to retain its powerful affective and subjective connotations. In this way, the photograph is continuously decoded and recoded in the serial and collage structure of the family slide show and the videotape.

The Photograph as Paradigm for Green's Critical Practice

The ambiguity of the photograph in Green's videotape parallels the ambiguity of the subject in her work. Miwon Kwon criticized site-specific work, such as Green's, for reintroducing the importance of the author-subject: "A nomadic narrative requires the artist as narrator-protagonist."[62] But *Partially Buried*

Continued actually opens up the artist-subject and renders its status indeterminate. Unlike Mr. Green's first-hand accounts, an anonymous narrator with a British accent describes the artist's experiences. Green is careful to distinguish herself from the artist here, finally referred to in the videotape, although the man in the videotape is her father and the personal history referenced is informed by her personal history. The artist in the videotape is a persona that loosely mirrors Green herself, and we are never sure if the mirror image is accurate. Like the subjectivity presented in private snapshots, which is refracted through the conventions of snapshot photography, artistic subjectivity in this work is presented to us as mediated — only in the form of representation. This parallels perhaps Amelia Jones's arguments about the presence of the artist's body in performance art.

The same is true of the photograph. Connected by the common format of the slide show, the images produced by a black soldier in Korea in the 1950s, a white avant-garde artist in the 1960s, a black site-specific artist in the 1990s, and by implication ours are brought together in a dialog with images used in mass culture and knowledge disciplines. In Green's videotape, the private snapshot becomes one among many recording practices. Placed in the montage structure of the video, we see the photograph as document, memory, and fiction.

The slide show sequence in *Partially Buried Continued* is the metaphor for Green's broader critical practice, as we are made aware that we encounter these sites, histories, and subjects only as representations. Using the strategies of collage and serial structures, the video foregrounds the processes by which history is conveyed while drawing our attention to the processes by which site is represented via photographs. The nostalgic pleasure we now derive from the slide show in Green's video enables us as viewers to identify with these pictures and stories and thus engage in a critical reflection on the production and consumption of history and memory.

The Photograph as Link in *Code: Survey*

Green's recent work titled *Code: Survey* demonstrates how the structures of collage and series are used in the context of a digital database to raise questions about the meaning of photographs and other forms of documentation. Green has made other digital archives. The first was for her installation *Import/*

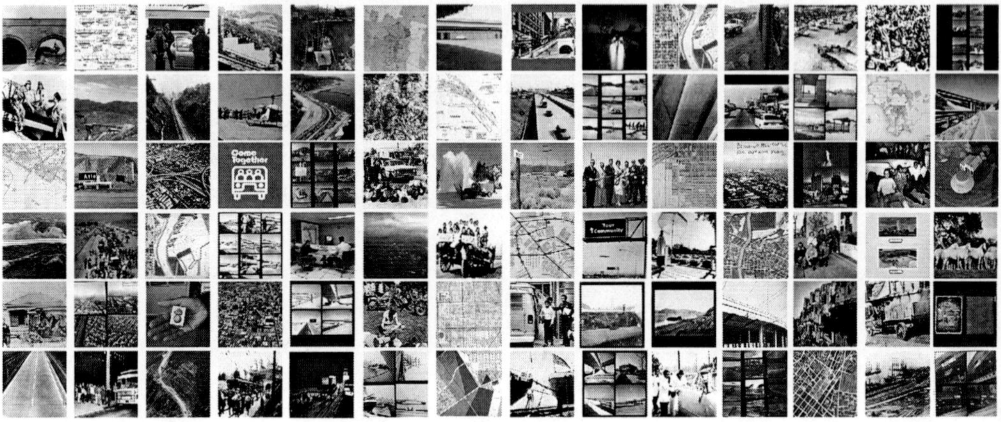

FIGURE 2.5 Renée Green, *Code: Survey*, 2006. *Courtesy of the artist and Free Agent Media.*

Export Funk Office, which was put together while Green was teaching at the Academy of Fine Arts in Vienna. *Code: Survey* (figure 2.5) from 2006 was commissioned by the State of California and takes the form of a collection of images, texts, and recordings of memories and experiences associated with expressways in California.[63]

Code: Survey clarifies that the photograph, in Green's work, is a complex object whose meaning changes based on the words attached to it or the way it is framed by the images that precede and follow it. The piece takes various forms, but it is organized in a grid with each space in the grid bearing an alphanumeric code tied to an image. These separate images are linked to various keywords, which in turn are connected to other images, texts, maps, and recordings. A single image can be attached to various different texts.

For instance, one photograph dating from around 1920 described as "Nettie Perry on a Jenny biplane" shows a black woman standing on the wing of a biplane. The image is accompanied by the tag words "aviation, history, Exodus, flight, movement, travel, women." These words are linked to texts and sound recordings of individuals recalling memories or explaining things, which illuminate one or another aspect of the image: women empowered by freedom of movement, the African Diaspora, the history of airplanes, and so on. The viewer can choose to read all of the texts or follow a different thread of images and texts. While in Green's videotapes and films the protagonist

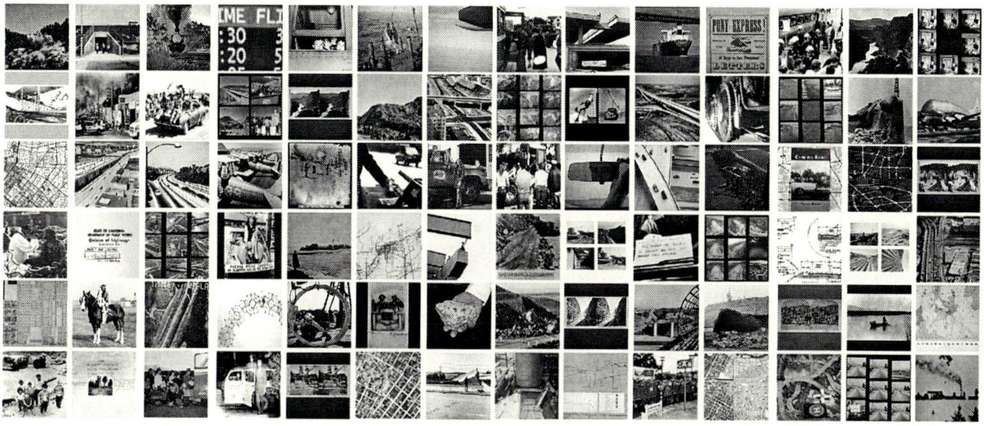

guided the viewer through the various images and texts, in this piece, as in her installations, the artist turns more control over to the viewer.

The title of the piece *Code: Survey* refers to two different activities that take place in the development of an archive of information: surveying and then organizing that information so it can be retrieved again. There are many references to surveillance in the images and texts themselves including aerial photographs of jammed highways and images of control centers where workers monitor traffic patterns on video screens. Although these images speak to the use of surveillance to control the movement of traffic, the term also suggests that photographs viewed as documents, as in an archive or any system of information, have the power to objectify and control the individuals that are its subject matter.

Code: Survey, as described by Green, explores California's romance with the freedom of the road provided by car culture. In reading through these images and texts, the browser discovers that the seeming limitless freedom of movement in our culture has been managed, guided, and curtailed. For instance, images tied to the word "immigration" show the internment of American citizens of Japanese descent during World War II. This image links to a photograph of a Chinese American pilot in the 1930s, a faded postcard of boats anchored in the harbor, and so on. Anchored within series organized in a grid, the photograph's meaning is made more complex. We are given readings and counter-readings of the image based on the relationships established by the archive.

The grid and the series, as the visual analogies for the archive, also emerge as the quintessential structures for organizing information. The grid and the series organize the modern systems of streets, indexes, buildings, maps, graphs, and tables. Rosalind Krauss in her analysis of Eugene Atget's body of work argued that, because his work was organized as an archive, it dispelled the notion that Atget was a kind of fine artist.[64] In conceptual art of the 1960s, rational systems of organization, such as the archive, were used to reduce the artist's expressive contribution to the work. The viewer is invited to figure out the rules of the game, the formula that determined the work's structure in Sol LeWitt's serial sculptures or Hollis Frampton's alphanumerical films.

In Green's works we are also asked, as we move through the installations, to determine the connection between the objects and images, to analyze the stories being told and the way they are being told, as well as to think about those things that are overlooked. If Marcel Broodthaers's or Bernd and Hilla Becher's archives exclude certain material in order to convey a certain message, Green's focuses instead on having the viewer question how the document, the object, or the category is subject to the archival structure. Green's installations position the viewer as reader to question the rules and procedures of the archive.

Installations to Be Read

In the twentieth and twenty-first centuries, the various techniques of mechanical and electronic recording that are available have produced material memory. Green's work starts with memory as materialized in the form of an object to analyze. *Partially Buried in Three Parts* begins with questions about the documentation of a site-specific work and goes on to question how we evaluate documents of history and their relationship to memory.

The archive is the structure that contains this form of materialized memory and many installation artists have employed the structure of the archive in their work. However, Green often uses a narrative structure to lead the viewer into the work. The protagonist in Green's films becomes the person with whom the viewer identifies and follows through the film as archive. In the installations, the viewer becomes a kind of protagonist who sifts through the material of the installation. The viewer find threads that connect the materials — as the art historian Alex Alberro has noted — constructs narratives, and finds discrepancies.

The viewer, in browsing through the installation's materials, mimes Green's own research practice. The viewer is a critical reader who discovers that the significance and meaning of objects in the archives, and the memories and evidence of history in the form of photographs, documents, and objects, can change based on their relationships and arrangements. Green's work uses the structure of collage and series, grid and archive, to invite the viewer to question how meanings are produced from these materials. In that process, the photograph as document is revealed to be an ideological object whose frame guides our reading of it. Green's work is distinct among other kinds of site-specific installations that take the form of archives in that it involves the viewer in the process of reading, interpretation, and the production of history and memory.

THREE

the poetics of experience

ANN HAMILTON'S INSTALLATIONS AND PHOTOGRAPHS

The Picture Is Still

The building sits at the edge of a harbor presided over by submarines and destroyers whose flags wave in the breeze. The only feature that distinguishes this building from the dusty warehouses around it is the Chelsea-style frosted glass door. Pushing open the door, I feel first the relative coolness and darkness of the space. A slight tinkling sound accompanies my movement, as the breeze follows me into the building. It is dark because the ceiling is hung with lines of charcoal sticks dangling parallel to the ground from strings suspended above me. They hang in a thick cloud, causing an immediate sensation of claustrophobia, as my head penetrates the mass. The charcoal is also the source of the chiming sound, as the sticks, rendered crystalline in their transformation to charcoal, strike each other in the breeze.

It is difficult to determine the dimensions of the room because the light from the doors reaches only so far. But despite the gloom, one begins to sense the relative emptiness of this space, an emptiness underscored by a low, watery tone, almost like a whale signal. It echoes from the bare concrete floors and metal walls of two welded, metal tunnels and from the massive I-beams sunk in a trench that cuts across the floor. As they ascend to the ceiling, the I-beams disappear into the mass of charcoal. Once I walk among the strings of charcoal and look up at the ceiling, I realize that what initially seemed quite dense is quite sparse. And as you move through the charcoal, it is almost like walking through a swimming school of fish. The strings reach past my shoulders and the sticks ring as I walk through them. The entire space is not that large; the echoes make it seem much larger than it is.

The trench leads the viewer toward the tunnels. They are massive, made of steel and concrete, and they seem quite old. As I enter the musty right-hand tunnel, I realize the strange watery sound is coming from a video projection on the back wall. In the video, a camera pans over a black-and-white photograph of a person with an open mouth. It scans the contours of the head, mouth, and body. It is difficult to read the picture, and the camera lens, which must be tiny, distorts the image. A whispering voice narrates the camera's discoveries. To be in this space is like being underwater in the hull of a ship or an empty, dry tomb. The strange effect is deliberate. This eerie space, which was located in a small warehouse in the city of Yokosuka, Japan, is Ann Hamilton's installation *the picture is still* from 2001.

I chose this particular installation because it is one of the few by Hamilton that I have experienced first hand. Claire Bishop in her book *Installation Art: A Critical History* writes that installations depend on the viewer's presence in and direct experience of the space. This is true in many cases, but what happens when the majority of people see installation art, as in the works in the previous chapter, in photographs only? Seeing *the picture is still* in situ provides me with the opportunity to compare the first-hand experience of an installation to photographs of it to understand what is lost and what is gained in the photographic documentation of installation art.

Hamilton was invited by Akira Ikeda Gallery to make the installation. This unremarkable space intrigued her because of its notable history. When she first saw the building, which was leased by Akira Ikeda from the Japanese government, it had been fashioned into a regular exhibition space with white walls and concrete floor. She noticed that the welded metal tunnels were visible, rising above the floor, but completely ignored. She decided to inquire about the building's history. During World War II, she was informed, torpedoes were loaded onto ships through the tunnels. Learning this, Hamilton wanted to explore the site's connection to history — not to re-present it but to evoke the gravity of that history. *The picture is still* is one among a group of installations that Hamilton made in the 1990s that engaged with histories of particular sites in various ways. For *the picture is still*, she chose to uncover the original bones of the building and thereby expose the history hidden by the gallery's "white cube" format.

Like Renée Green, Hamilton begins her installations by doing a great deal of research. She knew that Colonel Paul W. Tibbets Jr., the pilot of the plane the *Enola Gay*, which dropped the bomb on Hiroshima, lived in her home town of Columbus, Ohio. Searching for connections to Tibbets, she looked through the photo archives at the Ohio Historical Society for images from World War II. In the process, she was struck by the way the photograph distances the viewer from the moment it depicts.[1]

The German critic Siegfried Kracauer had also noticed the distancing effect of photographs decades earlier. Looking at a portrait photograph, Kracauer described shivering at the reduction of a living person to a conglomeration of immobilized objects.[2] Roland Barthes, looking at photographs of his late mother, would later describe the photograph as "flat death," a concise description of the way the photograph flattens and abstracts that which it depicts but also preserves the moment now lost.[3] The title of Hamilton's installation speaks to the nature of the photograph and its connection to history. It is both *still* and *still here*, while the moment has vanished.[4] For Hamilton, the sense of loss she experienced in looking at the photograph leads to a desire to restore the fullness of that moment in order to understand it. "Something about this became apparent as I looked at more and more photographs — of the war — the atrocities on both sides — we can't understand from the pictures — we can't have that time back. Yet its very history is a constant and invisible presence in our time."[5]

Although Hamilton is writing about history in this quotation, her statement is also an accurate characterization of the tension between installation art that requires the viewer's bodily experience of the work and photographs of the work. For this type of installation art, the photograph is marked by loss. Installation artists who make works in this vein, like Hamilton, regard the viewer's experience of the installation to be of primary importance. The aim of Hamilton's installation work is to break down the distance that remains between viewer and artwork, to engage the viewer through the body and the senses. Photographs of the work, however, reduce the complexity of the bodily experience of it. Hence, photographs present a problem for Hamilton's work because they condition, as we have seen from chapter 1, how a work of art is perceived and understood for both its current and its historical audience. Hamilton's installation *the picture is still* grapples with this problem in the historical experience of war that has been forgotten. Hamilton chose to deal with photographic documentation differently from Green and other artists who work with and make archives and who seek to understand memory and history through these formats. Hamilton's installation tries, instead, to conjure the way the war continues to haunt the present through a corporeal experience.

Another body of Hamilton's work from the late 1990s pinpoints the moment an experience turns into image. To make these pieces, a willing subject must stand before Hamilton, in close proximity to her face, and stare at her mouth for an extended period of time. The artist holds in her mouth a small simple pinhole camera for which she uses her lips as a kind of shutter. The images that are produced look like eyes at the moment they open. The sitter's response to their experience is often plain in the image: discomfort, hilarity, and boredom. These pictures attempt to capture an experience of being in a body in the presence of another body in defiance of the flattening, abstracting, and stilling effect of the photograph. These works explore the tension between experience and image by taking a different route through the image.

Photography and the photographic condition are therefore threaded through Hamilton's work, but there remains a tension between photography and lived experience. Photography is a supplement to Hamilton's work, and for other installation works like Hamilton's, which are interested in various modes of direct bodily experience. These works produce their own supplements in the form of photographic archives and catalogs, which circulate in the networks of the international art market and provide symbolic status. The photographs of these pieces serve as documentation as well as providing an unacknowledged support for these works in an expanding art world. Bodily experience is made the explicit subject matter of this work precisely because it is set off by these photographic images. Hamilton's body of work is one of many that reveal a dialog between picture and experience in installation art. Although these kinds of works do not incorporate photographic archives, in an effort to deal with the ephemerality of these pieces, they inevitably produce such archives through the documentation of the works.

Hamilton's haunting installation of charcoal in *the picture is still* highlights the relationship between image and experience. Hamilton wrote, "For me a central experience is the twining of the collective and horizontal body overhead to the vertical singular shadow image of one's body in the work—this can be documented but is something that when you experience it is central to the structure and meaning of the project."[6]

This is not a new preoccupation for Hamilton but goes back to some of her earliest professional work. Hamilton began her undergraduate education in 1974, at St. Lawrence University, a liberal arts school, but then transferred to Ohio State University and then to the University of Kansas where she trained as a weaver. She graduated with a Master of Fine Arts degree in sculpture from Yale University in 1985.[7] In graduate school, Hamilton began making room-sized sculptural installations characterized by visual distortion. Her first major installation was *room in pursuit of a position* (1983) where cockeyed and fragmented bits of furniture were scattered across the ceiling, floor, and walls of a room. The piece played with viewing positions and perspective.

Hamilton had an interest in photography and the way the photograph renders the body, or parts of it, an object. She used photographs of her own body to create sculptures that rendered her experience of her body uncanny. This relationship between body, object, and image was explored in formal terms in Hamilton's series of studio photographs later called the *body object series*. Hamilton dressed herself with objects such as shoes, branches, or a door. In these images, the object and the artist's body are joined, confusing the division between subject/object, self, and other in the image that results.

In making these images, Hamilton said, she realized she wanted to not represent the experience but instead make the experience be her work. She was encouraged by David von Schlegell in Yale University's sculpture department to look at performance as an addition to her work.[8] Soon after, she made the piece *suitably positioned*, often described as "the toothpick suit." In this piece, Hamilton wore a suit bristling with toothpicks and stood for hours in a doorway. The suit activated the space around her and changed the encounter with other individuals who approached her, as Hamilton did not interact with them but rather offered herself as an object of the viewer's gaze. Joan Simon points out this connection between the *body object series* and *suitably positioned* and Hamilton's later use of performers who also are instructed not to interact with viewers but to behave as if absorbed in their own activities. She soon began making more room-sized installations that involved tremendous amounts of various kinds of material piled on floors and tables, and adhered to walls and other surfaces.

In the late 1980s, Hamilton's installations expanded to include several interacting elements and grew somatically intense. The installation also often included a performer who buried his hand in sand, sanded mirrors, or other simple activities. The environments were richly textured and often visually stark, including single figures or objects in vast fields of material. She also began using the "attendants" in the work. These were volunteers who spent all day performing a manual task, such as knitting or sanding objects in the installation. In the late 1990s, Hamilton's work shifted to pieces in which the viewer was the only human presence. Notably, in 1999, she was chosen as the U.S. representative at the Venice Biennale and constructed *myein*, an elaborate installation of many parts, such as a rack of knotted handkerchiefs in the courtyard and a mottled glass wall. The installation resembled an empty stage set in which pink powder fell from the ceiling in the U.S. Pavilion in Venice and dusted Braille that was embossed on the wall. After this project, Hamilton's work became simpler, relying on single devices, such as *at hand* (2002), where custom-made machines mounted in ceiling beams picked up and dropped papers, which fluttered to the floor, a feature she later repeated for *corpus* at Mass MoCA in North Adams, Massachusetts, in 2003–2004. It was the viewer's experience of these strange but absorbing spaces that became the heart of Hamilton's work. At the same time, she considered the photographs of these spaces to be important but subordinate to this aspect.

Studying Experience

Experience and the related ideas of participation, immersion, and spectacle have been a part of art discourse and of ephemeral artworks, such as installations, since the 1960s. Art writers describe experience as valuable. It is seen as transformative, as invigorating, as something that puts viewers in command of their surroundings and senses. For instance, installation-type work includes and activates viewers' and the artwork's space. As their bodies and the exhibition space are included in the experience of the work, viewers are guided to reflect on the process of perception or experience. In this way, they are put in command of the experience and led to a new understanding of the work of art and their selves.

Experience that contributes to the sense of self and shared experience is the foundation for group identity and community. Since the late eighteenth century undergoing experience has been considered the primary means of constructing the modern self.[9] As an example of this modern sensibility, Craig Ireland points to the late eighteenth-century development of the *Bildungs-*

roman, in which the novel's protagonist undergoes a journey that causes the character to develop. The novel in this sense reflects modern experience. The self in modernity is subject to change and capable of integrating experience as an inherent process of its formation.

The twentieth-century American pragmatist philosopher John Dewey in his book *Art as Experience* used the art encounter as a way to examine experience in general. Dewey described experience as a dynamic interaction between self and environment. He argued that all experiences resemble aesthetic experience insofar as they have a wholeness and integrity setting them off from the ordinary run of events. For Dewey, the subject could never be the same after undergoing an experience. Experience transforms the self.[10] This idea is typical of modernist notions of self-formation. The aesthetic experience, for Dewey, becomes the ideal way to *experience* experience, so to speak, and to participate in the process of self-formation that is necessary to modernity. Hans-Robert Jauss writes, "To experience art is an excellent way in which to experience the alien 'you' in its otherness, and, thereby, in turn to have an enriched experience of one's own 'I.'"[11] Martin Jay argues too that experience leaves changed the sense of self. "That is, an experience, however we define it, cannot simply duplicate the prior reality of the one who undergoes it, leaving him or her precisely as before; something must be altered, something new must happen, to make the term meaningful."[12] In this sense, experience is something that disrupts the horizon of expectation and is thus able to offer new perspectives on old ideas and social practices.

This characterization of experience taken more broadly can be seen as the foundation for social change, and other theorists have based their work on these ideas. Craig Ireland points to E. P. Thompson's appeal to common experience in the formation of a group consciousness (or in Thompson's case, working-class consciousness) as a foundation for political action. Thompson criticized abstract theorizing and turned to everyday experience as a way to resist dominant middle-class culture. His political ideas derived from his work as a historian who examined the history of social and work practices among the English working class. Thompson argued that the difference of working-class experience would provide members of this class the ground from which to question and criticize dominant culture.[13]

One of the points that Craig Ireland makes about E. P. Thompson's appeal to experience is that immediate experience is seen as something that falls outside of language. The body becomes the foundation from which an "outside" of ideology can be formed. The problem with this argument, as Ireland points out, is that it reifies the body, takes it outside of history and culture and naturalizes differences. From this ground an alternative politics and agency can be formed, a stance that has the potential to be liberating or coercive with regard to who can be included in the group and how the characteristics of the group are defined.

Movements including feminism, civil rights, and postcolonial politics have emphasized the importance of the difference in personal experience of the group for defining and articulating community identity and a sense of political agency.[14] Ireland argues that this understanding of experience came to the fore in the 1970s. It informed subaltern politics, such as the feminist movement ("the personal is political") and other cultural phenomena of the 1970s from the "back to the land movement" to the reemergence of handicraft as a form of resistance to industrialized, capitalist culture. At the same time, the appeal to experience in the 1960s and 1970s suggests that experience had become a curious and interesting topic, as if there was no longer certainty about what experience is.

Art as Experience

Perhaps it is because of the uncertainty concerning experience that it has become a prominent aspect of art practice and exhibition since the 1970s. As in the social movements, we can see the notion of experience appearing in feminist art practices in the 1970s where the appeal to personal experience is subject matter for art as well as the means for effecting social change. Discussing and displaying shared experience was a primary strategy in the feminist practices of Suzanne Lacy, Leslie Labowitz, Judy Chicago, and other artists. It is the central tenet as well of more recent community and activist-oriented "new genre public art." It has also been a significant aspect of the group of practices designated "relational aesthetics" as well as installation art, as Claire Bishop argues. Art institutions can provide a unique experience in the form of performances or installation art. Writers in the field of art criticism over the twentieth century have valued some types of experiences in art practice more than others. For instance, in his canonical 1939 essay "Avant-Garde and Kitsch," Clement Greenberg makes the case for valuing aesthetic experience over the experience of everyday life. He argued that fine art must maintain its autonomy from the experiences of a degraded capitalist kitsch culture. In doing so, the aesthetic experience provided by fine art enables criticism of modern culture in general.

Unlike the encounter with an everyday object, the encounter with a modernist painting, according to Greenberg, was a purely visual and instantaneous experience, distinct from any other experience in daily life. Painting, as a visual medium that emphasizes its own material limits, must address itself to the eyes. Michael Fried, Greenberg's protégé, described this experience of modernist painting as "presentness." "Presentness is grace," he wrote famously at the end of his essay 1967 *Artforum* article "Art and Objecthood," underscoring the sense that aesthetic experience in modernist art should be transcendent and specific.

However, in modernist painting, aesthetic experience is visual, and it addresses a disembodied subject. Modernist criticism follows a tradition in Western culture in which vision has been seen as the highest of the senses. Having no direct contact with its object, vision has traditionally been regarded as corresponding to the intellect, reason, or spirit.[15] The idealization of vision filtered into modernist art criticism of the midcentury, which, thus, reinforced the historical hierarchy of the senses. Later critics of modernist art and criticism in the 1960s and 1970s, such as Brian O'Doherty and Minimalist sculptor Robert Morris, describe the modernist aesthetic experience not as transcendent but as lacking. It is an experience in which vision is isolated from the other senses and cut off from the body. O'Doherty, as we have seen, argued that the modernist art gallery is constructed to deny any sense but that of the eye and, in doing so, makes seeing an intellectual activity rather than a holistic organic activity.

In the 1977 essay "The Present Tense of Space" Robert Morris noted that sculpture in the 1960s and 1970s was distinguished by an interest in direct experience that was bound up in spatial and temporal perception. Morris describes the work of artists such as Richard Serra and Robert Irwin as being part of new spatial arts, which are arts of the present tense.[16] The spatial installation-type work also produced new criteria for art in the 1970s. He argues that this work is directed at the subject in the mode of "I," the self caught up in the immediate moment of perception or lived experience. The spatial experience for this subject is infused with a sense of continuous time and is framed by the limits of the body. Morris separates this "I" mode from "me," which is a sense of self that forms in reflection on experience in judgment, in language, or in *memory*. With a typical modernist painting, where the viewer in theory grasps the static object immediately, the distance between the "I" and the "me" mode is quite short. In the new spatial work, Morris says, the distance between one and the other is much greater. The encounter with this type of art, he implies, takes more work. It requires something from the viewer and offers something to the viewer in return, in terms of the richness of the experience. Mary Miss and Suzanne Harris's work also seem to be based on this idea of the importance of direct experience.

For her part, Rosalind Krauss describes the subject that experiences the Minimalist art as differing from the biographical subject. The Minimalist subject is composed of distinct, intense moments of bodily perception that are merely strung together but do not necessarily develop or become integrated. These intense moments of perception could provide the ground for resistance to experience in industrialized culture, as Krauss says, but she warns they also describe the "postmodern" fragmented subject that is the product of late industrialization.

Krauss goes on to draw the connection between experience of the Minimalist object and broader social conditions:

> And thus this is, we could say, compensatory, an act of reparations to a subject whose everyday experience is one of increasing isolation, reification, specialization, a subject who lives under the conditions of advanced industrial culture as an increasingly instrumentalized being. It is to this subject that Minimalism, in an act of resistance to the serializing, stereotyping, and banalizing of commodity production, holds out the promise of some instant of bodily plenitude in a gesture that we recognize as deeply aesthetic.[17]

Mary Ann Doane says something similar about contingency. The contingency of the lived moment represents a kind of freedom in the face of structured and rationalized time in industrial capitalist culture. Other artists in the 1960s expanded the notion of aesthetic experience. Allan Kaprow thought the participants' experience of his environments, Happenings, and activities was central to his work. He studied Dewey, making notes in the margins of *Art as Experience*.[18] He seemed to read Dewey as suggesting that quotidian experience could be aesthetic experience. Kaprow's ritualized activities and environments were intended to focus the participant's attention on the everyday sensation, the simple gesture, and the routine task. As Kaprow wrote in 1958 in "The Legacy of Jackson Pollock," he believed artists of the 1960s would make the viewer

> preoccupied with and even dazzled by the space and objects of our everyday life, either our bodies, clothes, rooms, or, if need be the vastness of Forty-Second Street. . . . Not only will these bold creators show us, as if for the first time, the world we have always had about us but ignored, but they will disclose entirely unheard-of happenings and events, found in garbage cans, police files, hotel lobbies; seen in store windows and on the streets; and sensed in dreams and horrible accidents.[19]

In this article, Kaprow sees the artist as revitalizing the viewer's perception of the everyday world through distinct experiences. Clambering through Kaprow's hot tires on a summer day in *Yard* (1961) or shuffling through the newspapers and chicken wire to choose a fresh or fake apple in *An Apple Shrine* (1960), the viewer, the artist hoped, would rediscover a childlike awareness. For Kaprow, the art experience goes beyond the aesthetic sphere and transforms the viewer's and the artist's everyday experience. Kaprow's description of the subject's transformation of perception rhyme Dewey's notion of experience as a way of shaping the self.

Experience is a term that has been applied, therefore, in many different contexts in American art from the discourse on modernist painting to the reference to phenomenology in minimal art and performance. Claire Bishop's book *Installation Art* continues this discussion by enumerating the varieties of experience produced by installations of various sorts and the viewing subjects they construct. Minimalism, especially Robert Morris's writings, has clearly been influential in these revisions of the notion of aesthetic experience. The influence of Minimalism would also help to transform the nature of exhibition spaces after the 1960s. Rosalind Krauss describes a conversation she had with Thomas Krens about the moment he conceived of Mass MoCA, the grand, transformed industrial space in North Adams, Massachusetts, which showcases installation art. Krens thought of renovating the site for a museum after having seen a large gallery in Germany converted from a factory space. Krauss's anecdote is telling because it says a great deal about the exhibition context for installations in the 1980s, 1990s, and 2000s. According to Krauss, Krens said that the small-scale museum that tells the story of art history was obsolete precisely because of Minimalism's demands on the viewer and the space of the exhibition site, which

> would forego history, in the name of a kind of intensity of experience, an aesthetic charge that is not so much temporal (historical) as it is now radically spatial, the model for which, in Krens's own account, was in fact, Minimalism. It is Minimalism, says Krens in relation to his own revelation, that has reshaped the way we, as late twentieth century viewers, look at art; the demands we now put on it; our need to experience it along with its interaction with the space in which it exists; our need to have a cumulative, serial, crescendo towards the intensity of this experience; our need to have more and at a larger scale.[20]

Krauss's example for this type of exhibition space is a Minimalist exhibition at the Musée d'art moderne de la ville in Paris, in which the redesigned space and the interaction of the works (the light cast from Dan Flavin's light sculptures) with this newly grandiose and neutralized space are central, rather than the works themselves. However, Krauss goes on to connect these sites to a shift in the art market in which museums become like corporate entities. She points to Krens using the term "museum industry," which was perhaps an unfamiliar idea in 1990 but is now commonplace. The industrialization of the museum, she says, will require "the increased control of resources in the form of art objects that can cheaply and efficiently be entered into circulation. Further, in relation to the effective marketing of this product, there will be the requirement of larger and larger surface[s] over which to sell product[s] in order to increase what Krens himself calls 'market share.'"[21] Krauss is referring to the franchising of art institutions, such as the Guggenheim Museum. Installation art has become a dominant medium in these exhibition venues. Art historian Kate Mondloch notes in relation to media-based installations that the audience member who can walk through an installation and "window-shop" can determine the time of viewing, making this one of the appealing aspects of installation for contemporary audiences.[22]

Contemporary Installation Art as the Art of Experience

There are many examples of installations that emphasize viewer's direct experience of the work and are exhibited in these sorts of exhibition venues. In fact, one could argue that, because they focus on direct experience of various sorts, all of the pieces that Claire Bishop discusses in *Installation Art: A Critical History* could be included in this category. Almost any work that focuses on bodily experience, that engages more than the visual sense, or that transforms a space into an immersive environment would participate in this strain of installation art. These are works of art that focus on internal, present-tense experience.

The following short survey of these works falls into three basic categories that crystallize different aspects of experience. The first are installations that focus on immersive materiality and on engaging the viewer's senses of touch, smell, and even taste. These works focus on sensation in the present. Some of these pieces seek to avoid the domination of vision in Western culture and have their roots in works from the 1960s, such as Allan Kaprow's and Hélio Oiticica's. The second category includes works that seek to engage the observer in reflection on the processes of perception, such as sight or sound. These works ultimately derive from the sculptural practices of the 1960s and 1970s related to Minimalism, such as Robert Morris and Richard Serra's large-scale site-specific pieces. A third strain of work focuses on the materiality of objects and their relationship to the human senses to evoke memories and human experience. These works focus on how sensation helps in recollection of the past. The materiality of the work is intended to produce an atmosphere of charged emotion, such as the installations of Joseph Beuys and other artists who use materials symbolically.

One strain of work focusing on the senses and materiality comes out of Latin America in the 1960s. This would include work by Hélio Oiticica and Lygia Clark who emphasized direct bodily engagement with the work. A more recent example would be Ernesto Neto's large-scale, soft, sculptural installations. Originally from Brazil, Neto makes work that draws on the Neo-concretist sculptures of Clark and Oiticica. His work is often composed of soft, stretchy, polyamide polyps, which are hung from the ceiling and then filled with various materials, such as aromatic spices. The sculptures suggest an organic, living body and engage not only the visual sensation but also the sense of touch and smell. One well-known piece titled *Walking in Venus Blue Cave* was an entire room through which viewers could walk, exploring with their hands the fleshy orifices, and feeling the polyps stuffed with Styrofoam, spices, or other materials. Like Hamilton's, Neto's work seeks to immerse and to engage the viewer's senses.

Tara Donovan's sculptural installations could also be included in this category. Although Donovan does not focus on engaging the sense of sound or smell, her installations create a dramatic tactile space by the accumulation of simple materials such as plastic straws or pieces of tar paper (*Transplanted*, 2003). These materials are organized in a repetitive pattern that makes the material appear to be a growing organism. The work often requires a close look before the observer understands the materials being used, and for this reason, they are difficult to photograph. The large-scale works of Anish Kapoor have a similar materiality. Kapoor's pieces are often made of stretched cloth or carefully polished metal walls that create unsettling distortions. It is difficult to understand these works visually. Concave surfaces appear to be convex, while punctures in a wall seem to extend to infinity. In *Past, Present, Future* (2006) exhibited at the Institute of Contemporary Art in Boston, one-quarter of a sphere composed of a waxy, red substance was raked by a circular blade that over time created scars in the perfect circular form. Kapoor's work stages materiality and frames the act of perception on a grand scale.

Another type of installation work derives more directly from Minimalism, especially the large-scale works of the 1970s, such as Robert Morris's maze pieces and Richard Serra's ellipses and arcs. All of these pieces are about the experience of space and sensation in the "present tense." An early example would be the work of James Turrell whose installations make light seem palpable. In a well-known series of works, a viewer enters a gallery to see a large, brightly colored, practically glowing rectangle mounted on the far wall. However, when one approaches the rectangle, the space suddenly drops back, and the viewer realizes that this is an opening into another colorful light-filled chamber. The "mist installations" of Ann Veronica Janssens, such as *Whose Afraid of Blue, Red, and Yellow* from 2001, are perhaps the descendants of Turrell's exercise in illusionism. In this piece, the artist constructed a room-sized installation and created a colored space for viewers to move through by filling the room with smoke and then lighting it through colored filters. The light installations of Spencer Finch are another more conceptual example of this kind of work. Finch tries to re-create his experience of light in certain locations, such as Los Alamos, New Mexico, in *Blue (sky over Los Alamos,*

New Mexico, 5/5/00, morning effect). In this piece, he uses electric bulbs to re-create the effect of natural light for his viewers. Japanese sound and installation artist Ryoji Ikeda strikes a slightly different tone in his light pieces. In *Spectra II*, Ikeda made a work that recalls Bruce Nauman's *Green Light Corridor* from the early 1970s. In this piece, Ikeda invited an observer into a darkened room, which turns out to be a corridor. Blinded by the darkness, the sometimes-frightened viewer is confronted by a high-pitched tone that is connected to a strobe light. As the viewer's eyes adjust, a red laser appears at the end of the corridor, which the viewer can choose to walk toward or not.

More strictly sculptural versions of these kinds of works include the large *Torqued Ellipses* by Richard Serra located at the Dia Art Foundation's Beacon New York institution. Viewers must navigate these large-scale pieces and pay attention to both their perceptions of how the works mold space and create subtle variations in air pressure and sound and the way light plays on the rusting metal and produces shadows and highlights. In Julianne Swartz's work of architectural intervention *Line Drawing*, she punched round openings through the walls of the space. Swartz then used fans and mirrors to alter the perception of the space.[23] Her work derives from Michael Asher's alterations of galleries and many of the pieces that were exhibited in the *Rooms* exhibition, such as by Gordon Matta-Clark and Mary Miss or by Alice Aycock. Certain works by Carsten Höller function in the same way, including his metal slide pieces, which participants are allowed to slide down to experience the thrill of speed and gravity. All of these works rely on the observer's presence and experience of the space, as Bishop says.

A final category of installation art would be works that use space and materials to refer not to the present but to the past. In these pieces, sensuous materials are employed to evoke memory, human experiences, or stories. I would include Ann Hamilton's work in this category, along with artists such as the Colombian artist Doris Salcedo and French artist Christian Boltanski. For instance, in Salcedo's work, memory is concentrated in the form of dense sculptural works that employ a postminimal sculptural language. Using old wooden furniture that has been filled with concrete, Salcedo evokes not only the private interior of the home and the family but also the density of human bodies. Gathered together in large installations, these pieces refer to the effects of the civil war in Colombia. More recently, Salcedo has made works that utilize chairs to fill up architectural voids, such as her dramatic contribution to the 2003 Istanbul Biennial, where she used thousands of old chairs piled a few stories high to fill an empty lot between two apartment buildings in Istanbul.

Christian Boltanski uses objects to evoke a sense of dread and mystery. In Boltanski's *Les Habits de François C*, he photographed items of children's clothing in black and white, as if they were pieces of evidence. He then placed the photographs in deep boxes and mounted them on the wall in a grid formation.[24] The objects are uniform and grim and suggest anonymous and premature death — an allusion to the Holocaust. In another piece from the mid-1980s, titled *Chases High School*, Boltanski re-photographed the individual faces of students from a Jewish high school class that graduated in 1931 in Vienna. He enlarged the images, made them blurry, and rendered the sitters remote, setting them up under desk lamps that should illuminate but that obscure the images instead. These were then set on top of old tin biscuit boxes.[25] The viewer will know nothing more about the people in the photographs. The viewer is thus prevented from making any connection with the people in the image. This work relates to Boltanski's earlier archive-like inventory pieces and his general fascination with the question of individuality and death in mass culture. Joseph Beuys influenced all of these works, which use symbolically or culturally charged materials to convey ideas about spirituality and experience. Ann Hamilton's work falls into this last group of installation art.

All of these works focus on perception and experience in the present tense for individual bodies. They seem to elude photographic representation. However, it is in the attempt to grasp the present tense, Mary Ann Doane argues, that the archival impulse is born.

Memory, Experience, and Historical Images in Hamilton's Work

Ann Hamilton's interest in experience is due in part to her observation that the way we deal with objects and materials in everyday life has changed radically in modernity. She thinks of consumer culture as contributing to a decline in knowledge.

> Anni Albers talks about this predicament in her book *On Designing*. She writes about the fact that there is so much schizophrenic behavior in society because

we don't have contact with materials from a raw to finished state. In the kind of work we do every day, we engage midslot in something, from the way that we buy food to the way that we push paper around.[26]

More recently, Hamilton has written,

> We live in a world run by technologies that are invisible to us, a world in which materials are often disassociated from their source — in a world where the coat on our back no longer links in our mind to the fleece of a sheep. I am interested in how the tactile knowledge of material processes and systems remain relevant to our cultural imagination, in how embodied forms of knowledge pass forward without being categorized as anachronistic or nostalgic.[27]

Like Robert Morris, Ann Hamilton has thought carefully about the reasons she makes art focused on bodily experience. As the quotation above indicates, her interest in the body comes from a response to everyday experience in a media-saturated and technology-dependent environment. Her work tries to enrich a viewer's experience by encouraging them to focus on how and what we perceive through the five senses. Several of Hamilton's installations from 1988 through 1996 were constructed as intense, sensuous experiences in which the space buzzes with organic and mechanical rhythms. Viewers are invited to be aware of their perceptions and sensations in these spaces. Imagine crossing the threshold of *mantle* at the Miami Art Museum (figure 3.1).

The artist sits in a chair sewing the sleeves on wool coats. In the same room, shortwave radios broadcast news from around the globe and pungent flowers wilt on a long table. In this space, the observer is immediately aware of simultaneous movements, sounds, and smells, and is challenged to be attentive to these perceptions. In *mantle*, as viewers linger in the space, they attend to the smell of the flowers as they dry imperceptibly and collapse and to the quiet, steady rhythm of the artist sewing sleeves amidst the crackle from the radios.

Hamilton's work spans the gap between the simplifying aspect of photographic vision and the full-body immersive experience of her complex installations. I will argue in this section that Hamilton's work recalls, perhaps as a distant collective memory, the moment when modern methods of production supplanted craft or workshop production by means of photographic technology. It is the same era in history that the photographic impulse is

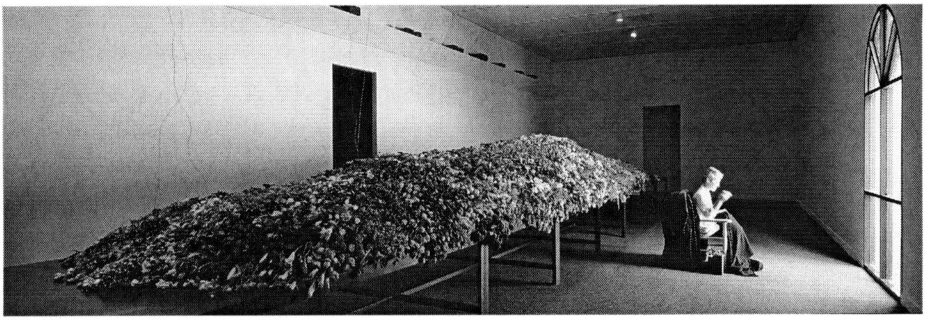

FIGURE 3.1 Ann Hamilton, *mantle*. Miami Art Museum, Miami, Florida, April 2–June 7, 1998. Materials: about sixty thousand fresh-cut flowers; eight tables (each 32 feet x 6 inches x 6 inches), connected to a length of 48; eleven various model shortwave radio receivers; shelf (72 feet long x 12 inches deep, mounted 13 feet above floor); broadcast voice; thirty-three 4 x 4 inch speakers; white-painted wood and wicker chair; figure; steel block; sewing implements; thirty-three gray, blue, and black wool coats. *Photo credit: Thibault Jeanson. Courtesy of the Ann Hamilton Studio.*

born. This historical development is staged metaphorically in the installations in which Hamilton employed an "attendant" to perform different kinds of work in the space. As we will see, these attendants embody the moment when the craftsperson was transformed into the worker via photographic methods of study. It is an activity that not only took place in the past but also takes place everyday when the consumption of images on screens displaces the use of the whole body and its other senses.

These workers are placed within the context of sensually complex spaces. For Hamilton, the attempt to stimulate all of the senses is motivated by a desire to produce an immersive experience for the viewer that engages all the senses including vision. Hamilton's work invites the viewer to surrender to the installation environment, to become absorbed in its surfaces via the sense of sight, smell, touch, and even taste. The walls of her installations are often covered with all sorts of edible materials, corncobs, cornmeal, and husks; sweet-smelling beeswax; eucalyptus; smoked pigskin; honey; bourbon-infused water; and mussel shells. The white, clean surface of the gallery space is complicated and made sensual, inviting a connection with the viewer's body. The architecture is "embodied" by engaging the viewer's body through all of the senses.

Hamilton, throughout her career, has been interested in producing an embodied architecture that calls for a response from the viewer's body and responds to it as well. Seen in psychoanalytic terms, it is an experience of bodily intimacy that recalls the infant's deep connection to the mother's body. Although Hamilton does not describe the work as strictly feminist, her installations and interest in the senses share some characteristics with feminist artistic strategies, following the theories of Luce Irigaray and Helène Cixous, as in Irigaray's *This Sex, Which Is Not One* and Cixous's *"Coming to Writing" and Other Essays* that emphasize the sensation of touch, smell, or hearing rather than sight as strategies for honoring the feminine. For Hamilton, this has taken the form of dislodging vision from its seat in the skull and confusing it with other senses. For instance, in *the picture is still*, Hamilton used a tiny camera that she had had specially designed to film a photograph with her fingers. As one watches the video, it is as if one is both seeing and caressing the image at the same time. Her videos often conflate the senses in this way. Her pieces reawaken latent bodily memories in such a way that the viewer can be both seduced and disturbed.

Hamilton's interest in body knowledge is informed by her training as a weaver in the 1970s.[28] For feminists in the 1970s, craft was a way to honor an unacknowledged art practiced by women in the past. By practicing craft, it was possible to recover the experiences of women in the past and to include them in the history of art. For Hamilton, agency is epitomized by the act of making. And it is the act of making that opens the subject to knowledge of material experience. Hamilton's work seems to follow this logic. Hamilton's interest in making has its roots in the work of artists such as Jackie Winsor, whose emphasis on handwork at a heroic scale set her apart from the Minimalists with whom she is often compared. In *Bound Square* (1972), Winsor recycled old rope and used its fiber to bind the ends of four logs together in the ancient construction strategy of wrapping. The piece, although simple, took hundreds of hours to produce. Anna Chave connects Winsor's interest in this type of work to the ingenuity she observed on the part of her mother who raised her children in Newfoundland and built a house, cooked, canned, and used all of the skills required to survive in a rugged rural setting.[29] Winsor's sculpture reflected her respect for labor and, as Chave notes, especially the unremunerated labor associated with women.

In her 1991 interview, Hamilton discussed her own interest in hand labor, which she connects to a neglected type of body knowledge that has been lost in a society where the primary gesture is the pushing of buttons or touching screens.[30] New technologies and new types of work practices have changed our engagement with the material world. A similar dismay accompanied the change wrought in social and bodily practices by factory production. As the Marxist theorist Georg Lukács explains it in *History and Class Consciousness*, the object produced by the factory is not the product of an organic work process where a single hand is involved from start to finish but instead the result of many different automated processes. In the factory product, the traces of labor are erased, as the worker flicks his hand over the product as it moves down the line. Walter Benjamin relates the same movement to the flick of the gambler's wrist, or that of flipping on a light, striking a match, or pushing a button on a camera — the gesture produces no real experiences for the person who performs it. Theodor Adorno and Benjamin argued that, in the transition to modernity, experience was stripped to those essential features necessary for functioning in an industrialized world.[31] As in the movement of a second hand on a clock, unrelated and identical instants accumulate with each automated gesture. Factory time is fixed into moments, not stories. Time is rationalized in modernity. No knowledge or experience is activated in the motion, as push-button technology circumvents the need for embodied knowledge.

E. P. Thompson in his vivid accounts of weavers' lives describes what advocates of the "craftsman ideal" believed they were losing in industrialization.[32] Thompson's accounts focuses on a moment of transformation when hand-weaving was replaced by weaving mills in England. His writing provides glimpses of a work practice that allowed enough flexibility and leftover energy for collecting, writing poetry, making music, and gardening. While sitting at the loom, a weaver could prop up a book and read or talk with fellow workers. Thompson's images conjure dreams of preindustrial contentment and security. He gathered anecdotes of weavers' reactions to factory production and concluded, "They resented, first, the discipline; the factory bell or hooter; the time-keeping which over rode ill health, domestic arrangements, or the choice of more varied occupations."[33] There was a desire in the nineteenth century to establish a movement to return to a system of production based on medieval practices of craft and guild organization and these tendencies continue into the twenty-first century. These advocates of the "craftsman ideal," as the scholar Eileen Boris calls it, such as members of the arts and crafts movement, set up workshops and schools to teach soon-to-be-forgotten methods of handicraft.[34] Artists and critics, such as the English artist William Morris and critic John Ruskin, hoped to undo the alienation that occurred in the industrial production of commodities.

The "craftsman ideal" continues in the twentieth and twenty-first century. It is a reaction against capitalist "one-dimensionality." The Marxist philosopher Herbert Marcuse warned against a society of one-dimensional men, by which he meant a society of those trained with one or two specialized skills in order to fit into an integrated system of industrial production.[35] Craft and hand labor were perceived by some to be a way of getting outside these conditions. The handmade product represents the possibility of resistance to modern capitalist culture. E. P. Thompson wrote his piece "The Weavers" in the early 1960s in Britain. In the 1960s in the United States, there was a movement, with motivations similar to that of the arts and crafts movement, to return to craft-based forms of production as a way of escaping 1960s corporate and industrial culture. And these ideas continue in the DIY (do it yourself) movement that views the ability to make things by hand as a way to resist the control of everyday life imposed by corporate culture.

Hamilton is careful to distinguish her work from the desire to valorize craft as artists did in the 1970s. Hamilton's installations validate the process of making without producing much in the way of long-lasting handmade objects. Instead, in Hamilton's work, the process of making is opened up and transformed into its various experiential modes: material sensations, traces, and actions. It shifts the interest from a permanent object to the components of an experience that, perhaps, disrupts everyday experience in a push-button technology culture. In this way, it seems to be connected to Doane's idea of the contingent in modernity.

A primary difficulty for Hamilton's works lies in conveying an *experience* of craft and the body knowledge to an observing viewer without asking the viewer to make something. The artist initially tried to solve this problem by framing the gestures of hand labor. Hamilton's large-scale installations of the early 1990s, which often involved the gathering and assembling of large amounts of material, also marshaled large groups of volunteers. They nailed metal tags to floors, folded shirts, and sewed silk panels. Hamilton's installations, like Judy Chicago's *Dinner Party*, were accumulations of large amounts of hand labor. Even *the picture is still* involved the work of many volunteers tying and hanging branches of charcoal by hand from the ceiling of the space. The tasks to which Hamilton set her volunteers were valuable for the artist because they engaged her participants in the process of making.

These aesthetic gestures take the forms of the worker's repetitive movements in the installations, of gestural marks left in the heavily worked surfaces, and of video images of hands knitting, sewing, and so forth. In Hamilton's installations, when an attendant stages a gesture, it is integrated with the working body. The defenders of the craftsman ideal claim that craft production enables a type of knowledge and an experience of the material world that is lost in machine production by engaging the body more fully in work. The holistic understanding of materials and processes that a craftsman knows is reduced to a gesture or a series of simple gestures in assembly-line production.

This process is figured in the image of the simple work diagram in which a series of movements is reduced to a set of visual signs: a two-dimensional image. Bruce Kaiper describes the result: "Instead the engineer includes us [the workers] as a part of the construction problem to be abstracted. Our movements including our skill, the time we take and our work relations are made into symbols, signs, mathematical equations and lines."[36] The gesture sets off a whole series of minute, complicated motions in the machinery into which the hand's gesture disappears.

The trace of the hand is reduced to a click or flick. In the factory-produced object, the traces of labor and the time it took to make are illegible. Plastic and metal do not accept the trace of a unique hand. The flick of the worker's hand over the product takes, ideally, only a moment, and the trace of one hand working over the entire body of a commodity was replaced with the movement of many hands. Industrial production fragments the making process so that individual workers no longer see the product of their efforts. Instead, their gestures are scientifically measured and specific to the task at hand, as this is the most efficient means of production. In this process, the body of the worker is integrated into the work process.

The reduction of the work gesture to a click immediately calls to mind the reduction of bodily experience to image via the click of an opened camera shutter. And this is partly how these more efficient processes of production came about. Frank B. Gilbreth, who was the pioneer of time-motion studies to improve the efficiency of workers in production, studied the motion of workers via film and photographs. He did so to break down the complex movements of a work into clear units and then to choreograph the gestures of workers so that they would accomplish their tasks in the most efficient manner possible.

Following the pioneering work of Étienne-Jules Marey and Eadweard Muybridge earlier in the nineteenth century, he filmed workers doing their work against walls with a grid painted on them and, using a specially calibrated clock, he timed their movements. He also attached light to workers' hands and set up a camera for long exposure, thereby attaining a continuous line that could be viewed in three dimensions in a stereograph. He then devised ways to save movements and time. For instance, he turned the lines of the stereograph into static, wire models that workers could use to learn how to move.

In his classic study of bricklayers, Gilbreth follows a procedure of carefully delineating all the variables that enter into efficient production.[37] They range from the "brawn" of the workman to his contentment and to the weight and size of his tools. He also studied the human body carefully and determined the easiest and most comfortable gestures for a worker to make in the process of his work. Gilbreth had great concern for the bodily comfort of the workers. He advocated free food, good lighting, and frequent periods of rest for the most efficient work. But this comfort was intended to make easier the abstraction and integration of a living being into the process of machine-based factory assemblage to save money. Gilbreth aimed to make the human into a machine in the best way possible. He studies the human body as if it were a machine, making comparisons such as the following, where he discusses a worker working on a machine and makes no distinction between the two bodies: "Motions should be on the fore and aft vertical plane passing through the body. It is so necessary to have the motions similar that often counterbalances and springs can be installed to reverse motion, thus also causing the hardest work to be done in the most convenient direction."[38]

In Gilbreth's films and photographs, we see workers seated at worktables or standing at workbenches. The camera is positioned so that it is possible to see the hands at work on the tabletop, which along with the walls, has been carefully covered with a grid. Gilbreth placed a timer, his microchronometer, in the foreground of the film frame. It is black with white hands that turn continually as the worker works. Gilbreth constructed his promotional films with sequences of before and after the application of his methods. Before the methods are applied, the workers' motions are halting and hesitant. After the application of his methods, in the newly brightened space, the workers' hand motions are synthesized to the repetition and rhythm of the work. There is no hesitation or fumbling to the gestures. In essence, the idiosyncrasy of the gesture, the worker's individual attempt to adapt to the work environment, has been diminished, and the motion has been generalized and abstracted—a process of abstraction symbolized by the gridded photograph. The gesture becomes automatic and universal and requires a certain kind of limited attentiveness on the part of the worker. This attentiveness seems different from what is required of the craftsman. Photography in this instance had an effect on the experience of everyday life for these workers. Gilbreth's work is a perfect example of the way that Henri Bergson asserted that science attempts to capture the complexity of vital experience, thereby simplifying it.

In the context of Hamilton's artwork, the people that she calls the "attendants" represent her ideal viewers. These "attendants" are the silent individuals who were put on display in her installations and performed simple tasks such as knitting, sanding mirrors, or sewing over the course of the exhibition. Hamilton's term "attendant" means "one who pays attention." The poet Rainer Maria Rilke regarded attention as the remains of a "lost ideal of artisanal absorption in work, now exiled to the margins of a mechanized and routinized world."[39] Authentic experience from Rilke's perspective is one component of now-lost artisanal culture. For Hamilton, attentive making can be the remnant of a collective experience that as an aesthetic experience approximates what has been lost in industrialization. Hamilton has said that the person who best understood her installation *myein* at the Venice Biennale in 1999 was in fact the museum guard who, while protecting the work, spent hours on end in the space observing the subtle changes of light and movement. In the exhibition of their handwork, Hamilton frames the attentiveness that these workers brought to their tasks. It is a curious thing to put attentive labor on display in this way.

Gilbreth's photographic methods might seem completely antithetical to Hamilton's presentation of work by "attendants" because they drain the in-

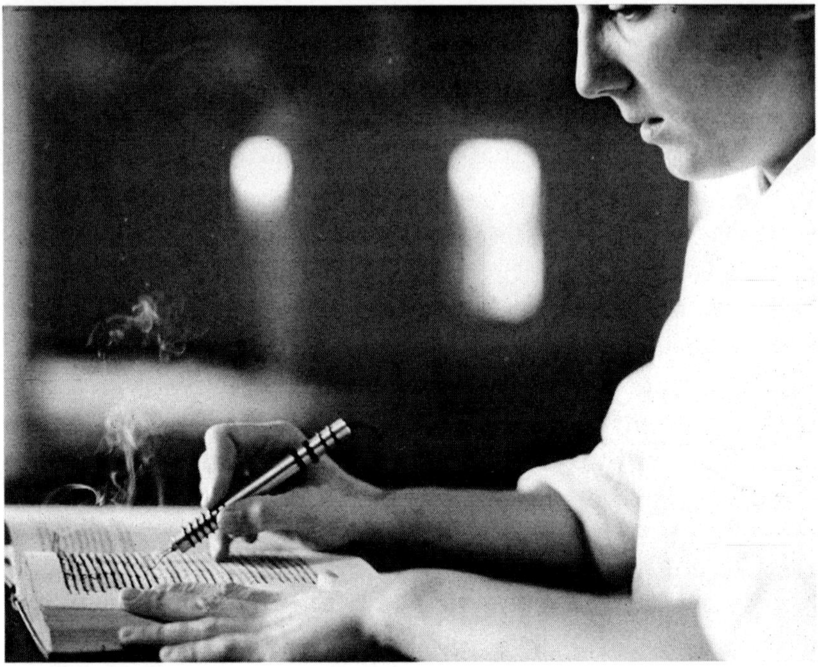

FIGURE 3.2 Ann Hamilton, *tropos*. DIA Center for the Arts, New York, October 7, 1993–June 19, 1994. Materials: translucent industrial glass windows, gravel topped with concrete, horsehair, table, chair, electric buren, books. Recorded voice: audiotape, audiotape player, speakers. *Photo credit: Thibault Jeanson. Courtesy of the Ann Hamilton Studio.*

dividual experience of work, abstract it, and generalize it. However, there are remarkable visual similarities between the two. "Attendants" have been included in ten of Hamilton's pieces since 1989. An attendant is often standing at a table, seated at a table, or on a stool doing a repetitive motion. Their work, as in Gilbreth's films, is presented for the inspection of the observer without acknowledging their presence. For instance, the mirrors to be worked in *aleph* are lifted from the worker's left side, sanded until they are useless, and then moved to the right. The same maneuver occurs in each of Gilbreth's factory studies, such as one scene where a woman worker stands at a table and polishes glycerin bars. It is clear that Hamilton's attendant's motions have also been carefully scripted; they are not halting or hesitating but smooth and repetitive. Like the factory worker's, their work is an abstraction of the pro-

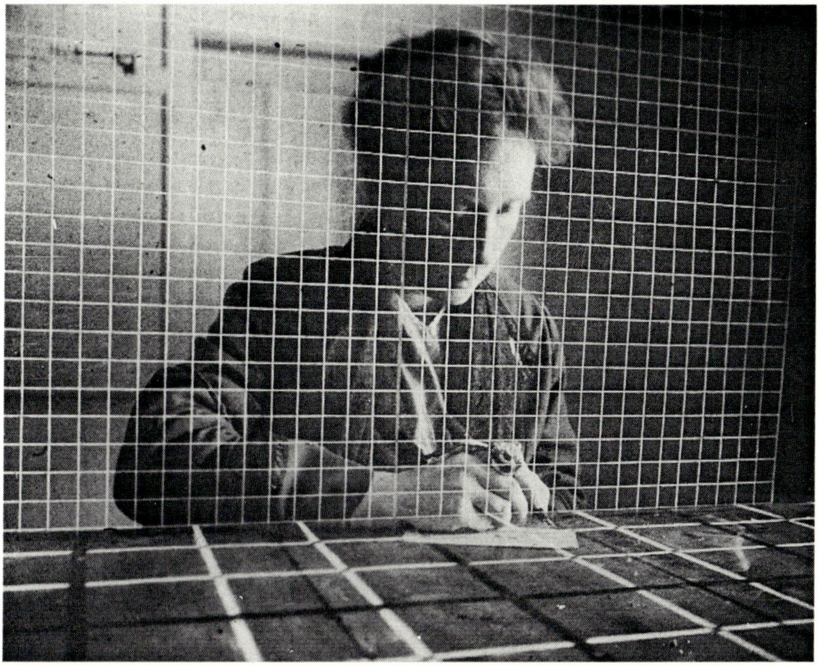

FIGURE 3.3 Frank Gilbreth, *Lillian B. Gilbreth in Motion Study*. *Frank and Lillian Gilbreth Collection, Archives Center, National Museum of American History, Behring Center, Smithsonian Institution.*

cess of production, and their work has been photographed and filmed, albeit for catalogs and CD-ROMs. And in the process of moving, Hamilton's attendants would look more like Gilbreth's workers, whose motion, with the help of the camera, has been better integrated into the overall system of factory production and whose bodies have been assimilated to the working rhythm of machines.

Hamilton's installations of the 1990s do not simply yearn for the fullness of a preindustrial mode of production. Instead, they allow for a play of tension between "craftsman ideal" and factory labor rendered efficient by means of photographic technologies. Both aspects of the history of labor are evoked in these works. Hamilton's pieces, just like the former factory spaces in which many of them take place, hark back precisely to that moment in the late nineteenth century when hand labor was disappearing in the face of machine labor, when photography enabled scientists and artists to analyze the body and its rhythms. There is therefore a complexity in Hamilton's work that is often ignored when it is characterized as a return to preindustrial experience. The question of relationship between image and experience is referenced historically via the history of labor evoked in Hamilton's installations.

Hamilton's work naturally responds to some of the spaces in which it has been exhibited. These are often the old industrial spaces of cities taken over when industrial economies faded or changed. In the late 1960s, Reesa Goldberg has noted, for instance, that the space of exhibition for avant-garde art in New York was transferred from the intimate, home-like atmosphere of the galleries of the Museum of Modern Art to the industrial warehouses of marginal parts of the city that were found for alternative art spaces.[40] In these spaces, the artists used the materials they found left over from the buildings' previous lives as small factories, or a disused school in the case of PS1. Hamilton's work seems to pick up on the memories embedded in the bones of these buildings of the nineteenth and twentieth centuries.

Documenting Hamilton's Work

Many professional photographers have documented Hamilton's work, but these images have rarely conveyed the experience of her spaces. And it is important for these images to communicate the work accurately. For an installation artist in the last thirty years, photographs in magazines, in books, in art history lectures, or on the World Wide Web signify the artist and represent a body of work in a global context. Large-scale installations are also expensive to produce and often require institutional support, which is generated by publicity produced by such images.

Hamilton's work exemplifies the shift in the relationship of installation art to photography. Catalogs have accompanied many of Hamilton's exhibitions, and she also has an archive of photographs of each installation that includes prints and negatives of her installations, although not every one of her pieces was documented in this manner. When discussing the documentation of her work and the catalogs that have been published, Hamilton points to budget and time constraints. Because installation art does not have the profit margin of something like painting, independent galleries are less willing to invest in it. The production of a catalog often depends on the resources of the hosting institution. And often, by the end of a project, she said, the documentation of work becomes another project in itself.[41] The installation produces its own archive. All of these factors shape the documentation of the work, the pictures that are taken, and their circulation in the art market.

Hamilton considers any interpretation of her work a type of collaboration, as evidenced by her close working relationship with commentators on her installations, such as scholars Susan Stewart and Joan Simon. Simon, for instance, spent years not only going to all of Hamilton's installations but also putting together a catalogue raisonné of her work in consultation with Hamilton. The Paris-based photographer Thibault Jeanson is Hamilton's preferred photographer of her installations. Jeanson often photographs architectural interiors for catalogs and magazines. While working in Europe, Hamilton saw published in a magazine some photographs that Jeanson had taken of a house in Uppsala, Sweden. The photographs inspired her to take a three-hour train ride out of her way to see the house. Some time later, by chance, Jeanson's representative submitted photographs to the Dia Art Foundation in a bid to photograph Hamilton's installation *tropos*. When Hamilton saw the photos, which included the Uppsala photographs, she knew that he was the person to photograph her piece. He has since photographed many of her installations, including *the picture is still* and *mantle*.

For *tropos* (1993–1994) at the Dia Art Foundation in the Chelsea neighborhood of Manhattan, Hamilton emptied the gallery and turned it into a light- and sound-filled space. She covered the floor in layers of horsehair and set an attendant at a small table in the center of the room. The attendant had a heated wire wand and burned away lines of text from a book. As the attendant worked, the recorded voice of a person with aphasia moved from speaker to speaker in the space, "turning" observers as they followed the sound.

When Hamilton met with Jeanson at Dia, he said they sat down in the horsehair and talked about various things for an hour or so.[42] Then Hamilton left, and Jeanson recalled that he realized, "We didn't talk about the piece. I don't know what she wants from me. I don't know where I'm supposed to go." Hamilton stated that it is important in interpreting her work that the writer or photographer both understands her intentions but also makes the work his or her own.[43] She wants the photographic or textual interpretation to in a certain sense become, not a contingent object, to use Martha Buskirk's phrase, but something that stands on its own. In this way, the artist might assert, the photograph becomes someone else's work and is clearly distinguished from her own.

In describing his work in Hamilton's installations, Jeanson made a distinction between making a document, which he connected to signification, and producing an illusion. He described his effort to make images of Hamilton's work as the effort to capture a dream. The ever-changing atmosphere and the emotions evoked by Hamilton's space for the photographer are more important than the record of concrete objects in the space. Using the metaphor of tying himself to the mast of a drifting boat, Jeanson said that as a photographer he floats around in the space and watches what happens.

The photographer's experience in Hamilton's spaces seems very similar to the way that Hamilton describes her initial encounter with the site in which she is going to make a piece and the way she hopes a visitor will encounter her installations. "My site visits have an enormous influence on the work. I have to walk a site's impression into my body in order to begin working. I need to register silently all of the impressions your body registers (temperature, smell, light) as felt impressions before I can work. This plentitude of atmospheric information has an enormous influence with how I perceive and register the words spoken, or the sounds heard."[44]

Jeanson, in photographing the space, essentially follows the same process of attentive awareness as Hamilton's attendants. But Jeanson's descriptions of his photographic process in Hamilton's work make it clear that he is trying to capture an experience that encompasses more than mere vision. It is also clear that the photographs try to go beyond the limits of camera vision.

Jeanson said that, in Hamilton's installations, within the constraints of time and money, he would spend the first day without the camera. Then, as he got to know how the space changed under given conditions of light, he would take out the camera and begin making exposures. He uses a large-format camera with an additional viewfinder because the viewfinder on these large-format cameras does not give an accurate sense of the final image's framing. He waits for the "perfect moment," the moment that will encapsulate the installation as a whole, and then opens the shutter, depending on the lighting conditions, for up to forty-five minutes. Given one day of work, he could take seven to eight exposures.

He photographed *the picture is still*. Hamilton's installations at the time used minimal light. For instance, *ghost: a border act* of 2000, which was mentioned in the introduction, was located in a recently vacated factory space in Charlottesville, Virginia. The installation comprised two "rooms" made of silk screens, which were suspended from the ceiling and seemed to float in the space. A long table, a single chair, and a rotating digital projector were inside each room. The projector cast the image of a pencil drawing a line on the silk screens and the walls of the factory. The only light in the space was what came from the projectors. A similar situation took place in *the picture is still*, except, in that instance, the only light in the space came from the frosted glass windows at the front of the gallery, which rendered one side of the space very bright and the other dark. Although eyes could balance the contrasting light, the camera couldn't. For Jeanson, these were difficult conditions in which to photograph, and so, for two of the images, he was forced to light the space so that the image would picture the space the way the eye sees it. Despite his efforts, Jeanson was unhappy with the images that he took and returned to Japan later to try again.

Jeanson always uses a panorama format when photographing Hamilton's pieces because, he said, he thinks of them as landscapes rather than interiors. His use of this format links Hamilton's installation art in interesting ways to the panorama paintings of the eighteenth and nineteenth century. This wide-angle format, even on a photographic scale, encourages viewers to imagine themselves enveloped within an environment. Panorama photographs reproduced at a small scale do not have the same impact. However, these images approximate natural vision because they include peripheral vision. In the Jeanson photographs, the viewer gets the sense of being placed in a specific position within a large illusionistic space.

Panoramas, theorists have argued, are enjoyable because they place the viewer in a position to command the space. Painted panoramas of the eighteenth and nineteenth centuries were large, often circular structures painted in great detail with 360-degree views of cities or battlefields.[45] For viewers, the sensation of having the world spread out before their feet is part of the pleasure of looking at these paintings. These image-spaces reconstitute the centered subject that installation, in some accounts at least, seeks to subvert. When a photograph is read as the naturalistic depiction of three-dimensional space it, in effect, opens up the visual field and allows the viewer to command that space visually. In this situation, rather than being immersed in the space of the installation, the division between the subject (the person looking at the photograph) and the object (the space of the installation) is reinforced. There is a small difference between many of Jeanson's panoramic photographs of Hamilton's installations and these images. While panorama paintings place the viewer at a high point in relation to the scene depicted, Jeanson's photographs tend to place the viewer in the thick of installation, the camera lens always at the height of a body standing upright. In this position, it is as if the viewer were immersed in the installation. It produces the illusion that we are eyewitnesses, so to speak, in the space.

It is not so different to photograph an installation than to photograph architecture. Architectural photographers have choices in the interpretation of an architect's work. Some make an effort to understand the architect's intention and original vision. When documenting a work, they emphasize the essential formal qualities of a building. Often, this involves editing out incidental signs of use and context, such as vegetation, furniture, and automobiles. The image condenses the formal qualities of the architecture. Photographers may have a heavy hand in interpreting the architecture in formal terms for the viewer but at the same time see themselves as stepping out of the way and letting the architect's work speak for itself. Other photographers prefer to emphasize not the concept but the building as a space that has been lived in and persisted through time, including signs of wear and tear and neglect. Often the photograph becomes a strong and subjective interpretation of the photographer's reaction to the aura of the space.

In a special edition of *Architecture California* devoted to the relationship between architecture and photography, Wolf Prix points out that photographs of architecture are inherently inadequate to the experience of a building because viewers cannot sense or see what is "behind" them. In a photograph, one's vision is narrowed and fragmented.[46] And because the photographic print is two dimensional, the elements in that print are organized according to the logic of a flat plane or visual field. Photographs always flatten and abstract.[47] In looking at a photograph, the viewer is always aware of the distinct qualities of that two-dimensional object but, if the proper visual signals are there, suspends the limitations of that format enough to imagine the lived quality of what the scene depicts.[48] Some photographs, of course, do this more emphatically than others. To frame the issue in semiotic terms, the viewer could read certain signs in the photograph as naturalistic, as if the photograph represents the space of the artwork, as one would experience it first hand. At the other extreme, one could read the photograph as pure, flat surface. Such images tend to emphasize the formal qualities of the space and avoid imitating natural vision.

Put simply, all photographers face choices about how they will manipulate the material conditions in order to make an image. Modernist photographers of the early twentieth century were delighted with the prospect of divorcing vision from its seat in the human body. As in modernist painting, some modernist photography acknowledged the flat surface of the photographic print, producing abstract images with no illusionistic space. These are images that correlate with monocular rather than binocular vision. Modernist photographers also produced images that in their depth of field exceeded the limits of natural vision in all-over clarity. The camera's ability to capture visual phenomena that the eye couldn't see, to fragment the visual field, and to flatten and abstract the visual world opened up aesthetic possibilities for these photographers. But it also produced a kind of disembodied, machine-like vision.

Photographs that imitate natural vision carry the cues that invite the viewer to read them as depicting three-dimensional illusionistic space. These cues can include clear orthogonal lines, natural lighting, and a sense of uncalculated immediacy to the image. The analog photograph is physical evidence of the conditions of a certain time and place, or a "that has been," as Roland Barthes says. For this reason, the photograph has a certain amount of authority as document, even as it marks absence. Most installation photographs are regarded in this way. Although Hamilton uses the term "document" to describe the images of her installations, they don't have the aesthetic of documentary photography, although most can accurately be described as naturalistic photographs.

The Catalog For *The Picture Is Still*

The Akira Ikeda Gallery sponsored the publication of a catalog for *the picture is still*, which came out in 2003.[49] The book, in keeping with Jeanson's photographs, has a panorama format of 12 by 15 inches. The photographs are arranged as a walk-through of the space, opening with an extraordinary image on the first pages that a viewer to the space probably would not see. It is a shot of the doorway in which the frosted glass doors have been opened completely.

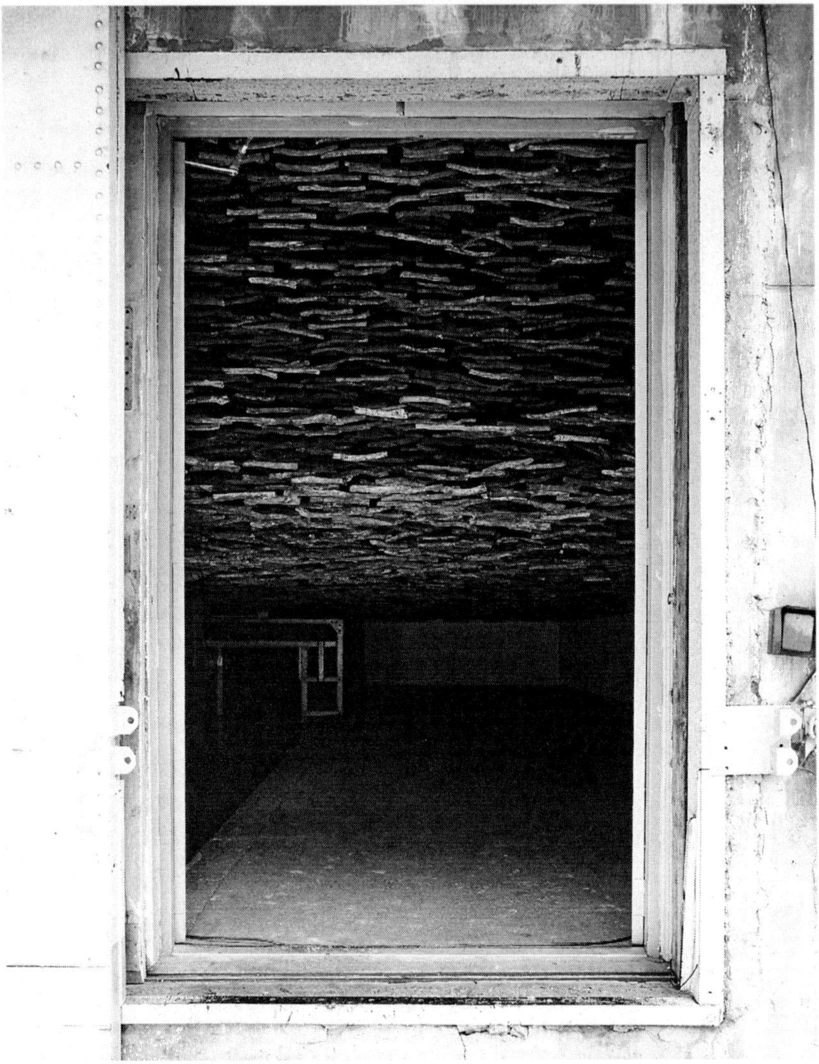

FIGURE 3.4 Ann Hamilton, *the picture is still*. Akira Ikeda Gallery, Taura, Japan, May 19, 2001–May 18, 2002. Materials: projected video image: 35½ x 46 inch steel grid, thread, charcoal, video with sound, speakers. *Photo credit: Thibault Jeanson. Courtesy of the Ann Hamilton Studio.*

The exterior walls of the warehouse building are flush with the surface of the page, and within the gap produced by the opened door, the exposed cloud of charcoal branches and the torpedo tunnels recede in the gloom.

The average viewer of the installation did not have this perspective on the piece, but it is an apt visual metaphor for the artist's intentions for the installation. There is the startling contrast between the ordinary building and its gloomy, almost eerie interior. It is a visual metaphor for excavation and discovery, the sense of a past that is present but invisible. As the image abstracts and encapsulates the meaning of the installation, it also divorces itself from the bodily experience of the space. In this sense, the photograph reveals its function as an opaque signifier, even as it appears to be a window. The startling opening of depth within the flat surface of the page is reminiscent of a Gordon Matta-Clark piece *Pier In/Out* (1973). It is also a suggestion of what will be a play of tension between abstraction and naturalism in photographs of the site.

Not all of the photographs in the catalog function this way. The opening photographs work to give the catalog reader the sense of having just entered the space. On the second title page, a panoramic photograph of the branches of charcoal by Tetsuo Ito fills up both pages. The shot has been taken from the depth of a torpedo channel looking up at the mass of branches from below, while a steel I-beam has been positioned to be in the page's gutter. The branches are densely packed, filling the limits of the picture frame, going from edge to edge, and thereby flattening out the image. This is a space that the viewer cannot imagine entering. It is a visual space.

Another functions to give viewers a striking sense of a great space opening up before them. The entire space from the head of the channel follows the steel I-beams as they recede into the space. Strong orthogonals guide the viewer's eye into depths of the left tunnel where the video projection is just visible. The viewer is drawn irresistibly into an illusionistic, three-dimensional space.

The images by Jeanson move the viewer from the position at the front of the gallery down the side of the channel, with the camera hovering just below the mass of charcoal. The images, in panorama format, are all in black and white and take up both pages. In each, the branches look as if they are a solid form in the space. The final image of this trio shatters this illusion. The camera looks across the gallery space again, but this time it has been placed among the branches of charcoal, which swarm around it.

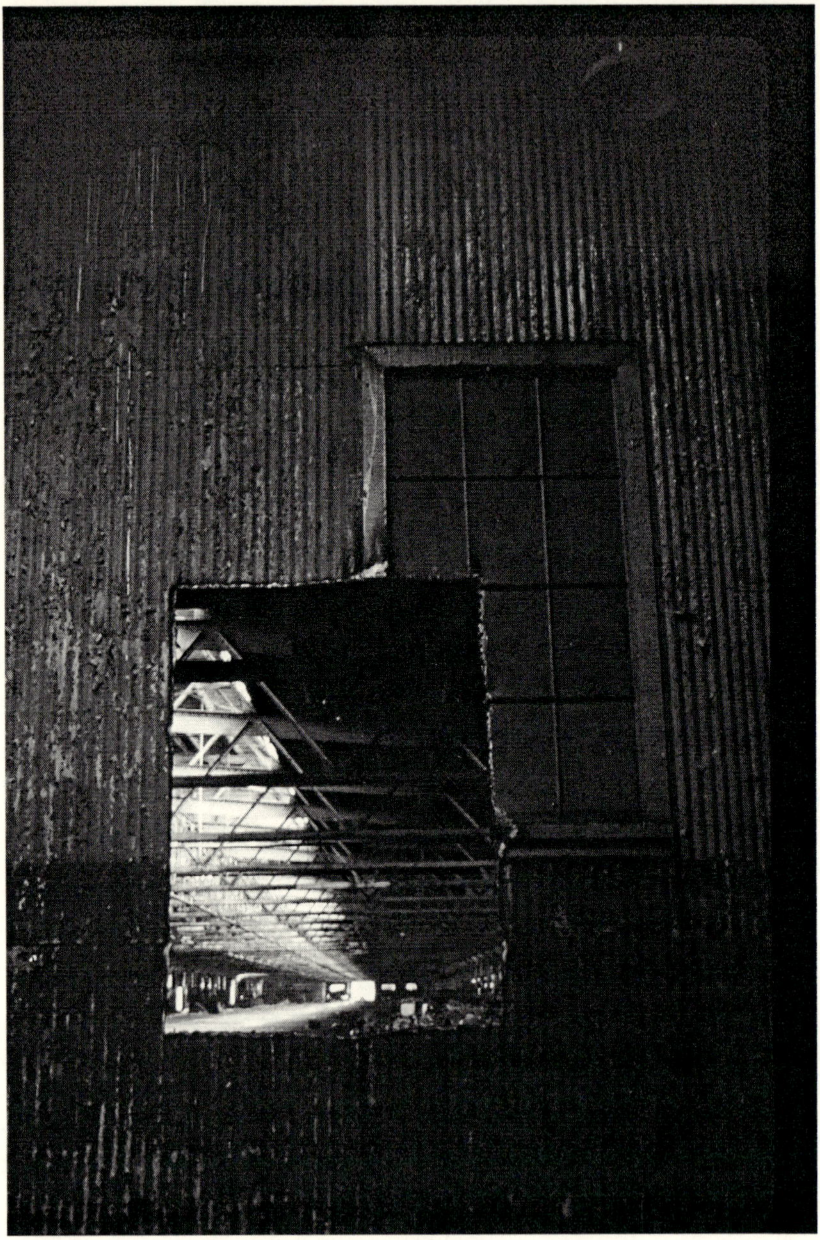

FIGURE 3.5 Gordon Matta-Clark, *Pier In/Out*, 1973.

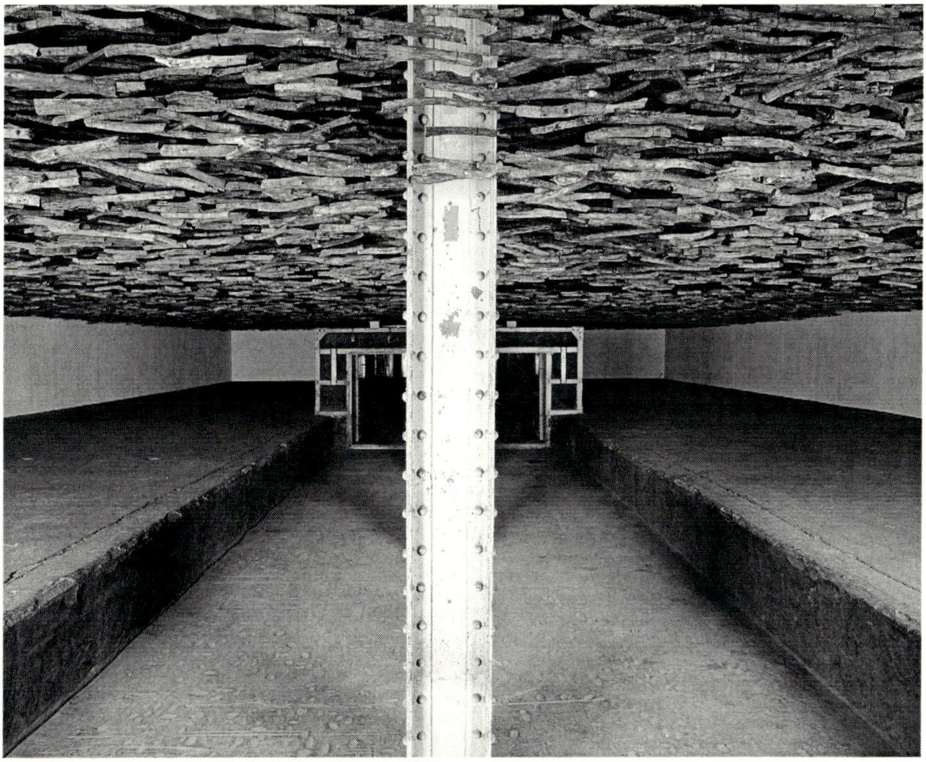

FIGURE 3.6 Ann Hamilton, *the picture is still*, Akira Ikeda Gallery, Taura, Japan, May 19, 2001–May 18, 2002. Materials: projected video image: 35½ x 46 inch steel grid, thread, charcoal, video with sound, speakers. *Photo credit: Thibault Jeanson. Courtesy of the Ann Hamilton Studio.*

In this image, the camera is surrounded, and only a few of the branches are in focus, almost like natural vision. It is the kind of picture that gives the viewer the sense of being immersed in the space. Jeanson, at times, decides to make a bad picture because it more accurately captures the experience of the space. In this sense, the image signifies an embodied vision, which has limits. In *the picture is still*, he allowed some of the images to be burnt or overexposed on the sunlit side of the space, while the darker side flattened out with the branches turned into an inky, black pool. These images do mimic the appearance of the space when one looked to the bright door from the dark side of the room.

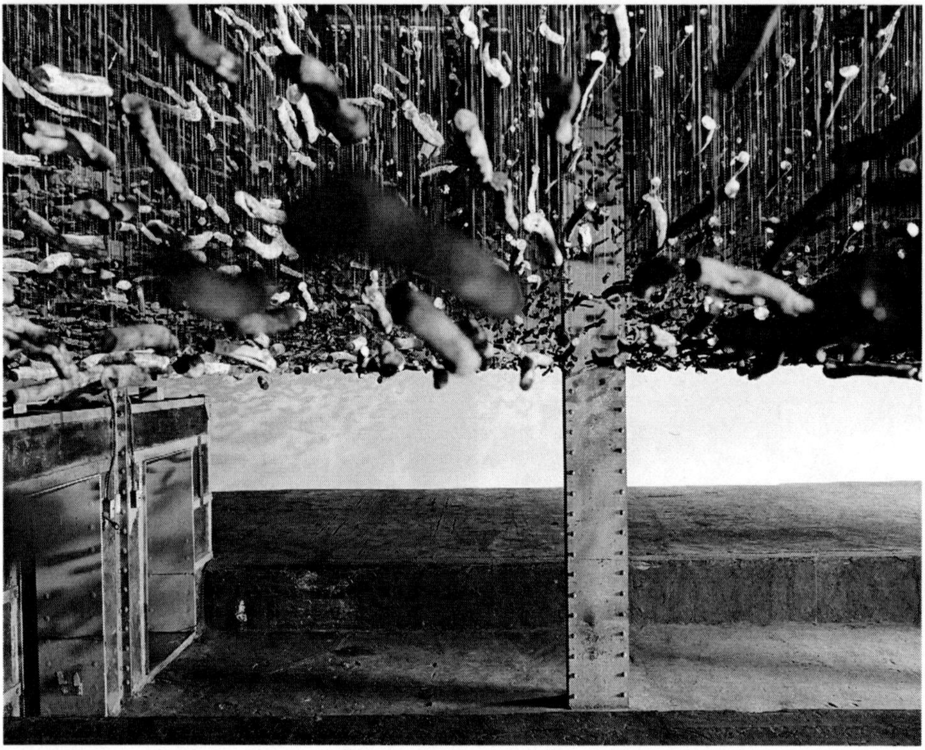

FIGURE 3.7 Ann Hamilton, *the picture is still*, Akira Ikeda Gallery, Taura, Japan, May 19, 2001–May 18, 2002. Materials: projected video image: 35½ x 46 inch steel grid, thread, charcoal, video with sound, speakers. *Photo credit: Thibault Jeanson. Courtesy of the Ann Hamilton Studio.*

Jeanson's description of his process seems quite similar to Hamilton's ideas and descriptions of the ideal viewer's experience in her work. Hamilton attempts to anchor viewers in their bodies, to make them aware of their sensations and the way the body uses those sensations to interpret a space. In the effort to capture that experience, camera vision also tries to become embodied. However, it never quite works that way. In the catalog, the photographs shift between emphasizing the depth of field, the openness of space, and the sense of being immersed, and drawing out those formal qualities of the installation that make interesting pictures, that is, the formal play of horizontal and vertical lines that work with or against the frame and flatness of the printed page. Where Gilbreth's use of photographs and film sought to simplify the complexity of lived experience, Jeanson's photographs try to recapture that complexity.

These are the photographer's, catalog designer's, and the artist's deliberate choices in photographic styles. There are a remarkable variety of photographic strategies designed to give the viewer an authentic sense of what it was like to be in the installation. Compared to the catalogs for the *Rooms* exhibition and even Matta-Clark's *Splitting*, the photography and design of the catalog for *the picture is still* is far more complex. Like the PS1 catalog, the photographs lead the viewer through the space, giving a sense of the passage of time. And like Matta-Clark's, they mimic the way one turns one's head in different directions as one moves. However, there are more ways of depicting these aspects of a space in the Akira Ikeda catalog. The higher-quality color photographs and their size enhance the variety of photographic strategies.

The difference between the *Rooms* catalog and *the picture is still* catalog marks a shift in the requirements of the art market in the 1970s and the 1980s. The conventions of catalog photography dictated the style of the photographs of her installations. As installation art has been taken up into better-funded art institutions, the style and quality of photographs have changed considerably in the last thirty-five years. One can compare the catalog of *the picture is still* to that produced by PS1's *Rooms* in 1976. The *Rooms* publication with its grainy, low-production, black-and-white images look as if they could be reproduced in a newspaper. The images of Hamilton's installation *the picture is still*, by contrast, have the quality of a photographer's book or the high-quality layouts of architectural magazines.

Because most of the installation art of the late 1960s and early 1970s was produced by young artists whose work was not yet sought after by mainstream galleries, it was not as subject to commercial pressures. Along with their interest in de-aestheticizing art practice, many artists in this position had little reason to spend the money to document an installation extensively. And, for some artists, ephemeral work need not be preserved to the same extent because the experience itself was the focus. As Allan Kaprow argued, what could a photograph capture about such an experience?[50] For the small group of insiders who saw the work in its original state, the photograph or the video serves merely to jog personal memory. But for those who come after, the photograph becomes an iconic sign of an exclusive event.[51] It becomes a contingent object that signifies a moment in time within the institution of art history. This realization on the part of art institutions and galleries has placed pressure to produce exhibition catalogs that sustain interest and represent an artist's work accurately.

And Yet, Photographs Are Never Enough

It is interesting that Hamilton's inspiration for *the picture is still*, and her exploration of the issue of agency, came from looking at a photograph and concluding it is impossible to understand history from an image. It is something that she deals with in her installations all of the time. Because she never repeats an installation, the majority of her audience encounters images of her work before it ever sees one of her installations in the flesh. Each of her pieces is usually specific to and inspired by the site in which they have been made. Only parts of her work, such as mechanical objects or individual tables, have traveled to different venues. The photographs of Hamilton's installations are documentation, according to the artist.[52] And almost every one of her installations has been beautifully photographed.

Installation art, for the most part, seeks to produce an immersive, embodied experience and, not only an immersive experience, but also a situation in which the boundary between subject and object is nearly breached. For her part, Hamilton points out that much of her work has been about exploring boundaries and investigating the possibility of their rupture. In order to appreciate this aspect of her work, it is necessary to be enveloped by it. Photographs can't achieve this effect of being enveloped in a space, nor can they imitate the sound of charcoal chiming in the wind.

This is the inherent defect of two-dimensional images as documentation of three-dimensional spaces in real time. Robert Morris notes that, in viewing a photograph, one is always removed from the moment in which it was taken while, at the same time, one's body is outside the place that it depicts. One must always project oneself into the photograph and connect the two-dimensional object to the three-dimensional space it depicts. Photography, as Amelia Jones notes, is never enough. For Morris, "spatial arts," in which I would include installation art, should elude the stifling grasp of the photograph. "It is of course space- and time-denying photography that has been so malevolently effective in shifting an entire cultural perception away from the reality of time in art that is located in space."[53] Morris sees photography as homogenizing experience, transforming it into easily consumed units. In the new "spatial arts," by contrast, the viewer is surrounded by the work. The experience, which engages the "I" mode, is imageless. It cannot be pictured or represented, or can be so only in a way that deceives.

For Morris, the "I" aspect of the viewer in one of his pieces is the self as it is poised at the tip of "time's arrow." This is the self in the moment of direct experience without memory, language, or reflection. Any reflection, judgment, or associations that emerge after that initial moment shift consciousness into the "me" aspect.[54] Morris, in this essay, favors the "I" mode of experience, and his simple objects of the early to mid-1960s with their uninflected dull surfaces and simple shapes are intended to discourage viewers from thinking about metaphoric relationships or allusions and to engage them instead in a reflection on their immediate perceptions. Morris describes the shift into the "me" mode of engagement, into transformative representations, such as language and images, as the entrance of "noise" into the system. Immediate, lived experience would seem to be experience before it is social, before it circulates among different people. The "me" mode is the beginning of the representational process that transfers this direct experience into memory, language, and pictures. It is the stage at which direct experience is grasped by social structures and, E. P. Thompson might argue, becomes ideological.

This is one of the reasons photography was troubling to Allan Kaprow. Kaprow thought the photograph could not capture the actual experience of an event, and he also believed they could only be rather weak substitutes. And like many artists working with ephemeral objects and experiential art forms in the 1960s and 1970s, he understood the photograph as extraneous and superfluous to his "real" work. Photographs appear as integral parts of a few of Kaprow's Happenings and gestures but often in a way that points out the inadequacy of the photograph. He noticed that it was impossible for people in his events and activities to refrain from posing for the photographs, which disrupted the spontaneity of the Happening.[55]

Kaprow spoofs the photographic document in his piece *Transfer* (1968). In *Transfer*, Kaprow directed participants to stack oil and chemical barrels in various configurations at sites around Middletown, Connecticut, and spray paint them a different color at each site. After each construction and painting, Kaprow had participants pose in an obvious way for a "triumphal photograph." According to Jeff Kelley, Kaprow was pointing out the art world's need for photographs and images of these events that were meant to be experienced. These images, which are set-up, hokey reactions to the Happening, play up the distance between experience and image that Kaprow wanted to avoid in his work. Roland Barthes describes the process of being photographed as one in which the subject is mortified and rendered an object, even a museum object.[56] Kaprow's later projects were often deliberately unphotographable or, at least, unsatisfying as images, involving slow and invisible processes, such as wetting and drying stones, breathing into a partner's mouth, or exchanging buckets of dirt.

Kaprow also used the photograph to point out the absence that is an inherent part of the photograph. In *Six Ordinary Happenings*, Kaprow used the photograph as evidence of a tiny event that had already taken place. For *Giveaway*, a part of *Six Ordinary Happenings*, stacks of dishes were arranged in impromptu still-life groups on street corners and then photographed. The next day, the empty street corners were then photographed. In this project, absence (of dishes) was embedded in the structure of the photograph. But this particular Happening also pointed out the absence of lived experience in the photograph itself or the transformation of experience into something else. The photograph becomes a poor substitute for the original activity.

Rather than avoiding having her work documented by photographs, however, Ann Hamilton has chosen to explore the representation of bodily experience in photographs in a new project.

Embodied Images: Hamilton's Photographs

> The photograph's desire is not to signify at all costs; nor to witness or inform. It is more of a shock or illusion. Or a disappearance as well, because if something wants to be come an image, it is not to endure but to better disappear. (my translation)[57]
>
> —Jean Baudrillard, from *Sommes-Nous?*[58]

In the Jean Baudrillard quotation above, from a chapter in a recent book of contemporary photography, he argues that photography is not about witnessing. He proposes that things want to be photographed not so they endure but rather so they can better disappear. In photography, the body disappears behind the image. It becomes a specter. As demonstrated in the catalog by

Akira Ikeda, photographs of Hamilton's installations tend to be naturalistic images that imitate illusionistic space or formal abstractions. Each style represents a form of disembodied vision, in the mode of flat, visual space or monocular vision. Can the more ineffable aspects of bodily experience be captured in a photograph?

Hamilton explores this in a series of portrait photographs titled *face to face*, which she began in the late 1990s. The project consists of a series of pinhole photographs of close associates. Hamilton has made a series of these images using friends, family, and people with whom she has worked on projects. This group of pictures combines images and experience in a way that illuminates the complicated relationship between representation and experience in Hamilton's work.

These images explore the limits to representing bodily experience in photographs. They do so by embedding the chemical and even the mechanical process of photography in the body and rendering the experience shared by the sitter and photographer. For the sitter, the process involves the uncanny sensation of being stilled and observed by another. In a certain sense, these photographs are like her installations in that one gains a unique perspective on them by experiencing them first hand. In this case, first hand means being photographed by the artist.

Hamilton photographed me in a grungy parking lot in Charlottesville, Virginia, in 2000, when she came to the University of Virginia to make the installation *ghost: a border act*. The experience was acutely uncomfortable as it involved staring at the artist's mouth at close range for thirty seconds or more. For this series of images, Hamilton made a set of simple pinhole cameras by poking a hole in a plastic film canister in which she had lodged a single frame of unexposed film. She then put the film canister in her mouth and had me stand directly in front of her only inches from her face and opened her lips in order to expose the film. Because I am slightly taller than Hamilton, I had to hold still and peer down into her mouth for what felt like an extraordinarily long time. Once the exposure was complete, Hamilton closed her mouth/the shutter, then removed the canister from her mouth, and covered the small pinhole with a piece of tape until the film was ready to be developed.

In some ways, the experience of being photographed in this manner was probably similar to what it was like for those first daguerreotype sitters who had to be restrained by devices long enough for their images to be captured by the sensitized photographic plate. However, the experience in this case was made more uncomfortable since I was placed in close proximity to another human being. I was not looking at her eyes but, in fact, staring at part of her face that one usually doesn't look at for very long. In this sense, I was both in the presence of another being and looking at her in an objectifying way. I was also aware that she had an equally good view of my face. In fact, she had time to study my face and to realize, I felt, that I was trying to act relaxed and hide my posture but failing miserably. Needless to say, it was amusing but uncomfortable.

When Hamilton showed me the result of the exposure, she said she was pleased with it because my uncertainty and vulnerability was plain to see on my face. In the image, it seems as if I am peering with trepidation into a watery, eye-shaped hole. Hamilton explains that the human figure, the sitter, in the image takes the place of the pupil in the eye. Hamilton writes, "The resulting image is a trace presence of the time of standing or sitting 'face to face' with a person or landscape. The figure or landscape becomes the pupil in the eye shape created by my mouth, much the same way as one sees a tiny image of oneself in the reflection of another person's pupil."[59] The image is blurry and ringed by the smudged outline of Hamilton's lips, which happen to look like the edge of eyelids. In each print, the image is distorted as the light rays were bent by the pinhole. Some images are clouded. Others are sharp, depending on how much the sitter moved as the film was exposed. Some people smile. Others stare. In other images, you can tell that the two participants couldn't keep from laughing.

Each is the record of the encounter between two bodies and, more than just bodies, two faces. The length of time for each exposure and the tension that builds up during that time seem to be infused into the image. At the same time, the images illustrate one of Hamilton's principle interests — the transposition of the senses. In this case, eyes become mouths and mouths become eyes. In essence, she is trying to make the notion of embodied vision literal by embedding vision in a part of the body that touches and tastes but does not see. Hamilton's photographs slow down vision by anchoring it in the body, creating the illusion that one can see someone seeing. We are both "inside" the seeing subject and outside at the same time. These images thicken the flat surface of the photograph in the process, so that the image conveys in

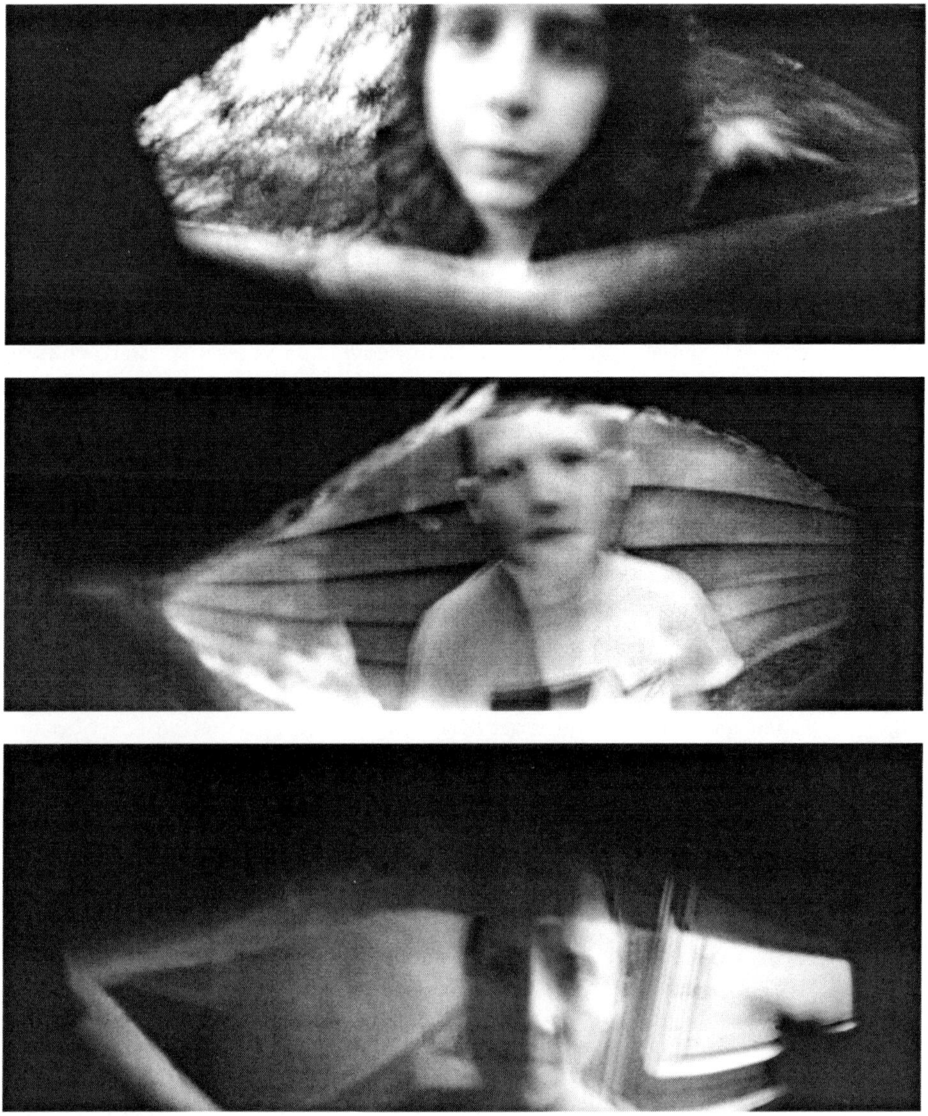

FIGURE 3.8 Ann Hamilton, *face to face*, 41, 51, 58, 2001. Medium: pigment print in wood frame. Edition: 3 with 2 Artist's Proofs (each). *Photo credit: Courtesy of the Ann Hamilton Studio.*

some sense the experience of seeing and being seen. In this way, Hamilton's pinhole photographs work against the disembodied, instantaneous quality of vision found in most photographs.

In her recent book *Self/Image*, Amelia Jones describes photographic practice as emerging from the desire "to see and know from a single point of view." She then goes on to connect this to the modern ideology of the singular, centered, male artist as genius.[60] The photograph as document is connected to the production of this subject in Western culture, as it satisfies the demand to see and know. In this relationship, the object of photographic vision is rendered legible according to the knowledge disciplines of Western culture, while the viewing subject is invisible and illegible and, therefore, escapes the grasp of these disciplines.

However, Jones argues that Western philosophy is incorrect when it identifies a dichotomy between perceiving subject and perceived object insofar as it ignores the ways that subjects are produced through images. The Western subject, she argues, is produced in the structures of representation that developed during and after the Renaissance, including photography. She points to Jane Copjec's argument regarding Renaissance painting in which she argues that classical Renaissance painting, which depicts a clarified three-dimensional, illusionistic space based on one-point perspective describes not the visual world per se but rather the drive to see. For this reason, not only is vision in this space not disembodied, but also the image includes and constitutes the body, and vice versa. The viewer/subject emerges from within the image. The boundaries of subject and object, in images, are woven together in complicated ways.

Jones extends this argument to new imaging technologies, such as video. Working from the psychoanalyst Jacques Lacan's theory of the screen, Jones describes the video screen as embodied or as fleshed. In performance art documented by video, the screen becomes a point of physical contact between the viewer's body and the artist's. In the work of someone like the Swiss video artist Pipilotti Rist, the strict division between subject and object is broken down as one watches the video. The viewer and the artist's body are both immersed and subsumed by the screen.[61] Video, Jones argues, becomes a form of haptic visuality or the mixture of sight and touch.[62]

In Roland Barthes's late work *Camera Lucida*, he examines photography from the point of view of the desiring viewer rather than the critic: "Every time I would read something about Photography, I would think of some photograph that I loved, and this made me furious. Myself, I saw only the referent, the desired object, the beloved body."[63] Barthes describes the photography as fleshy, something that captures experience and evokes affect. *Camera Lucida* is a phenomenological study of the photograph as an object that engages the body—from the mechanical clicking sound of the camera shutter release to the sensation of being pierced by the photograph. The *punctum* is the detail that ruptures the ordinary reading of a photograph drawn from the cultural codes available to the viewer, which Barthes describes as the *studium*. It is the *punctum* that penetrates the viewer's body, while the *studium* remains respectfully at a distance: "What I can name cannot really pierce me. The incapacity to name is a good symptom of disturbance."[64]

Barthes suggests that there is an ineffable aspect of experience that the image *can* capture. He links photographs, in this way, not only to desiring bodies but also to death. In a famous passage, Barthes describes the way that photographs mortify the body by demanding the sitter pose for the camera. In the process, he observes, "the Photograph (the one I intend) represents that very subtle moment when, to tell the truth, I am neither subject nor object but a subject who feels he is becoming an object: I then experience a micro-version of death (parenthesis): I am truly becoming a specter."[65] In the process of becoming image, one shifts from subject to object.

Hamilton's photographs involve the experience of the gaze of another from the position of the person looking and the person being looked at. In the case of Hamilton's pinhole photographs, the photographer and the sitter share these positions. The tension between subject and object is heightened in this work. The photographs record the oscillation between subject and object in the act of capturing the image. Hamilton sees her work shift and turn on the point that Barthes describes where bodily experience shifts to image, subject turns to object, and experience becomes sign. It is the same point beyond which Robert Morris did not want the spatial arts to go. Hamilton's work in this way is distinguished from Morris's spatial arts. Hamilton's work explores the limits of these positions, trying to uncover what is held in common when these boundaries are breached.

This is perhaps why Hamilton cites Helène Cixous's 1991 book *"Coming to Writing"* as one of the works that has been most influential for her. Cixous's essay is a poetic recounting of her experience as a woman who has an almost physical urge to write. The urge is expressed precisely in the multiplicity and fragmentation of language. In her work, the body and the senses are taken apart and transformed into text:

> Maybe I have written to see; to have what I never would have had; so that having would be the privilege not of the hand that takes and encloses, of the gullet, of the gut; but of the hand that points out, of fingers that see, that design, from the tips of the fingers that transcribe by the sweet dictates of vision. . . . Writing to touch with letters, with lips, with breath, to caress with the tongue, to lick with the soul, to taste the blood of the beloved body, of life in its remoteness; to saturate distance with desire.[66]

Writing for Cixous is an acknowledgment of distance and desire, but it is at the same time the process in which subject becomes material object and the object produces the subject. In the marks on the page, a new body is created, which encompasses and surpasses her identity as a Jewish woman. Hamilton's pinhole photographs in displacing the senses seek to intertwine viewing subject and viewed object in a manner similar to what Amelia Jones suggests in her analysis of self and image. Hamilton's pinhole photographs make sensible, rather than just visible, the process of seeing and the desire to see. As Mary Ann Doane noted, "But it is finally in the new representational technologies of vision — photography, the cinema — that one witnesses the insistency of the impossible desire to represent — to archive — the present."[67] In the moment one tries to grasp the present, the moment of seeing, the archival impulse emerges. Hamilton's images reinforce the fact that vision is always embodied and limited. But they also reveal how much bodily experience is intertwined with and framed by images.

Experience and Image

This chapter has looked at installations that appeal to an experience that is available through the body and that requires the viewer's direct experience of the piece. Installation art that requires the viewer's direct participation and bodily presence partakes in a notion of John Dewey's description of experience. According to Dewey, in the dynamic interaction between observer and environment, each shapes the other. And in the process, each is transformed, having gained something new. The development of installation into a familiar global genre in art is linked to the interest and desire for extraordinary experiences. Ann Hamilton's explanation for the appeal of her work might be that her installations ground the viewer's consciousness in her body in a way that our culture and contemporary environment no longer requires but for which we long.

Installations such as these that focus on bodily experience, including Ann Hamilton's, Richard Serra's and others, seem to defy recording by photograph. Something is missing in the images of these works and, in that lack, the viewer longs for the full experience. Hamilton's work is interesting because it explores the tension between image and experience. And in some ways it is because these works cannot be captured adequately in photography that they are fascinating and alluring. Like Benjamin's ideas of the ritual objects and the power of aura, these works require pilgrimages to really see them. Thus, even as the experience of these works escapes capture by images, it never completely excludes or ignores the photograph but is in fact framed by it. Each of these works produces an archive that represents the desire to grasp lived experience.

The installations that appeal to direct bodily experience ultimately produce their own archives, in the form of photographs and catalogs.[68] The catalogs and images of these works bring them into the realm of art history. The photographs will ultimately be the memory of these installations, will provide the jumping-off point for future histories of this genre, and as we saw in chapter 1, they will shape our understanding of these installations in the future. In the next chapter, we will look at installations in which the now-outmoded media of analog film and photography have become part of the subject matter of installation art.

FOUR

camera obscura

MEMORY IN FILM AND VIDEO INSTALLATIONS IN THE 2000S

For me, making a film is connected to the idea of loss and disappearance.

—Tacita Dean

The installations in this chapter address the sensuous aspects of outmoded analog media and raise questions about how these forms of technology have shaped experience and now shape memory. These installations are archival in the sense that they interrogate the representation of history and memory, but they also draw on the materiality and sensuous aspects of these now-outmoded forms of recording. In Renée Green's work, the slide show and other outmoded forms of media, such as vinyl LPs and Super 8 footage, have been used as part of the material of her installations and films because they mark certain time periods. According to Andreas Huyssen, "The issue of media is central to the way we live structures of temporality in our culture."[1] These forms of media fascinate at the moment of their obsolescence because they mark a shift in the way we remember and in the archival objects we produce.

It may be useful to consider these materials using Sherry Turkle's notion of "evocative objects." She defines evocative objects as those things that because they are so integral to daily activities have become part of our emotional and thinking lives. "We think with the objects we love. We love the objects we think with," she asserts.[2] The fascination with outmoded media in the form of film and recordings of various kinds represented in these installations is due to the fact that these media, which produce anxiety and excitement when first introduced, have now become familiar and beloved objects. Their appearance as art objects also suggests an interest in how time is measured and memory is experienced at the end of the twentieth century and into the twenty-first — this moment when analog photography is giving way to digital.

Tacita Dean's film *Kodak* presents the artist's feeling of melancholy at the passage of analog film. Nostalgia may be the word to describe this curiosity with the outmoded, but nostalgia has been a disdained response to change in modernity. However, these works suggest that the nostalgia evoked provides a way to think about the transformations of technology and memory and the social effects of these media at the end of the twentieth century. The works discussed in this chapter engage the viewer's body in the materiality of these now-obsolete media, inviting us to reflect on memory and ephemerality through our affective reaction to these materials. Analog film and photography now spark bodily memory. I will be discussing the work of Tacita Dean, Matthew Buckingham, and Tony Cokes. In the film installations of Matthew Buckingham and Tacita Dean, the emphasis remains on the sensuous experience of film as a now-outmoded medium. In the video installation of Tony Cokes, however, the flattening effect of digital photographic media is used to create a distanced perspective from which the viewer can reflect on the social effects of technology.

Endings: Tacita Dean's *Kodak*

Tacita Dean's film *Kodak*, produced in 2006, is a meditation on the passing of 16 mm film as a widely available medium. Dean takes as her subject matter the production of Kodak film at one of the few remaining plants in France, which was scheduled to cease production shortly after she made her piece. Running at forty-four minutes, *Kodak* consists of shots of three to four minutes in which the camera is fixed and focused on a piece of equipment or a corridor in the plant. The only sound is the ambient sound of the plant — the hiss of the air ducts, the slosh of chemicals in vats, and the whir of the rollers that guide the plastic film as it moves through the machines.

Dean's film begins by showing us the factory as if it were an empty stage set. She composes the shots in a manner that recalls photographs by Charles Sheeler or Walker Evans[3] or perhaps Bernd and Hilla Becher, the pair of salvagers who sought to preserve the industrial architecture of Western Europe in their photographs. We see a large drum and a sloping piece of metal. A line of fluorescent lights cuts across the top of the frame. The image is static and conveys the sense that these monolithic machines were intended to be there for centuries. However, we know that they will soon be idle ruins. And "ruin" is one of the key terms used to describe Dean's fascination with her subject matter.[4]

Kodak folds in on itself, as the artist uses some of the last film produced by the French Kodak plant to make it. The work in this way is a film that elegizes its own disappearance. The piece also has a classical structure, as it takes place over the course of a single day of production at the plant. This is the same structure found in pieces that record their own production, such as process art where the time and procedure of the work's making is inscribed into the body of the work.

Dean's film has a sense of melancholy that reflects her reluctance to let this medium of art making go. She was born in Canterbury, England, in 1965 and attended Falmouth School of Art and the Slade School of Fine Art. She came to filmmaking early, having been given a Standard 8 camera when she was a child.[5] Filmmaking was part of the family history, as Dean's grandfather Basil Dean began the Ealing Film Studios. Perhaps because of this childhood history, her 16 mm films focus on history and the passage of time, such as the film of the setting sun (*The Green Ray*, 2001) or the contradictions of history, as in the strange relics of a futuristic boat of the 1960s (*Teignmouth Electron*, 2000). And, like Green, Dean too has addressed Robert Smithson's work in her pieces.

In surprising ways, the subject matter of Dean's work parallels that of Renée Green's. As Hal Foster noted, both artists' works can be considered a form of archival practice. Serial structures appear in each artist's work. In fact, Dean's artists book *Floh* (2001) is dependent on a serial structure and the ability of the viewer to produce meaning from a set of photographs. If Green's work employs the serial structure of the slide show as a memory ritual, Dean's employs the photo album, another quintessential format for displaying private photographs. But where the photographs in Green's work have a personal history to which we as viewers are privy, Dean's photographs are homeless and silent.

The pictures in this book were collected from flea markets and junk shops while Dean was traveling. We see in them the same patterns that one sees in all family snapshots: images of prized possessions, vacations, and notable moments—the kind of things that we as consumers have been taught to photograph, as I noted in chapter 2. But we also have a sense of what catches

Dean's eye, which includes strange images, such as a butterfly resting on a snow bank or photographs of the singing group The Osmond Family taken from a television screen.[6] As in Green's work, the sequence seems to be important—but we struggle to draw the connections from one image to the next. Sometimes they seem formal, sometimes thematic, and at other times the only connection seems to be stark contrast. Dean's work invites us to draw connections between the sequences of images. But these are *unheimlich* images—so familiar but also inexplicable. They form a kind of uncanny archive that records an image of the human world, as Jean-Christophe Royoux says.[7]

Both Renée Green and Tacita Dean are interested in how history and memory are made and the effects of each. Both spin narratives that bring their artistic personae into play as protagonists. Each of them has made a work about Robert Smithson's work in which the notion of pilgrimage and ruin is involved. Dean chose *Spiral Jetty* and made a sound piece that recorded her search for the piece (*Searching for Spiral Jetty*, 1997).[8] However, although she is an archival artist, she rarely produces installations that mimic archives the way Green has done. Instead, the installation format enters her work mostly via film and film projection, and as with all of the pieces discussed in this chapter, sound is an important aspect of her work.

Endings are a perennial theme in Dean's work.[9] She focuses on the end of futuristic dreams in the 1960s and demonstrates how strange it is to see the failed or obsolete future in ruins—something like Walter Benjamin's notion of the "wish image." Walter Benjamin's concept of the wish image represents the unfulfilled collective hopes for the future latent in a manufactured object. The wish image arises in response to dissatisfying social conditions and is created by reaching back "to a more distant past in order to break from conventional forms." It is when the wish images' future-oriented nature is not realized—when, as Susan Buck-Morss says, it remains unconscious, a dream—that the wish image turns into a fetish. In the fetish, the wish is perceived by the collective to have been actualized, and the impetus for change is nullified.[10] It is the strangeness of the historical artifact, its evocative quality, that intrigues us and allows the viewer a moment to reflect on historical changes—and endings. Hal Foster writes of Dean, and the others he names archival artists, "Archival artists seek to make historical information, often lost or displaced, physically present."[11] This physicality is the important aspect of these pieces, as they call on bodily memory.

Although Dean's works themselves are fragments, they have a unified structure and focus on a single event, which has a beginning and ending. In studying single objects, a single phenomenon, site, or person, Dean's films and other pieces have a wholeness that Green's does not pretend to have. There is too in Dean's work an unapologetic melancholy that Green's tends to eschew.

The film *Kodak* exemplifies the qualities of unity, silence, and melancholy in Dean's work. At certain points in *Kodak*, the factory seems to be a window on the past. The plant itself is dated, and we can see in the bones of its old machines and outmoded control boards that what had been considered the latest in twentieth-century technology is now archaic. The factory fills with technicians who move carts around and arrange plastic sheets on spindles to transport to other parts of the factory. At one point, the camera focuses on a man wearing a white jumpsuit. Gloves are shoved carelessly in his back pocket while he is performing some kind of operation at a console among a field of illuminated buttons. The scenes in the factory, such as this one, have the atmosphere of the 1960s—that moment in time in which the utopian future seemed just at hand, when modernity seemed to have triumphed. In this realization, there is a surprising recognition that this time of hope has passed. This surprise includes the way labor is depicted in the film. The skilled factory labor that goes into making the film product, the carefully regulated breaks taken by workers, and the rhythm of production at the factory, which moves at an unfamiliar pace, seem alien to the twenty-first-century, middle-class art viewer.

However, it is the materiality of the raw plastic that seems to intrigue the artist most. At certain points, the movie shifts to color. The factory is darkened. Light shines through the back of layers of plastic as they move over the spindles. The edges form shimmering lines like pink water rippling in the air. In the darkness it is the sounds that take over: the rhythmic squeaks of the equipment and the air rushing through the vents. The camera dimly observes people moving in the dark and focuses on workers. An employee takes a reel of film base off the equipment and replaces it with an empty spindle. As the plastic moves across rollers and from one machine to the next, it looks like water cascading down a surface or a field of glowing color fixed in the air. In its early stages, the plastic is thick like taffy and at points takes on a bright cerulean hue that looks like pure color.

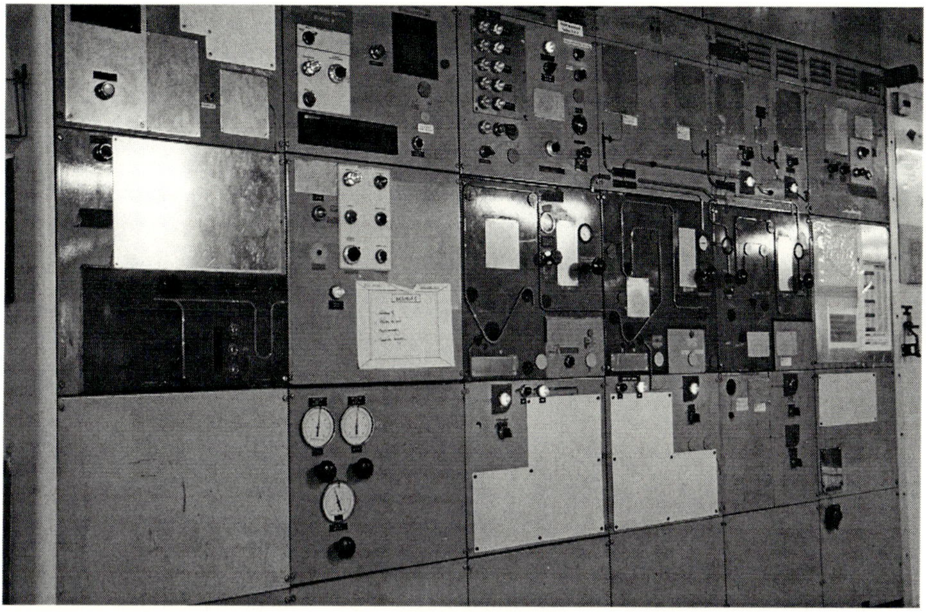

FIGURE 4.1 Tacita Dean, *Kodak*, 2006. Film installation; 16 mm color and black-and-white film. *Courtesy of the Marian Goodman Gallery, New York.*

Then, suddenly, dull, brown paper replaces the film. The space changes from transparent and glowing to dull, strict, sculptural lines. It turns out that Dean has chosen one of the days in the year in which the factory lights are turned on and paper is run through the equipment. The paper shoots down across the spindles, revealing how fast the plastic was actually moving. In a long shot, it descends down into the depths of the factory like a snake flying through the machine, going into the depth of the factory space. In another sequence, shot in black-and-white film, the viewer sees the paper edge on. It transforms back into a transparent substance that once again resembles water streaking down the surface of the screen. The pink reemerges, returning color to the dim space, as the paper slips away.

Then the workers seem to be withdrawing from the factory space. This is the end of the workday. In the corridor, people are passing and chatting. Some have coats on. Some give kisses on both cheeks to their fellow employees. As the corridor fills up, we can hear people whistling and punching their time cards. They are going home.

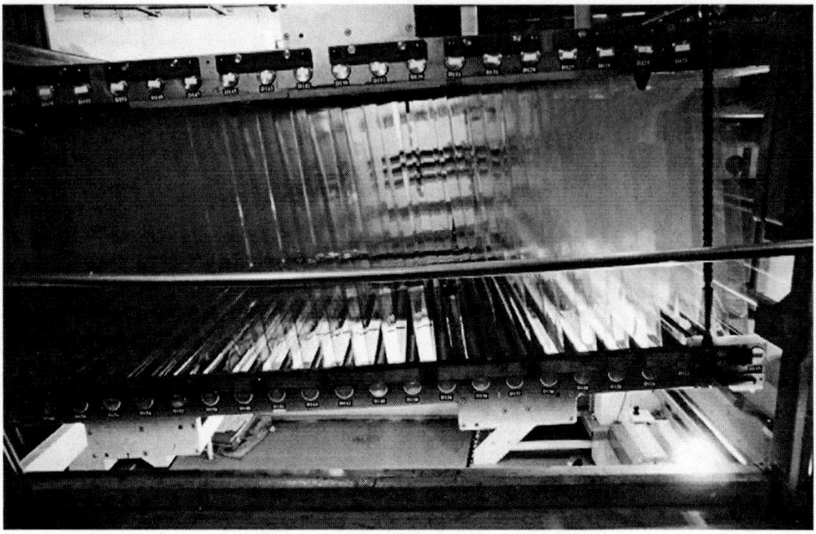

FIGURE 4.2 Tacita Dean, *Kodak*, 2006. Film installation; 16 mm color and black-and-white film. *Courtesy of the Marian Goodman Gallery, New York.*

Soon the factory is empty. The machines are still. The camera focuses on a deserted loading area with arrows painted on the pavement. Abandoned office chairs range across a vacant hangar with faded numbers on the wall. Broken signs hang on chains from the ceiling. Unwound from spindles, film bits litter the floor. We see a dirty production area, an empty, illuminated corridor. The arrows painted on the walls lead us out of the factory and to the end of the piece: a room littered with odds and ends of film and debris. Film itself has become waste material, as the screen goes dark.

In first decade of the twenty-first century, the Kodak Company has begun to cease or scale back the manufacture of various products related to analog film and photography, as digital media have begun to take over. During the 1990s and 2000s, various corporations released new versions of digital scanners, digital cameras, and digital projectors with increasingly high resolution and color quality. In response, in 2004, Kodak ceased the manufacture of film slide projectors, and in 2005, the company ceased making Kodachrome Super 8 film. Meanwhile, Kodak has also begun making digital products and acquiring companies that do so. In 2009, the company stopped making Kodachrome 64 film, which is the last of the Kodachrome products. Development services for this film were only available through December 2010. Although 16 mm film is still available, it will be only perhaps a specialty product, relegated to the realm of fine art.[12]

Dean's film is a point of reference for this chapter because it demonstrates how our relationships to the technologies that were seen to transform experience and memory at the beginning of the twentieth century have now changed. The viewers' responses to these outmoded media references a once-familiar, scripted social experience that has become defunct. The works discussed in this chapter, which include Tony Cokes's *Headphones* (2004), and Matthew Buckingham's *Situation Leading to a Story* (1999), present different possibilities for involving viewers in the physical encounter with analog media that are now part of the experiential aspect of installation art, to reflect on the shaping of memory in the twentieth century.

When the film *Kodak* was exhibited at the Guggenheim Museum in 2007, it was displayed in a home-like atmosphere in a room with carpeted floors and soft armchairs. As James Quandt notes, Dean deliberately places the projector in such a way that one can hear the sound of film as it whirs through the machine, "a sound oddly antique."[13] Dean, he notes, refuses to show her films in a traditional cinema format. Instead, she prefers installations where viewers can move around. At the Guggenheim Museum, the projector was placed in a room separate from the projection, but one could still hear the fan and the sound of the projector as it moved. The arrangement highlighted the flickering quality of 16 mm projected film in an atmosphere that was dark and inviting, familiar to those of a certain generation, but also somber because the work represented the passing of this recent period in history, the era of analog. Even the practice of watching an analog film will soon be relegated to the arena of fine art.

Moving Images as Installation Art

> In the closed space of cinema there is no movement, no circulation, and no exchange. In the dark, visitors sink into their seats as though sinking into bed. The cinema becomes a cocoon, inside of which a crowd of relaxed, idle bodies is fixed, hypnotized by simulations of reality fixed on a single screen. This model is broken apart by the folding of the dark space of cinema into the white cube of the gallery.
>
> —Chrissie Iles, *Into the Light*

The film or video installation of the 1960s and 1970s drew on the interests of Minimalism to bring the work of art into the viewer's space and to engage the viewer's body. In the process, the viewers become mobile bodies invited to reflect on their perceptions of the space, to take different viewpoints, and to take note of the architectural situation as well as the physical qualities of the image. In other words, ideally, the projected image installation allows for the kind of reflection on perception in real time that Robert Morris advocates in "The Present Tense of Space." Kate Mondloch has written about this aspect of installation art. When one considers the body in these media installations, the screen emerges quite clearly as a material object in the installation space that sets off another array of experiential factors that must be acknowledged. She describes screens as ambivalent objects — both material objects in the viewer's space and virtual windows through which the viewer looks. This focus on screens allows her to describe various modes of viewing structured by the inclusion of these objects in art contexts. These installations are designated "screen-reliant" because the screen is something with which the viewer must interact.[14]

The presence of the moving image and screen surface also makes the experience of time more complicated in film and video installations. Margaret Morse has argued that video installation is both an art of presentation (installation) and an art of representation (photography, video, and film). Unlike the traditional film, in an installation that includes moving image media, there is no clear separation between the viewer and the material on display. In the works discussed in this chapter, the film projector is often also a significant object in the installation. In the installation format, the viewer is able to move through the space and to examine the image in a way not permitted in these other formats. Several rhythms of time are experienced at once in film installations, including the pace of bodily experience, the movement of film through the projector, and the time of the film story.

The installations that are discussed in this chapter are all interior spaces — rooms. The Latin word for room is *camera*. The original camera obscura, developed in the Middle Ages, would have been a room in which a hole was made in a wall in order to let light from outside be cast inside. A screen or sheet could be hung to intercept the light, and on that sheet, a perfect but reversed and upside-down image would be projected.[15] The technology was soon used both as a kind of entertainment as well as a scientific instrument, to view solar eclipses safely. Of course, camera obscuras are the basis for the modern camera. This is a minor connection between the origins of photography and the development of room-sized, film-installation exhibition spaces, but it is interesting to ponder. The contrast with the cinema space in these old camera obscuras is significant. Where traditional movie theaters have viewers seated, these camera obscuras would have allowed the viewer to move around. And interestingly, these camera obscura spaces and installation art spaces represent more closely the setting of early cinema exhibitions where the film projector itself was an object of fascination for the viewer.[16] Before 1907, viewers behaved more like they were in a space of leisure, walking in and out, talking loudly because the films were mostly silent and the length of the projection was very short.

The image is made material and physically present in these modern installation works. One of the works that represented a breakthrough in the phenomenological or sculptural presentation of the projected image was Anthony McCall's *Line Describing a Cone*.[17] In this very simple 1973 film, McCall made the beam of projected light from the projector the focus of the viewer's attention because it occupied a volume in space. Made by filming and playing back in slowed-down time a circle being drawn on a surface, the cone emerges from a line of light over the course of half an hour. As this process unfolded, viewers could walk through the space, walk through the cone, and observe the projector as it cast the light. Time, the viewer's body, and perception are brought to bear in this work. "[The gallery] is rather the ground over which the temporalized space of the installation breaks."[18] In this situation, the image takes on a materiality and a presence in time and space that does not happen in cinema.

Make Your Camera the Family Historian! Matthew Buckingham's *Situation Leading to a Story*

Matthew Buckingham was born in 1963 in Iowa and graduated from the Art Institute of Chicago. He received an MFA from Bard College and also went on to attend the Whitney Independent Study Program. He has focused on film and photography throughout his career, and he shares the same fascination with memory and history as the other artists discussed in this chapter. For instance, in *Image of Absalon to Be Projected until It Vanishes* (2001),

Buckingham used a photograph of an equestrian monument to a bishop named Absalon (Absalon participated in the Crusades and used his plunder to commission a history of Denmark). The title of the work describes the piece accurately. The slide is to be projected until the film fades completely due to exposure from the heat of the slide projector.[19] Although the project comments on the ethics of commemorating historical figures such as Absalon as heroes, it also speaks to the fragility of photographic media. The work is again a type of process art into which decay becomes part of the structure of the work.

In 1999, Buckingham produced the film installation *Situation Leading to a Story*, in which he walks viewers through the process of gleaning a history from material fragments. In this case, the fragments consist of four 16 mm home movies that the narrator discovered discarded on a street in New York. Each has a different subject matter: a garden party in the 1920s, the renovation of a car garage in the 1930s, a bullfight, and a film that documents the building of a tramway in the Andes. The *story* comes out of the author's attempt to connect the films to each other and to their origin. In the course of narrating the films, Buckingham outlines the possible circumstances in which they were made by telling the story of the marketing and sale of Kodak home movie cameras.

The story begins at the end of the films' lives. One evening, Buckingham was walking on Eighth Street in New York City after watching a film at the Independent Film Center. He noticed a small box labeled Best and Company, a now-defunct department store, lying on a sidewalk next to some trash. The box contained four reels of 16 mm film nestled in labeled canisters. When the artist opened the film cans, he noticed that the films were brittle and had a strange odor, which is indicative of "vinegar syndrome." Acetate film breaks down over time, releasing acetic acids, which cause the plastic and emulsion to erode. The reaction produces a vinegar smell. Because of the films' condition, Buckingham decided to transfer the images to a new film.

The new film stocks were then spliced together. The sequence begins with a film labeled *Garden*. It shows a white, middle-class family dressed in the style of the 1920s at home on a summer day in a country house. The men wear jackets and hats and shoot arrows at targets or play golf. The women swing on garden swings or walk through the garden smoking cigarettes.

A little girl watches her older relatives shoot arrows. In one sequence, the camera operator films birds leaving a nest in the eaves of the house. The sec-

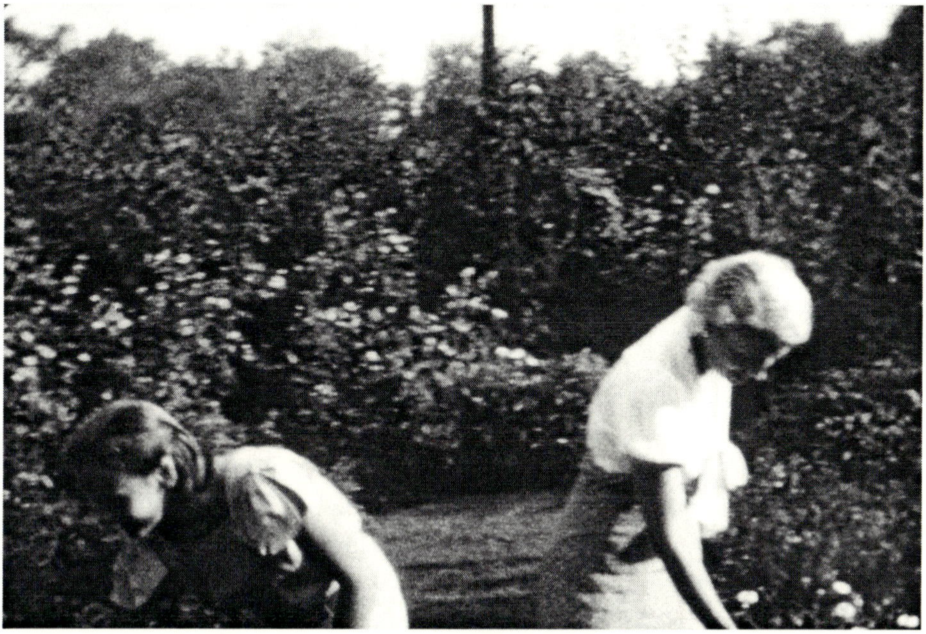

FIGURE 4.3 Matthew Buckingham, *Situation Leading to a Story*, 1999, Film still. Film installation. *© Matthew Buckingham. Courtesy of the Murray Guy Gallery.*

ond film shows the building of a cable car network in the Peruvian Andes. There are stunning shots of the mountains as clouds roll by them. White people make surveys while Peruvian locals pull on long cables or train horses and mules. Horses are shown carrying the materials of the tramway up the mountain. The third film shows the excavation of the yard at the country house and the building of a four-car garage. The final film shows a bullfight in Mexico in which the camera is turned on and off while the matador and bull sweep around the ring in the setting sun.

In the midst of describing one film, the narrator says, "I only remember certain words from the French I learned in school. One of those is *maintenant* or now, which derives from the Latin words for 'hand' and 'held' — to hold in the hand. I wondered who held the camera in the present tense, recording the moment." For the camera operator, the filming is here and now. For the viewer, the film represents paradoxically the "there and then" in the "here and now." It is in the process of trying to discover that unknown operator that

Buckingham begins to read one film against the other—to brush history against the grain, to use Walter Benjamin's phrase.[20] In Buckingham's film installation we find ourselves at the end of a chain of events, in which these once-innovative forms of material memory have become ruins. To understand why film and other old media became part of the content of installation art in the last fifteen years, it is important to understand how we have come to think about memory in the twentieth century.

Consumers of the Latest Memory-Making Technology in 1923

It was an exciting possibility to make one's own moving pictures and to display them at home in the early twentieth century, but the technology had to be worked out first. Kodak wanted to exploit a new market of home moviemakers, but the first step to doing this involved producing a film base that was not as likely to burst into flame as the highly inflammable nitrocellulose film used by professionals. At the beginning of the century, Kodak began work on an acetate-based 35 mm "safety" film. By 1909, they had found a usable formula that involved combining cellulose with acetic hydride, which would slow the burning of the film.[21] George Eastman insisted the CinéKodak Model A camera use only the new safety film. The first Model A was produced in 1920, and it was finally marketed to the public in 1923 with an advertisement in the *New York Tribune*.[22] The Kodak Company sold the cameras and film as part of a complete home movie production kit, including screen and splicer, for $325, which is only slightly less than a Ford car cost at the time.

Like the family slide show later in the twentieth century, the home movie was a new memory ritual that would bring the family together around the home movie screen. According to Mary Ann Doane, while still photographs could render a moment into a visual object, film was able to preserve the experience of duration in time itself. "What was registered on film was life itself in all its multiplicity, diversity and contingency."[23] People wanted this marvelous technology to preserve their family's special events. Buckingham notes in his commentary that within a few years over five hundred thousand movie-making kits had been sold. In researching the production codes found on the edges of the film he finds, Buckingham discovers that each of the film stocks was made in the early 1920s and early 1930s. We can assume then that the family that produced the films was able to afford a home movie camera as soon as it came out and to use it to record the banal moments of a summer afternoon and an overseas vacation.

The fact that the family who made these films owned a home movie camera in the 1920s indicates both how wealthy they were and that they used their wealth to buy the latest technology. To buy such products marks the consumer as up to date and sophisticated. The theorist Jean Baudrillard observed that there is an obligation for consumers to buy the newest and the latest.[24] Having the knowledge and power to buy the most innovative products is the means by which consumers differentiate themselves from others. The middle-class man who was able to buy the latest movie equipment distinguished himself from his less technology-sophisticated peers and was rewarded both with a sense of individual superiority and with the novel and liberating effects of the new technology.

The result of such enthusiasm, based on a desire to preserve memories and to distinguish oneself socially, had predictable results: an ever-growing cache of recordings, films, and images made by amateurs. As I have noted earlier, cultural observers commented on the accumulating pile of photographic records in the twentieth century, which burst the dams of memory and rendered mnemonic technology useless for the individual. Memories were soon relegated to various kinds of archives, administered by institutions, or left to rot in attics and basements. The transfer of memory to machines represents simply another example of new media technology.

Memory had become a kind of problem in the early twentieth century, and this understanding is reflected in the way it is described by writers. For Walter Benjamin, the new technology of photography and especially film had transformed memory and experience. He discerned a duality of memory, which turns on the relationship of technology to the body. The first type of memory is rooted in the body and based on perception. It is woven out of the threads of sensuous experience. The second type of memory corresponds to the photograph and other forms of recording media, such as film. This duality is also reflected in the two kinds of installation, the bodily/experiential and the archival, that this book has been discussing.

Bodily memory, for Benjamin, is exemplified by Marcel Proust's iconic scene of the tasting of the madeleine cookie in his book *Remembrance of Things Past*.[25] Proust, after trying and failing to recall his childhood, takes a bite of the sweet cookie and immediately relives a moment from his childhood when he ate these treats while drinking tea at his aunt's house. This happy moment returned to him with all the complexity of a live experience, engaging his senses and imagination. Bodily memory is a fleeting sensation of wholeness and pleasure in what is Proust's otherwise dull exercise in recollection. Bodily memory is a cluster of associations that cling to a perception. In bodily memory, one becomes aware of the network of memories and sensations that are tied to this perception. It is an experience of memory that declines as the function of remembering is taken over by photography, sound recording, and film, according to Benjamin. The transformation of memory is emblematic of the transformation of experience in the modern world. Genuine experience according to Benjamin can now only be evoked distantly via art in poetic "correspondences," which are the fusion of sound, sight, smell, and touch possible through art. The type of memory that Benjamin associates with "correspondences" is ephemeral. Poetry is one way of achieving this fusion, but perhaps Benjamin would have seen installation art as another means.

To contrast bodily and archival memory, Benjamin refers to Proust's dissatisfaction with his attempts to recall his experience of Venice. He describes the retrieved memories as a collection of photographs. Photography records all of the visual information of a past moment without any other sensuous data, thus freezing and isolating it. The takeover of the practice of memory by photography and film, for those early twentieth-century critics, is a symptom of the decline of genuine experience in modernity. Photography in Benjamin's argument is symptomatic of mechanization, the one-touch action of the modern world, and of the growing anonymity of the masses. All of the social and cultural relationships and experiences symbolized by the experience of bodily memory dissolve as the more anonymous realm of archival and photographic memory expands. However, photography also distances us from the past in a way that we can question it. It also serves as a foil to the powerful effects of ritual, which Benjamin sees as a means of unthinkingly holding in place certain beliefs, customs, and rules.

In Buckingham's film installation, *Situation Leading to a Story* (1999), he notes that the Kodak moving picture manual urged its readers to understand that "your movie camera exists to preserve life not to destroy it." In the late nineteenth and early twentieth centuries, the anxiety and excitement generated by industrialization was exemplified by the response to the possibilities of photographic technology.[26] Photography was seen as something that preserves but also destroys. In the photographic portrait, the individual, already absent, is reduced to the parameters of a spatial situation. In an old snapshot, it is not the actual individuality of the person depicted but the clothing and jewelry the sitter wears, the conventional and socially determined posing, and the spatialization of a moment of time. The photographic portrait is only an array of things. In photography, as we have discussed in reference to the documentation of installation art, an experience that includes all of the senses is reduced to a visual document bounded by a frame. It is an evocation of death.

The transfer of memory and experience to material records has had a profound impact on our culture. If history is conceived as material residues, the social relationships that form history are hidden within the concrete we walk on, the clothes we wear, and the books and stories we read. These objects do not appear as historical evidence of social relationships because we have forgotten their true origin as the work of other people. Whether from the madeleine cookie or the old arcades, the fragments of text from the past reveal in their materiality these barely remembered social relationships. The decline of bodily memory represents a loss of a certain kind of access to the past that requires work to recover. Film and photography, therefore, were the new technologies that spelled the end of certain ways of experiencing and remembering.

The person who encounters a film, the Buckingham work suggests, must go through the effort to redeem this material for history. As Mary Ann Doane notes, film records events indiscriminately and therefore risks opacity and meaninglessness by gathering a heap of useless historical details.[27] The films Buckingham finds seem to have this quality of randomness. The narrator of *Situation Leading to a Story* explains the efforts that he made to put these film fragments together and to render them meaningful, historical materials. The effort involves not only the preservation of the film and the research about its production but also the search for the places and individuals connected to it. The films must be placed in their original context to be meaningful — a context that involves a web of social, economic, and material relationships.

To that end, Buckingham visits an address in upstate New York in Ossining near the legendary Sleepy Hollow. In the process, he encounters various forms of history, both its revival and its erasure. He meets a miserable historical

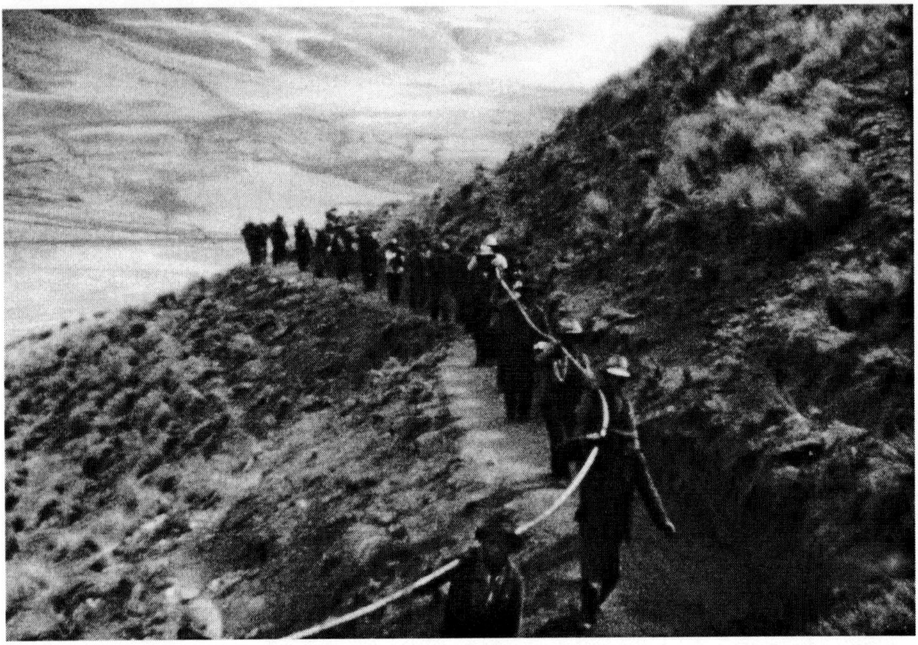

FIGURE 4.4 Matthew Buckingham, *Situation Leading to a Story*, 1999, Film still. Film installation. *© Matthew Buckingham. Courtesy of the Murray Guy Gallery.*

reenactor employed at the author Washington Irving's home. And he discovers that the town of Ossining, New York, changed its name from Sing Sing, which derives from the Native American name for the place, in order to distance itself from Sing Sing Prison.

Buckingham goes deeper into the background of the intriguing film titled *Peru*. The narrator is able to analyze these films in such a way that, through them, we see the relationships among individuals in the past.[28] He tells the story of the Cerro de Pasco Company in Peru, which was organized by a group of wealthy New York business people in 1901, around the time that the Kodak Company was conducting research on "safety film." They bought up bankrupt copper-mining companies in Peru and produced a powerful American-run business. The film shows the company and its local employees building a tramway through the Andes in the 1920s. The film could have been used to promote the company in some capacity. The harsh working conditions at the mine, we learn, inspired the organization of labor unions, and the company poisoned the land and water around the mine and then profited by buying it up for reduced prices. We follow the story of this company up until the 1970s when it becomes nationalized by a new revolutionary Peruvian government. Buckingham's narrative does the work of uncovering these social relationships embedded in the film. He never connects it directly, but the narrator's research again raises the question of whether this too is the source of the happy family's wealth in *Garden*.

Because he can't find direct historical connections, Buckingham finally wants to track down someone who would remember the connection among the films. In the end, he searches in the Manhattan phone book for Harrison Dennis, whose name he found on the films, and, much to his surprise, finds him. The narrator wants to describe the films to Dennis, to jog his memory. But when he gets on the phone with him, the man hurriedly states he doesn't remember the films, then becomes annoyed, and hangs up the phone. The only thing that connects these films for certain, finally, is that they were thrown away. Someone wanted to forget them and perhaps the memories that connect them. Despite the effort to recover this history, the person whose memories would connect to this history refuses to own them.

Buckingham's story, full of fits and starts, remembering and forgetting, and discoveries and disappearances, demonstrates one way of trying to uncover the social and cultural relationships embedded in every artifact of history. The unresolved quality of the story suggests that it is far more difficult to knit a story together out of fragments than one would expect. At one point, he says, "Narrative is a chain of events in a cause and effect relationship occurring in time and space. The plot of an event is selected from the events of a story." The home movies, he says, do not constitute a narrative, and in a certain sense, the narrator's story is far too fragmentary to make one either. Therefore, the films have become mute materials, subject to decay as much as any other kind of historical artifact. These materials, used to preserve individual memory, have enabled that memory to be disavowed and "forgotten." The transfer of the task of recording memory and experience to machines and materials represents a kind of forgetting. The theorist Theodor Adorno explains his concerns about the effects of industrial production, mass production, or reification on society to Walter Benjamin in a 1940 letter in these terms: "For all reification is a forgetting: objects become purely thing-like the moment they are retained for us without the continued presence of their other aspects: when something of them has been forgotten. This raises the question as to how far this forgetting is one that is capable of shaping experience, which I would almost call epic forgetting, and how far it is a reflex forgetting."[29] If the evidence of history is found in the materials and objects we use everyday, the technique of machine production allows this evidence to be forgotten. And what we learn, ironically, from Buckingham's work, is that the materials and practices of new photographic technologies, which once threatened the disappearance of traditional forms of memory, must now be rescued and preserved.

Pierre Nora, a French historian, wrote the article "Between Memory and History: Les Lieux de Mémoire" in 1989, and his assessment of the challenge of archival memory seems to ring true for an earlier moment in the century. Nora's memory is one of ritual and tradition that is now mostly gone. The little that is left remains under pressure from archival memory. Natural, collective memory has been pressed into and maintained in areas and objects Nora describes as *lieux de mémoire*. The conclusions of Buckingham's work contradict those of Pierre Nora. He claims that memory is endangered, pointing to the recent scramble in academia and the broader culture to examine memory in all its forms. And it is in danger from archival memory. But archival memory too is in danger of disappearing and requires preservation and redemption. Buckingham and Dean's filmic archives and films for archives suggest that film, recording materials, and still photographs, rather than threats to memory, have become endangered "evocative objects."

Outmoded Media as "Evocative Objects"

That film has become an "evocative object" is suggested by the installation arrangement of Buckingham's work. The installation of *Situation Leading to a Story* had a distinctive setup that Buckingham designed in order to encourage viewers to focus on the outmoded, material qualities of the film technology. The film projection and the film projector were placed in two different rooms. In the 2009 exhibition of the piece at the Museum of Contemporary Art in Denver, the artist used an Eiki Slim Line projector with the film reel held on a horizontal platform above the projector with two flywheels extended in either direction. In this arrangement, it was possible to watch the 8 mm film as it threaded its way from film reel through projector. The viewer could examine the individual frames of film as they passed. The very fascination of the film projector as an object, as in Dean's work, suggests that it is no longer an everyday piece of equipment but has become an artifact of history.

The arrangement of the installation is significant because it frames the different encounters with the film apparatus differently: sound, equipment, and image each have their own space. Buckingham explained that he arranged the components of the piece so that one would hear the audio on the film first, then encounter the film projector as it ran, and finally turn a corner and see the projected image. In the installation, a small window was cut close to the bottom of the wall through which the projector cast its relatively small projection. When viewers walked down a short hallway and entered the projection room, they saw that the film was projected in the farthest bottom corner of the room. The artist explained that he wanted people to enter the room in a line, stack up to watch the film, and then follow the same path out. In the exhibition in Denver, the speakers were not outside the room but inside and facing toward the projection. In this arrangement, viewers seemed to be reluctant to move past the speakers. Instead, they watched the film projection from a distance, as if the space was truly a private space in which only certain people were allowed to watch the films — like a home movie. Nevertheless, Buckingham is always amused that when people are comfortable they want to stand in the light of the projector in *Situation* and to cast shadows on the film projection.

Sound too is key to these works. As Tacita Dean remarked, "When I put the sound of a dog barking or a motorbike passing at dusk, I am so aware of the feeling of abandonment that it can create. It's incredibly powerful, sound."[30] The sounds in the installation reveal the difference between the digital present and the recent past when film was an ordinary event. It isn't possible to observe as well how a digital projector works, and although there is always the roar of the fan in a digital projector, the distinctive click, click, click of the film sprockets is absent. In writing about an exhibition of Tacita Dean's work, James Quandt quotes her as saying, "Analog, it seems, is a description of all the things I hold dear."[31] As explanation of this, Quandt goes on to say that digital imagery is "insubstantial, endlessly transmutable, there but not there." In Tacita Dean's work and in Buckingham's, the sound of the projector and its fan is audible in the projection room reminding viewers of the material presence of the media.

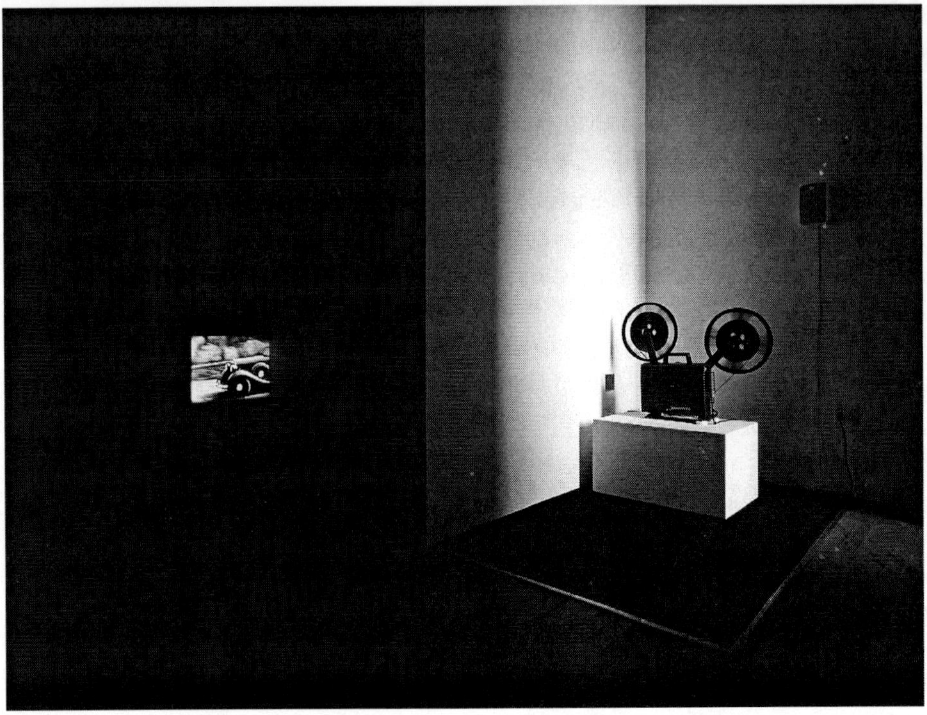

FIGURE 4.5 Matthew Buckingham, *Situation Leading to a Story*, 1999. Installation view at PS1. Film installation. *© Matthew Buckingham. Courtesy of the Murray Guy Gallery.*

Sound is also a key component in many of Renée Green's works. If Green's works seem to embody a photographic archive, they also comprise a sound recording archive. Green's installations and films are studded with various sound experiences. *Partially Buried in Three Parts* addressed the intersection of personal memory and history in the 1970s via music. She shot a video to accompany the installation. It opens with sequences of found footage, a fairground carousel, Green's Super 8 film footage of Cleveland, video clips of protesters in Berlin in the 1960s, and scenes from a 1970 Mick Jagger film. These shots are interspersed with images of record album covers and the sounds of music of the period.

The section of the installation *Partially Buried in Three Parts* titled *Simulated Vinyl Diary* included a set of record albums from the 1970s, a turntable, and headphones The arrangement invited viewers to relax and enjoy the music of the 1970s while coming up with their own memories and associations with the time. The title of this section suggests that this music forms the soundtracks and memories of millions of lives. This produces a sense of identification among viewers that has implications for understanding the formation of identity in the last few decades.

The most striking example of this in Green's video *Partially Buried* is the several-minutes-long sequence of music by Jimi Hendrix and Buddy Miles that accompanies a shot of a person looking through albums. The film then cuts to images of the hill where students were shot at Kent State University in 1970. The music represents the collective idealism of the 1970s, for which many are nostalgic, while the images recall the extinguishing of those collective hopes. The sequence represents the tension inherent in Benjamin's notion of the "wish image." In Green's video and installation, the enjoyment of pop music is connected to mass protest and political revolution and its aftermath in the 1970s. *Partially Buried in Three Parts* stages the tension between individual memory and collective history, as well as the nostalgia evoked by the material qualities of mass-produced objects in the twentieth century. The film is also full of sounds typical of the 1970s. The tick and whir of film moving through a projector accompanies Green's Super 8 footage of the Kent State University campus. The distinctive sound of a record needle dropping into a vinyl groove is heard accompanied by pops of static as the needle moves across the surface of an album. The inclusion of such characteristic sounds in the video emphasizes the material and sensory encounter with objects produced and used at an earlier period of time. The sounds embody and evoke for many the sense of idealism of that time.

The *madeleine* of the twenty-first century may be the sound of a needle dropping on a record or film ticking through a projector. The connection that we have to these mass-produced objects through our bodies points to the fact that we were trained to use them in a consumer culture that now deems them obsolete. These mass-produced consumer products shaped daily habits, social practices, and finally the memories of countless individuals. As we have seen in Dean's film *Kodak* and in Buckingham's *Situation Leading to a Story*, it is in the passing of certain media that they become interesting again — strange but hauntingly familiar. This turn toward the past has inspired some observers to suggest that nostalgia may now be a form of critique in art.[32]

Buckingham's films are silent but narrated with the story of their recovery, that is, the artist's efforts to research their origins and his failure to knit together this history. In the process of listening to this, the viewer realizes that Buckingham reads one film against the next—opening up possibilities for historical coincidence and connection, drawing together places such as upstate New York and the Andes, and emphasizing these materials' origins in specific times and places. In this way, *Situation Leading to a Story* shares qualities with Renée Green's video piece *Partially Buried Continued* as well.

History and Memory as Sensory Experiences

Thirty years after McCall made *Line Describing a Cone*, he was in a roundtable discussion with Matthew Buckingham on the occasion of Chrissie Iles's exhibition of projected image art at the Whitney Museum of American Art. At one point in the discussion, McCall noted that most of the artists who worked with film in the 1960s were completely self-taught, having come out of backgrounds in sculpture and painting. "And we approached it as material, much like one would approach the use of any sculptural material."[33] Buckingham responds to this by saying how his generation of artists was educated in the history and theory of film. For him, this education and background led him to read in history and in other fields that related to documentary film. It is clear that the generation of conceptual artists and their interest in the materiality of film had an impact on Buckingham's work. But Buckingham's film installations, like Dean's, highlight the materiality of film not simply as a medium but also as a historical object. His work appeals to the viewer's sense of smell, touch, and hearing, as much as to the sense of sight. While he engages the viewer's senses with his work, Buckingham hopes also to get viewers to reflect with him on the process of constructing a narrative history from material remains.

As I noted earlier, the projected image installation brings together present and past. The video installation, Margaret Morse argues, is the strange combination of the here and now of the viewer's body with the there and then of the photographic image. It is in the examination of the break between the two that the viewer begins to ask questions about memory and the way experience has been shaped by photographic media. It also turns the viewer's focus from the image alone to the entire moving image apparatus (projector, image, sound, and the space in which it is shown). The object that had been considered two dimensional and visual, the photograph, becomes three dimensional and haptic, tactile, aural, and even olfactory in the installation context. In Dean and Buckingham's works, this examination sparked by a bodily experience raises questions about obsolescence in technology and how obsolescence shapes the perception of history. These installations make historical objects physically present, as Hal Foster says.

The philosopher F. R. Ankersmit argues that in nostalgia the past and present are experienced in the same moment and in the same space. Nostalgic historical experience is the individual *sensuous* experience of the past in the present. Ankersmit calls this a "sublime" experience of the past: "Historical experience pulls the faces of past and present together in a short but ecstatic kiss. Historical experience is, in this way, a 'surface' phenomenon: It takes place on the surface or interface where the historian and the past meet each other."[34]

The encounter of the past in the "meeting of surfaces" suggests that the sense of touch, smell, and sound are more important than sight. When one experiences the past in this way, one undergoes the same sensations experienced some time in the distant past. History as surface in Ankersmit's reading does not render the past a shallow, hollow phenomenon but instead represents physical contact with the past that overcomes the gap between subject and object, history and the present, through bodily memory. Experience takes place in the contact between the surfaces of things. It is the aural, tactile, olfactory, and even visual contact with outmoded objects that provokes the sense of nostalgia. It is the intensity and emotional tinge of the experience of nostalgia that intrigues Ankersmit. He even argues that nostalgia provides the most authentic experience of the past.

Nostalgia is at the same time a powerful experience that is easily used to manipulate for the purpose of selling products, to create false allegiances, or to soothe prematurely worries about present conditions. And it is startling to realize that many collective experiences of nostalgia in the last part of the twentieth century are inspired and organized around the consumption of mass-produced consumer goods. In the era of mass production and mass media, millions of individuals are likely to have used objects, such as cassette tapes, home movie cameras, and vinyl LPs, in the same way at the same time. Our bodies and senses have been shaped by the collective engagement and use of mass-produced objects. Nostalgia is a sensuous experience, I argue, following Ankersmit, that involves the body of the viewer who uses the mass-produced objects that Adorno disdained as vehicles of forgetting. Activities such as putting headphones on one's head, hearing film pass through the sprockets of a projector, and smelling slide film heat up as it is warmed by a bulb become ways of reflecting on the passage of time.

All of these sensations are produced by the material qualities of objects that have been mass produced. Millions of people have experienced these sensations when using these objects. It is because of this that, when encountering these objects and materials once they become outmoded, we tend to respond with a pleasant and surprising feeling of recognition — a recognition that can even span differences among cultures and classes in contemporary society. This nostalgia reveals something about the viewer's relationship to the past and to other individuals.

The installations described in this chapter, including Buckingham's function as frames for evocative objects, or *heterotopia*—as I discussed in the introduction—spaces in which disparate places and times intersect via the objects and materials they contain. Michel Foucault names, as examples of heterotopia, museums, archives, and libraries where "time accumulates," a phenomenon that he argues is unique to modernity.[35] But he also includes the movie theater, which encapsulates both different places and times in the form of film. By producing an intersection of times and places using these outmoded forms of media, these installations reveal that photographic media, which Benjamin had described as a foil to bodily memory, can, when they become outmoded, engage viewers' senses and bodies and become experiential mnemonic devices. Analog film and photography now evoke bodily memories.

Media Nostalgia in Contemporary Art

There have been many examples of artists using media as a device for memory and nostalgia in recent exhibitions. In 2005, the Guggenheim Museum in New York acquired Slater Bradley's *Doppelganger Trilogy* (2001–2004), which was a sentimental and nostalgic piece about the artist's childhood heroes. The video installation took several rooms and focused on the artist's fascination with 1980s pop stars. Each of the videos imitated the various media in which the pop stars were originally filmed — from Super 8 film to the grainy videotape of portable, handheld cameras in the 1990s. Another exhibition the same year at the Baltimore Museum of Art focused on slide projectors and slide shows in art practice. The exhibition presented works produced in the last part of the twentieth century, from Dan Graham's *Homes for America* (1966–1967) to a recent work by Peter Fischli and David Weiss using slides of flowers and mushrooms displayed by timed projectors.

The 2006 Whitney Museum of American Art Biennial provided examples of media nostalgia as well. Many of the selections for the year included film installations in which the projector was placed in the installation space. Examples include Diana Thater and T. Kelly Mason's *Jump* (2004), which featured two happy things from Thater's childhood: the Bob Dylan song "Subterranean Homesick Blues" and jump roping. The work included a film projector, colorful bulletin boards, and recorded music. The same edition of the Whitney featured Rodney Graham's *Torqued Chandelier Release* (2005), a single-room film installation that displayed an elaborate film projector projecting a nearly still image of a crystal chandelier.[36]

As these exhibitions were taking place, as I have noted, Kodak and other companies were eliminating the production of analog film. The use of old film and slide projectors, vintage video, and other old recording media in works of art highlight the shift from the analog to digital media. These machines, tapes, vinyl records, and films have become fragments and ruins pointing to a newly estranged past. The transition to digital media in the 2000s seems to parallel the point in the early twentieth century when Walter Benjamin observed photography and film to have marked a decisive break with the older cultural forms of painting and the graphic arts. These analog media have colonized our unconscious, been objects of desire, and shaped our experiences. This new perspective becomes apparent in these installations that deliberately frame the material qualities of these media. We see in the late twentieth century that the viewer's encounter with these objects is more like Benjamin's bodily memory, which photography and film was supposed to destroy. Therefore, perhaps digital media has become a new foil to these outmoded objects and materials, as photography had been for traditional forms of memory.

Tony Cokes's *Headphones*

How do we regard nostalgia and old media in the period of transition to digital and downloadable media? Tony Cokes's video installation titled *Headphones* from 2004 demonstrates the way nostalgia in the 2000s illuminates this transition most clearly. His videos focus on the culture of pop music, and they often combine recorded music and textual elements. Cokes was born in 1959 and received an MFA degree from Virginia Commonwealth University. He also attended the Whitney Independent Study Program in the 1980s. Cokes has worked for two decades in video art and is well known for the video work of X-PRZ in the 1990s.

The video piece titled *Headphones* represents Cokes's interest in the way technologies have organized groups and social identities. It combines pop music and vintage marketing films by the music recording industry, which in the context of his video, should enlist the affective power of nostalgia kindled by these pop culture artifacts. However, the material qualities of the media he uses seem to be downplayed in this piece. Hence, if nostalgia is a sublime and tactile experience of the past, Cokes's work seeks to thin that experience or, perhaps, to filter it in order to encourage the viewer to reflect on the past and its relationship to the present. Cokes uses digital video and processors to create a sense of distance between the viewer and the powerful elements of the outmoded media in his work. The piece uses archival RCA Company promotional films and text by music theorist Jacques Attali in a layered structure. Although the vintage films inspire nostalgia in the viewer, the video frames that nostalgia in a particular way.

Cokes uses nostalgia to examine the way group identity is formed in the context of consumer culture and how such identities have shifted over the decades in the twentieth century. In nostalgia, one can perceive collective identity produced by consumer technologies that was obscured by the isolating effect of using the technologies at the time. Via the visual structure of his video, Cokes uses this awareness to invite viewers to think about the isolating effect of current technologies and the possibility of collective hopes, the "wish image" that they now obscure.

As the scratched, crackling film begins in *Headphones* we are invited into the home of an American family of the 1950s, just sitting down to listen to the latest in audio technology.

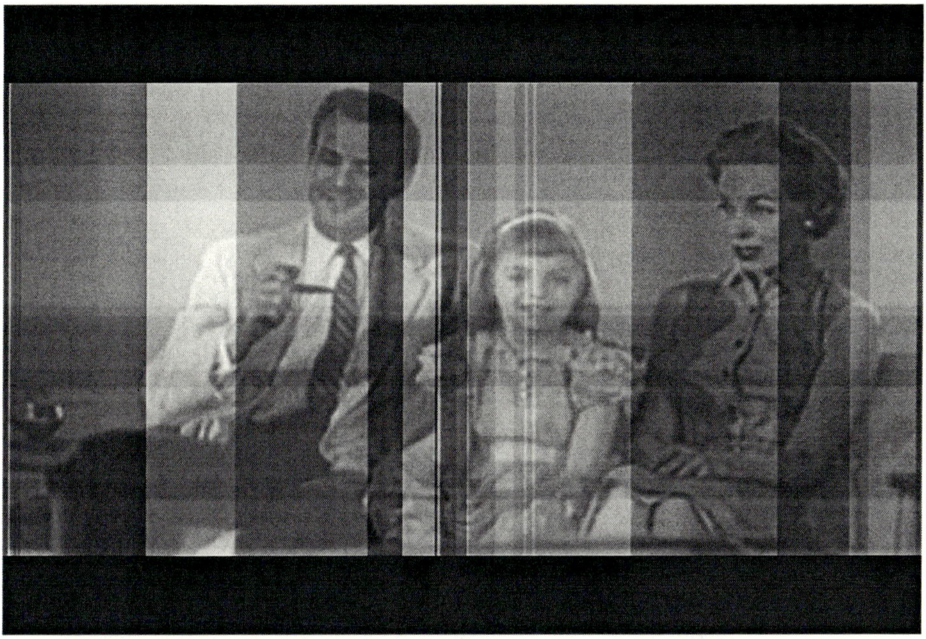

FIGURE 4.6 Tony Cokes, *Headphones*, 2004, video still. *Image: Scott Pagano for Tony Cokes 2005. Courtesy of the artist.*

They are white, middle class, and beaming with excitement. Father, mother, and daughter sit in a sleek and modern living room. As dad gives a large cassette to his young daughter to play on the tape player, the music swells and the narrator gushes over the simplicity of the new recording technology. The film, dating from the late 1950s, is a promotional piece made by the production company Jam Handy for the RCA Company's then innovative audio-recording cartridge, and it presents this scene of idealized white and middle-class normality as if it were made possible by consuming the latest in electronic products. As with most cultural artifacts intended to exhibit the latest in technology, the vintage film is now strongly marked as outmoded and naive.

The advertisement for RCA's cassette-recording device that begins Cokes's video seems most archaic because it suggests that a family would sit down in the living room *together* to enjoy a piece of recorded music. This archaic social practice points to Cokes's real subject matter — the social effect of recorded music. Recording has transformed music from a collectively enjoyed, performance-based medium to a medium that millions of isolated individuals with headphones consume. The video emphasizes that this is made possible by mechanical, electrical, and now digital reproduction.

Nostalgia is usually considered an individual experience, which might be the reason to discount it as a means to access collective historical experience. However, nostalgia reveals the connections between individuals that had been possible in the context of mass media and mass culture in the twentieth century. It does so in at least two ways. First, nostalgic experience shows us that we have been organized into groups with common interests by the products we consumed. Nostalgia is a means of consolidating an individual sense of self.[37] However, one of the characteristics that Elizabeth E. Guffey notes about the consumption of outmoded objects is that subcultures often form around these products. When various consumers of such products were interviewed about their interest in old things — ranging from those who buy vintage clothes to those who frequent Irish pubs — they continuously cited social connection and identification as one of the primary pleasures of nostalgia. In the realm of consumer culture, nostalgia conjures a sense of connection among people who watched the same TV shows, bought the same things, or listened to the same music. Having defined themselves through the products they consume, consumers in turn identify with each other through those same products when they are old. Thus, the product by which we distinguish ourselves from others when it is new becomes the product by which we identify with others as we get old.

Second, it also directly involves individual bodies. Individuals had to learn to use new technologies or to appreciate the latest music. It was necessary to train one's hands and ears to enjoy vinyl records or to project films at home. As Tony Cokes points out, many of the products for which we are now nostalgic were used to make certain strange, new activities, like watching home movies or listening to music in your living room, normal and expected.[38] The intensity of the experience of nostalgia in consumer culture derives from the bodily experiences and feelings produced in consuming these objects of mass culture. The training and practice to use these objects has transformed them into "evocative objects."

In Cokes's video, the father turning over his domain of the use and enjoyment of high-tech objects to a little girl is meant to underline the simplicity of this piece of home-recording equipment. It also symbolizes the way the paternalistic recording industry has given naive consumers the power to record their *own* music. The use of these consumer products reinforced social stratification and division, even as they produced groups. As the first piece of film ends, the title *Headphones* comes on screen with the words "transcription of a transcription . . . copy of a copy." As an extension of this mythical story of Promethean distribution, Cokes emphasizes that each film and piece of music in his video can be found as an individual downloadable copy on the Internet available to millions, and the artist includes the digital file names for each.

This introduction leads into another piece of archival RCA promotional film by Jam Handy titled *New Dimensions in Sound*, which dates from the late 1950s and promoted the company's innovative stereophonic sound systems. Both pieces of film come from a time in RCA's postwar history when it was aggressively expanding its market in home musical equipment and recordings. In 1949, in response to Columbia Music's development of the 33⅓ rpm vinyl record, RCA came out with its own 45 rpm extended-playing vinyl record and followed it with a turntable that could play records of both speeds. In 1958, RCA developed the technology for stereophonic sound.[39] As each new technology was released, the corporation had to build a new market for it and teach consumers why it was better and how to use the new equipment.

In this twenty-minute monaural film, an affable hidden narrator talks to several middle-class white men, all played by the same actor. As each character looks almost exactly alike, the film suggests that, even as consumer culture isolates individuals, it encourages a type of conformity. The narrator interrogates each man, who is alone and listening to music in his living room, about his obsession with high-fidelity, home-recording and playback equipment. The last few minutes of the film, however, shows a flight over the Grand Canyon that has no soundtrack. The producer intended the music for this segment to be supplied by the projectionist on new RCA home stereophonic equipment. The flight over the Grand Canyon aims to seduce the viewer with pleasant, new sound quality and images that, combined, suggest freedom through new technology.

Cokes chose only these last few minutes to include in his video. In one version of the work, it was projected onto a screen in a gallery on an average-sized wall at the scale of a large landscape painting. Projected at this size, the film of the Grand Canyon creates the illusion of flying along with the music, soaring over the rock ridges and floating over the river thousands of feet below, moving freely through open air. The images, in fact, would have complemented the stereophonic sound, which unlike monaural sound, seems to come to listeners in three dimensions. The film and sound would have generated a sublime sensation of moving through open air that consumers would associate with RCA's new stereo technologies, encouraging consumers to associate them with transcendence and, perhaps, even the possibility of escape from the pressures of modern, middle-class life. We see in this film clip a convincing example of a wish image, which expresses the hopes of freedom and happiness through consumerism and technology.

Of course, the vinyl LP, the turntable, and the cassette tape have now become mostly obsolete — dispatched to the realm of novelty — as have analog photography and film. After dominating the recording industry for several decades, the vinyl LP was challenged by the introduction of compact discs in the 1980s, and compact discs have now been challenged by the introduction of MP3s and downloadable digital files. Although vinyl records have recently experienced a revival with sales increasing by double digits in the last few years,[40] they seem now to be a connoisseur's object. Vinyl LPs are art objects in the work of Christian Marclay and others. For instance, an exhibition of work by contemporary artists who use records opened at the Institute of Contemporary Art in Boston in 2011. These are now evocative objects rich enough in terms of cultural memory and nostalgia to inspire works of art.

The Complexity of Nostalgia

For viewers in the twenty-first century, the RCA film is kitsch, nostalgia, or perhaps in the context of Cokes's video, what the design historian Elizabeth Guffey calls "retro." In the last half of the twentieth century, as in the nineteenth, there has been a preoccupation with preservation. But rather than the great monuments of the past, the interest in preservation now extends as well to the ephemeral aspects of popular culture and fashion. Old styles, like old movies, return to satisfy the thirst for authenticity.[41] This interest stepped up in the 1970s. For, rather than blindly consuming whatever was newest on the market, consumers in the 1970s and after demonstrated an awareness of the quick turnovers of styles, commodities, and designs and reacted to it. Elizabeth Guffey distinguishes pure nostalgia from what she calls "retro," which she designates as a fondness for the past that is tempered by self-awareness. The word "retro" first appeared, according to Guffey, in the context of the most future-oriented program in the 1960s: the American space program. It was a word used in association with John Glenn's dangerous space flight in the Mercury capsule in 1962 in which he had to use "retro" rockets to slow the descent of his capsule to earth. The word "retro" entered common speech in the early 1970s when cultural observers noted disillusionment with modernism's focus on "futurism." In retro, there is an awareness and self-consciousness about one's historical position in relation to outmoded styles and objects.

If nostalgia represents for Guffey a self-aware consumption of "retro" products, for Fredric Jameson, nostalgia is symptomatic of a problem. Jameson's description of nostalgia differs from Guffey's and from Ankersmit's in that it represents a failure of cultural memory and a giving in to the forces of consumerism. He was responding to the wave of nostalgia that swept through American society in the 1970s and 1980s. It was a time, in fact, that sociologist Fred Davis described as a nostalgia epidemic. He cited the revival of fashions from the 1920s and 1930s, as well as popular nostalgic films such as *Butch Cassidy and the Sundance Kid*, *The Last Picture Show*, *Amarcord*, *Jules and Jim*, and to some extent, *Bonnie and Clyde*.[42] In the 1970s, it seemed every era of history was available for appropriation by the TV drama.

Fredric Jameson seemed to despair of the critical power of cultural memory at this time. He argued that films such as *Something Wild* and *Blue Velvet* are not stories about people so much as they are "allegorical narrative(s) in which the 1950s meet the 1980s."[43] In such films, the historical context of the eras is stripped and packaged into easily consumed stereotypes.[44] Rich historical narrative was reduced to the melodrama of stock figures signifying different historical periods. The sense of time and history seemed to have changed under the influence of the mass media.[45] Mass media reduce memory to a thin surface phenomenon.[46] Rather than responding to authentic historical conditions, the postmodernist work of art used recycled recording materials of the past in a new antihistorical pastiche. And the postmodernist form of art, par excellence, according to Jameson, was experimental video.[47] Film, on the other hand, remains a medium that has the depth and richness to continue to harbor cultural memory.

For Jameson, video represents the evacuation of historical perspective. In video, he argues, it is not possible to obtain a sense of distanced perspective that is an inherent part of memory. Jameson designates this quality of video "total flow," where there is no pause or break left in the structure of video to allow for reflection. Nostalgia is the reduction of complex cultural memory to a thin, transient sign of history.

Critical Historical Perspective in Cokes's Video

Tony Cokes's *Headphones* seems to respond to this criticism of the immediacy of video by using the flexibility of digital video to create a formal and critical distance in the viewers' encounter with the 1950s film. The viewer is distanced from the seductive material qualities of the old promotional films by the video's layered structure. While viewers feel as if they are flying over the Grand Canyon, recent music by the electropop band *Static* begins to play, and text rolls across the screen emphasizing its two-dimensional materiality. The projection surface becomes a surface in the viewer's space. The music too disrupts the film, as it is slower than the film images suggest—there is no swell of uplifting orchestral music. In Cokes's video, we must look at several layers simultaneously, watching the digitized film images of flight over the Grand Canyon, listening to the contrasting soundtrack, and *reading* the scrolling text. We experience the sublime landscape by looking through and beyond words. The simple structure of layering presents a challenge to the viewer, as it is impossible to pay attention to more than one layer at a time. In this way, Cokes sets us in a distanced position to view the rhetorical tactics of the film, by rupturing its illusion of naturalistic, three-dimensional space via the flattening stream of Attali's text, and asking us to read the image.

The text in Cokes's video is based on Attali's 1985 book *Noise: The Political Economy of Music*, and it reinforces the visual structure of the video. It argues that music organizes sound in a manner similar to the way society is organized. In music, harmony is produced by the elimination of conflict. In society, conflict is eliminated by an organization of social hierarchies.

Marketing strategies emphasize the unique identity that one could obtain by consuming the newest and latest. These technologies on display in *Headphones*, however, have become nostalgic markers that situate the present in relation to the past. They don't absorb the viewer in an ecstatic sensory experience of the past, as suggested by the idea of a sublime historical experience, because the digital video flattens out the sensuous experience of the original film. In turn, this distance frames the old advertising films as ironic. In viewing these outmoded media through filters provided by Cokes, the viewer notes that the dream of collective transcendence that was promised to consumers by technologies was a dream. His use of these bits of archival film is ironic. We see a wish image revealed as an illusion, a false substitute for a desire. The advertisements are clearly manipulations of people's hopes. In Cokes's work, viewers observe their own response to these old media and think about it. It is in the awareness of common identity produced by nostalgia that one can see the ways that technologies organized and shaped the memories and identities of millions of people.

Analog Media

F. R. Ankersmit's idea of historical experience is a multisensory one in which the senses of touch, hearing, and smell are involved. This notion of historical experience contradicts the idea that the development of archival or machine-produced memory permanently escapes the investment of libidinal energies that Benjamin and others perceived in the outmoded objects of their day. If the camera replaces the storyteller, and the slide show replaces the village festival, the early critics of technology believed, the practices of remembrance would disappear. Both Fredric Jameson and Pierre Nora take this position. But these critics fail to note that the new technologies of the twentieth century generated their own rituals and practices that, in turn, developed new sorts of collective identity and evocative objects. It is important to note that these rituals, and memories are now generated and shaped by consumer culture and no longer solely by the social relationships among individuals.

However, rather than flattening and stripping the sensuous experience of memory permanently, analog media in photography and sound have shaped experience and memory in a way novel for the twentieth century. With outmoded, evocative objects, the experience of the past becomes a comparative practice. The brief and overwhelming sensuous encounter with the past in the form of an object, a sound, or smell is quickly followed by comparison of the past to the present. In this way, as the works discussed in this chapter suggest, outmoded media can provide both an intense experience of the past as well as the possibility for gaining a critical perspective on that past and the present. For instance, the sense of collective identity observable in the nostalgic response to these objects is felt often *only* in retrospect. This says something important about the effect of new media on social relationships and can lead to reflection on the current situation.

The development of a critical perspective depends, however, on how these old media are used in these works. If Jameson argued that video was too immediate and left little space for reflection, Cokes's piece manages to use digital video to encourage viewers to think about the relationship between the past and the present. One thing seems to connect Cokes's strategy to the way that Benjamin described photography in the mid-1930s. The photograph is materialized memory that addresses vision and excluded other senses, thereby providing the distanced perspective to examine a moment of past time. In digital media, we don't necessarily get the sound of film looping through a projector, or the smell of film stock heating up, or the crackle of a needle falling on a record. Certain material experiences of outmoded media disappear in digital media. Both photography and film in their time constituted the flattening and reduction of sensory and bodily memory, as does digital media in ours.

The Media Installation as Frame for Observing the Passage of Time

Eduardo Cadava provides a succinct image of how the photograph presented the means to reread history. The materialization of memory and experience in the form of recordings and mass-produced objects presents an opportunity. The stillness of the photograph, according to Cadava, is an advantage, as it seizes and holds time. This moment of history, frozen, can be brushed to reveal its constituents, the tensions that would otherwise remain hidden.

> Photography names a process that, seizing and tearing an image from its context, works to immobilize the flow of history. This is why, following the exigency of the fragment or thesis, photography can be said to be another name for the arrest that Benjamin identifies with the moment of revolution. . . . This caesura — whose force of immobilization not only gives way to the appearance of an image but also intervenes in the linearity of history and politics — can be understood in relation to what we might call the photograph's Medusa effect.[48]

Cadava later states that cutting the continuous flow of past to present and freezing it in object form "enables the rereading and rewriting of history." The freezing of time in photography is the reduction of lived and bodily experience to a visual artifact — a material object. It is this distanced view on lived experience that makes it possible to rethink such experiences. Note how Cadava's description resembles Henri Bergson's description of the modern scientific understanding of time as snapshots of lived experience.

However, Cadava and Benjamin draw a different conclusion about photography from Bergson. Where Bergson regards the reduction of experience as negative, Benjamin sees it as opening up possibilities. Benjamin argues that the uncertain nature of meaning, produced by the stilling of a moment in the photograph, "unsettles" viewers until they are provided with a text. It is the unsettled quality of the photograph and other recording media that enables the rereading of these forms of materialized memory.

The photograph is a framed object — separated from what surrounds it — that because of its structure, its stillness, allows viewers to reread history or to look at history in a different way. In a parallel way, the installations discussed in this chapter act as frames that provide the opportunity to question how memories and desires are shaped in the current centuries. The installations function as heterotopias, in Michel Foucault's terminology, as complex sites in which disparate places and times intersect. One of the things Foucault notes about heterotopias is that these sites are isolated spaces in society linked to it "by every point." According to Mary Ann Doane, the cinema engages many different temporalities: the mechanical rhythm of the apparatus, the temporality of the film story, and the temporality of the viewer's experience of the work.[49] In the installation space of the gallery in works such as Buckingham's and Dean's, viewers are asked to use their bodies and to engage in a fuller sensory experience. In Cokes's piece, the experience is enhanced not by an engagement with the viewer's body but rather by the extended time allowed for the viewer to read each layer of the video and to piece them together — something not possible in the traditional theater. The "white cube" of the gallery — one of those spaces seemingly separated from society — perhaps provides new dimensions to the experience of the projected image.

However, with film and video installation in the 2000s, there is rarely any questioning of the frame itself: the traditional gallery. This marks film and video installation as different from what took place in the 1970s where installation art was used to question traditional ways of exhibiting work. If this is an unfortunate concession to the conventions of the art institution, it also seems to allow the content of the works — the examination of memory in the form of material objects that engage our bodies — to come forward. The white walls of the gallery frame the film *experience* in Dean's and Buckingham's work and makes it out of the ordinary. In Cokes's piece, the work situates the action of comparison not so much among elements of the work itself but rather in the comparison between the film and its social and historical context.

If the gallery space presented a problem for those artists interested in breaking free of the strictures of modern art in the 1960s and 1970s, for artists working with projected images in the last decade or so, the gallery installation space seems to have provided a framework to experience these images and objects in a new way. As these media become obsolete, they acquire a powerful affect that underlines the difference between past and present.

Perhaps the 2000s are similar to the late nineteenth century, in which "documents, remains, survivals, ruins and edifices, fossils — in short, indexical traces that attest to a past by merging into it — achieved a kind of epistemological prestige in an era of intensifying time consciousness."[50] Different qualities of photographic media are highlighted in different contexts — meaning that the critical power of any medium is dependent on its timing and placement. The white walls of the gallery become a neutral frame once again to showcase the material qualities of these outmoded media and equipment. These installations as heterotopias allow viewers to become aware of the difference in our experience with contemporary and outmoded media. The film installation becomes the means of encountering the past in the present, allowing viewers to experience that past and to question how we represent it.

conclusion

INSTALLATION ART AND MEMORY

> There is only one Coliseum or Pantheon . . . but how many millions of potential negatives have they shed. . . . Give us a few negatives of a thing worth seeing . . . and that is all we want of it. Pull it down or burn it up, if you please.
>
> —Oliver Wendell Holmes

As Oliver Wendell Holmes noted in the nineteenth century, photographic archives preserve works but also make them mobile and available. Archives even present the possibility that the objects themselves could disappear and be replaced by their photographic replicas. In this quotation, however, Holmes does not grant that, once objects are part of archives, they are subject to the conditions and rules of these organizations of knowledge. Ultimately, archives shape our understanding of objects and events. As the photography criticism of the twentieth century has made clear, it is important to question these technologies of vision, these historical devices, because they shape our memories and our understanding of history as well.

Installations are often made to disappear, to become objects of history and memory. In this book, I have argued that installations produce their own archives. Lisa Le Feuvre puts it very well in her argument about the importance of photographs and texts to the work of Gordon Matta-Clark: "Robert Pincus-Witten, for example stated, 'You had to be there.' I would argue that the work is in fact all of these elements and, perhaps more importantly, it is also the spaces in between the pieces themselves."[1] She argues that works such as Matta-Clark's need to be considered in terms of their existence over time, even when the original works have vanished. Such an approach means considering documentation and ephemera as part of the work. Allan Sekula and John Tagg each argued photographic meaning is ambiguous. A photograph will reinforce whatever discourse in which it is used. Other artists that I have discussed in this book have made installations that encourage us to question how memory and history are constructed through objects such as photographs and archives. Renée Green for one has developed a politics of representation based on these ideas.

The heightened consciousness of ephemerality and history has been part of the understanding of modernity since the nineteenth century due to the rapid changes that are an inherent part of modernization. In the 1980s, Craig Owens considered the issue of ephemerality in the context of modernity: "If the modern artist was exhorted to concentrate on the ephemeral, however, it was because it was ephemeral, that is it threatened to disappear without a trace. Baudelaire conceived modern art at least in part as the rescuing of modernity for eternity."[2]

In his essay on allegory in postmodernism, Craig Owens offers the theory that modernism has always been concerned about the passage of time and, in the form of allegory, has brooded over it. Allegory, as Benjamin says, is one of the ways of saving things from disappearance in the passage of time. Following Benjamin's description of allegory, Owens connects allegory to the photograph. It is the photograph that preserves the ephemeral incidents of modern life. And therefore, allegory is closely connected to the archive.

Although site-specific art and installation art are not always identical, they often share the quality of ephemerality.[3] In the work of Robert Smithson, Owens connects photography and site-specific art, declaring Smithson to be an allegorist. Photography's importance in a work such as *Spiral Jetty* highlights the fragmentary nature of the work its own ephemerality and concentrates the desire to preserve the work. Photography and language in Smithson's work, according to Owens, are both extraneous and intrinsic.[4]

I have argued something similar in relation to the works discussed in this book. The book traces a constellation of relationships that are revealed when one considers photography and memory in the context of installation art. The relationships between installation art and its photographic representation, and the relationships between image, memory, experience, and archives, are present in the works in the 1970s. Installation art and site-specific art since the 1970s have raised questions about experience, memory, and representation. To paraphrase critic Ellen Handy, many installations are as sensitive to history and memory as painting is to light.[5]

Perhaps it is fair to say that these postmedium practices allow for contingency, in Mary Ann Doane's terms. Anything can be photographed; anything can be part of installation art, performance, and so forth. Installation art distinguished itself from modernist art by expanding the limits of painting. Allan Kaprow's environments were inspired by the large-scale paintings of American Abstract Expressionist Jackson Pollock. According to Kaprow, Pollock destroyed painting by pushing beyond the limits of the canvas to real life.[6] In Kaprow's characterization, Pollock enabled artists to put a frame around anything and to declare it art. The frame of Kaprow's art came in the form of institutional sanction of the universities for whom he worked and of galleries and museums administered via photography and language. The installation work that is discussed in the first chapter raises questions about the frame in the wake of Kaprow's and others' work in the 1960s and beyond. The works discussed take into account three principal elements derived from writings on Minimalism: the viewer, the artwork, and the space of exhibition. In many of the works discussed in this chapter, the notion of the frame of installation expands to include the space it is produced and exhibited in, to the temporal framework of the art object and viewer's experience, and finally to the institutional structures and systems of power in which the art is produced and viewed.

Chapter 1 argues that the catalogs and photographs of a work become an institutional frame for installations. The frame of the works of installation art in the form of catalogs and published photographs comes to replace the piece once the exhibition is over. The photographic documentation and catalogs inevitably shape our understanding of the history of these works. It is this aspect of photography that suggests that it is more important than mere documentation of installation art. I used Jacques Derrida's term *supplement* to capture the complexity of this relationship. The notion of the supplement reveals that there is a contingent quality to installation art as there is to a photograph: it can contain almost anything.[7]

Not all works of installation art take history and memory as their subject matter. But artists who *are* interested in them not only are concerned about "rescuing modernity for eternity" but also have used their installations *cum* photographic archives, collections, and even cinema spaces to ask questions about how contemporary society cultivates memory and constructs history. In installation art in the 1980s to the 2000s, memory and history are examined via critiques of subjectivity, identity, and institutional racism, as Jennifer González has argued. Art of this sort began to include social history, anthropology, and other disciplines.[8] Installation seems particularly appropriate for this work because it encourages viewers to ask questions about how they are seeing, the context of viewing, and what is being looked at.

This book takes this dimension of installation art into account in the works of several artists beginning in the 1970s. The representation and understanding of history and memory is one of the important themes of Renée Green's work, but it is also important in different ways in Ann Hamilton's installations, Gordon Matta-Clark's, Matthew Buckingham's, Tacita Dean's, and other artists discussed in this book. The time period of the 1970s where this book begins was a turning point in the interest in memory and history in art and other parts of the culture.

The four chapters of this book illustrate the different aspects of installation art that are revealed when photography is taken into consideration as an aspect of the work. Photography, as I have argued, supports the practice of installation but is also used as a critical tool in the context of installation art in the 1990s and 2000s. For instance, in the first chapter, I have considered what happens when photographs are all that remains of installation works, as in the works displayed in the exhibition *Rooms* and Gordon Matta-Clark's *Splitting*. In the catalog for *Rooms*, what is emphasized is not so much the individual works themselves but rather the qualities of PS1 as an exhibition space. The catalog showcases PS1 as a new institution with new ideas about exhibition. In Gordon Matta-Clark's work, the photograph becomes a way of framing time and space — marking the difference between lived experience and its representation. In the Artists Space exhibition, language takes over the role of photography in the catalog. The catalogs and artists books, as small-scale archives, have guided the history of these works.

In 1980, Craig Owens described site-specific art as hybrid and discursive. The work in the 1978 Artists Space exhibition is a good example of this type of work. The work of Adrian Piper, Louise Lawler, Cindy Sherman, and Christopher D'Arcangelo invited viewers to think about how they looked at art and understood art in the context of the particular art institution of Artists Space at a particular moment in time. Adrian Piper's piece used documentary photography in order to connect the fine art context to a broader practice of looking at and reading images that has racial consequences.

Piper's early participation in the conceptual art movement and her close friendship with Sol LeWitt were important to Green's work. And the influence of both artists' work can be seen in Green's interest in social interactions as subject matter for art as well as seriality as a formal device. Renée Green begins with the historical remains of Smithson's *Partially Buried Woodshed* and in her work asks the viewer to go beyond the traditional historical accounts of Smithson's work and the pivotal day of May 4, 1970, and place them in the context of personal memory and the culture at large. In the context of this installation as archive, she invites viewers to question how the photograph is read and how the photograph acquires meaning in particular orders. I situated Green's work in the context of a history of photography considered as evidence in the archive by noting how photographs were collected in the nineteenth century along with other kinds of artifacts in colonialist expeditions. These archives have had social consequences in terms of race and social relationships — but also in terms of our understanding of the nineteenth century. Photography and installation art are part of Green's critical tools. And her consideration of documentary remains in the form of photographs spurred an examination of the history of the 1970s.

The documentation of installation art, nevertheless, raises problems for installation artists. Images of installation must substitute for direct experience of the work. Ann Hamilton's work emphasizes bodily experience that includes the senses of touch, smell, hearing, and sight. The photograph represents a reduction of that multifarious and immersive experience to one of vision. For this reason, photographic documentation becomes a challenge. Nevertheless, the photographic documentation of ephermal, site-specific works of art, including performance and installation, allow them to circulate and gain status in a global art world.

I link Hamilton's work to Matta-Clark's for their mutual interest in the transformation of bodily experience to image. For Matta-Clark, this relationship becomes an important part of his work, out of necessity. For the most part, his works did not get exhibited in traditional art institutions and were destroyed soon after they were made. Hamilton's are similarly ephemeral, but for her the question of experience and its representation is also part of the content of the work. The documentation of the pieces is similarly careful. Other works of art interested in the present-tense, bodily experience raise similar issues in relation to photographic documentation.

In the moment where digital overtakes analog photography, photographs and film have become historical objects themselves. In the film installations of the last chapter of this book, a new understanding of photographic media seems to have emerged in the last few decades because of the slow passing of analog media. In the work of artists, such as Tacita Dean, Matthew Buckingham, and Tony Cokes, it is the media themselves that become objects of interest. In the 1960s and 1970s, which is the focus of Chrissie Iles's exhibition at the Whitney titled *Into the Light: The Projected Image in Contemporary Art*, the installation with slide projector or film projector did not inspire feelings of nostalgia or temporal dislocation. They represented instead tools for the display of art in spaces. It is in the context of contemporary installation art, however, that these objects become handles for nostalgia, and the artists mourn the passing of these media that were important to art in the twentieth century. By using the work of F. R. Ankersmit, I've argued that this of melancholy and nostalgia evoked by the ephemerality of these media can be used to gain a critical perspective on contemporary culture.

It is equally notable that each of the artists discussed in this chapter was also born in the late 1950s and 1960s and each has a different relationship to new media than older generations. In the work of artists who came of age in the 1980s and 1990s, the theme of history comes to the fore. Placed in the context of art galleries, in the classic white cube, film projectors and film become interesting sculptural objects. The film and the film projector are as sensuous as the beeswax or charcoal sticks in Ann Hamilton's installations. In the work of Tacita Dean and Matthew Buckingham, the film becomes both a carrier of the content of memory and a mnemonic device itself. It is the material qualities of the photographic media that trigger associations and memories in addition to the pictures they display.

Since the 1960s and 1970s, artists feel comfortable taking the risk of producing works of art that disappear. To take photography into account when considering installation art only enriches our understanding of the practice of installation art. This book adds a dimension to the study of installation art by considering its relationship to its supporting media. Photography of and as installation provides a lens through which to consider broader societal issues, such as how history was written and what memories are considered worth keeping.

Because of the problem of "epic forgetting," other members of the Frankfurt School have regarded memory as potentially subversive. In his 1964 book, *One-Dimensional Man*, Herbert Marcuse, one of the philosophers of the counterculture, writes of the resistance in consumer societies to understanding history: "Remembrance of the past may give rise to dangerous insights, and the established society seems to be apprehensive of the subversive contents of memory."[9]

Photographic media, which were thought to stop time and preserve faithfully moments of time in the photographic surface, are now seen to be subject to time and its passage as well. These objects have become ruins. Every dramatic technological change, historical trauma, and social shift seems to be followed by a period of reflection on history and memory—an effort to preserve and to understand these events. The last forty years have witnessed these kinds of changes in culture and art. As ephermerality intensifies at the end of the twentieth century with, for instance, the shift to digital technology, a keen interest in history and memory has emerged. It seems absolutely necessary to avoid the cultural problem of forgetting, and installation art has provided a space in which to come to grips with these the transformations and to question them.

notes

Introduction

1. Julie H. Reiss, *From Margin to Center: The Spaces of Installation Art* (Cambridge, MA: MIT Press, 1999), xv–xix.

2. Joan Gibbons, *Contemporary Art and Memory: Images of Recollection and Remembrance* (London: I.B. Tauris, 2009), 5. The art historian Joan Gibbons suggests that the interest in memory coincides with a shift from totalizing epistemologies of modernism to the more fragmented and subjective modalities of postmodernism.

3. Amelia Jones, *Body Art: Performing the Subject* (Minneapolis: University of Minnesota Press, 1998), 33.

4. Miwon Kwon, "One Place after Another: Notes on Site-Specificity," in *Space, Site, Intervention: Situating Installation Art*, ed. Erika Suderberg (Minneapolis: University of Minnesota Press, 2000), 52.

5. Walter Benjamin, *Illuminations*, trans. Harry Zohn (New York: Schocken Books, 1969), 159–60.

6. Mary Ann Doane, *The Emergence of Cinematic Time: Modernity, Contingency, the Archive* (Cambridge, MA: Harvard University Press, 2002), 13.

7. Both Joan Gibbons and Lisa Saltzman cite this passage in Proust as well.

8. Doane, *Emergence of Cinematic Time*, 9.

9. Henri Bergson, *Creative Evolution*, trans. Arthur Mitchell (1911; repr., New York: Henry Holt, 1926), 305–6. Bergson compares it directly to film.

10. Craig Ireland, *The Subaltern Appeal to Experience: Self-Identity, Late Modernity, and the Politics of Immediacy* (Montreal: McGill-Queen's University Press, 2004), 63–66.

11. The essay was reprinted in Clement Greenberg's *Art and Culture: Critical Essays* (1961; repr., Boston: Beacon Press, 1989), 6. Greenberg writes, "This

constraint, once the world of common extraverted experience has been renounced, can only be found in the very processes or disciplines by which art and literature have already imitated the former. These themselves become the subject matter of art and literature."

12. Greenberg, *Art and Culture*, 157.

13. Michael Fried, "Art and Objecthood," in *Art and Objecthood: Essays and Reviews* (Chicago: University of Chicago Press, 1998), 168.

14. Barbara Clausen et al., *After the Act: The (Re)Presentation of Performance Art* (Vienna: Museum Moderner Kunst Stiftung Ludwig Wien, 2007), 117.

15. Nicolas Bourriaud, *Relational Aesthetics* (Dijon, France: Le Presses du Réel, 1998).

16. Claire Bishop, *Installation Art: A Critical History* (New York: Routledge, 2005).

17. Claire Bishop, "Antagonism and Relational Aesthetics," *October* 110 (Fall 2004): 51–79.

18. Jones, *Body Art*, 35. Includes a direct quotation from Jacques Derrida, *Of Grammatology*, trans. Gayatri Spivak (Baltimore: Johns Hopkins University Press, 1978), 163. See also Douglas Davis, "Performance Photography," *Connoisseur* (March 1985):144–45; Anne M. Wagner, "Performance, Video, and the Rhetoric of Presence," *October* 91 (Winter 2000): 59–80.

19. Jones, *Body Art*, 37.

20. Clausen et al., *After the Act*, 7.

21. Clausen et al., *After the Act*, 19.

22. Martha Buskirk, *The Contingent Object of Contemporary Art* (Cambridge, MA: MIT Press, 2005), 59–107.

23. For instance, Philip Auslander in Clausen et al., *After the Act*, 25, and Babette Mangolte in Clausen et al., *After the Act*, 38.

24. For a more comprehensive account of the varieties of memory practice in contemporary art, see Gibbons, *Contemporary Art and Memory*.

25. Craig Owens, *Beyond Recognition*, ed. Scott Bryson et al. (Berkeley, CA: University of California Press, 1992), 40–87.

26. Owens, *Beyond Recognition*, 56–58.

27. James Meyer, "The Functional Site; or, The Transformation of Site-Specificity," in *Space, Site, Intervention: Situating Installation Art*, ed. Erika Suderberg (Minneapolis: University of Minnesota Press, 2000), 25.

28. Nick Kaye, *Site-Specific Art: Performance, Place, and Documentation* (London: Routledge, 2000), 1–2.

29. Kwon, "One Place after Another," 43.

30. Kevin Melchionne, "Rethinking Site-Specificity: Some Critical and Philosophical Problems," *Art Criticism* 12, no. 2 (1997): 40. Melchionne published an article that elaborated on the various types or degrees of site-specificity. One was "historical/political" and referred to works that recover history or political aspects of a site.

31. Fredric Jameson, "Postmodernism and Utopia," in *Utopia/Post-Utopia* (Boston: Institute of Contemporary Art, 1988), 14.

32. Jameson is not the only one who describes time in the late twentieth century this way. Baudrillard and Michel Foucault also describe time in these terms. Baudrillard and Foucault see the 1960s as a time of endings in which time has become materialized or spatialized.

33. Jameson, "Postmodernism and Utopia," 156.

34. Jameson, "Postmodernism and Utopia," 14.

35. Jean Baudrillard, *Simulacra and Simulation*, trans. Sheila Faria Glaser (1981; repr., Ann Arbor: University of Michigan Press, 1994), 8.

36. Grant Kester, "The Rise and Fall of Baudrillard," *New Art Examiner* 15, no. 3 (November 1987): 20.

37. Kate Linker, "From Imitation, to the Copy, to Just Effect: On Reading Jean Baudrillard," *Artforum* 22, no. 8 (April 1984): 47.

38. Thomas Lawson, "Forum: Generation In Vitro," *Artforum* 23, no. 1 (September 1984): 99; John Howell and Lisa Liebmann, "Forum: Retro/Trends," *Artforum* 22, no. 3 (November 1983): 73.

39. Lawson, "Forum," 99.

40. Linker, "From Imitation," 47–48.

41. Kester, "The Rise and Fall," 20–23.

42. Hal Foster, "The Art of Cynical Reason," in *The Return of the Real*, 99–127 (Cambridge, MA: MIT Press, 1996). However, Grant Kester critiqued the art world's fascination with Baudrillard by noting that the death of the real or the disappearance of history is only persuasive in a very few Western cities. Meanwhile, industry had moved on to developing nations where issues of production and collectivity are still very much alive and important.

43. Kester, "The Rise and Fall"; there are other cultural commentators who need to be mentioned in this regard. Andreas Huyssen, a literary and art critic, has written two books on memory culture, *Twilight Memories: Marking Time in a Culture of Amnesia* and, most recently, *Present Pasts: Urban Palimpsests and the Politics of Memory*. He links the interest in memory to questions and concerns about burgeoning archives and documentation but also to the interest in the Holocaust in Germany beginning in the 1970s. In addition, he cites the politicization of

memory and its use in documenting genocides around the world in the twentieth century. In his *Present Past: Modernity and the Memory Crisis*, Richard Terdiman, a literary critic with a new historicist bent, takes the thesis that a memory crisis in the nineteenth century produced specific approaches to literature and semiotics. Pierre Nora, a French historian, whose article "Between Memory and History: Les Lieux de Mémoire" appeared in the 1989 issue of *Representations*, is often cited by art critics in relation to the issue of memory. Pierre Nora, "Between Memory and History: Les Lieux de Mémoire," *Representations* 26 (Spring 1989): 7–24. Lastly, James Young wrote *The Texture of Memory*, a survey and critique of Holocaust monuments in contemporary Germany.

44. David Deitcher, William Olander, and Abigail Solomon-Godeau, *The Art of Memory: The Loss of History* (New York: New Museum of Contemporary Art, 1985), 50.

45. These ideas were taken up again in the collection of essays on photography *The Contest of Meaning: Critical Histories of Photography*, edited by Richard Bolton (Cambridge, MA: MIT Press, 1989), to which Solomon-Godeau was a contributor. Also in this volume, Benjamin H. D. Buchloh's essay "From Factura to Factography" addresses the ambivalence of photography in critical practice.

46. Mary Jane Jacob, *Places with a Past: New Site-Specific Art at Charleston's Spoleto Festival* (New York: Rizzoli Publications, 1991), 13–20.

47. Miwon Kwon, *One Place after Another: Site-Specific Art and Locational Identity* (Cambridge, MA: MIT Press, 2002), 105.

48. Lynne Cooke, Brian Curiger, and Greg Hilty, *Doubletake: Collective Memory and Current Art* (New York: Parkett, 1992), 23.

49. Cooke, Curiger, and Hilty, *Doubletake*, 26. Another European exhibition that used the topic of memory was *The Sublime Void: On the Memory of the Imagination* at the Koninklijk Museum in Antwerp in 1993. It included work by Rachel Whiteread, Jannis Kounellis, Juan Muñoz, Gerhard Richter, Jeff Wall, Michelangelo Pistoletto, and others.

50. Quoted in Ted Gott, *Don't Leave Me This Way: Art in the Age of AIDS* (London: Thames and Hudson, 1994), 57.

51. Douglas Crimp, "Mourning and Militancy," *October* 51 (Winter 1989): 17–18.

52. Gott, *Don't Leave Me This Way*, 34–51.

53. Gott, *Don't Leave Me This Way*, 69–70.

54. Lisa Saltzman, *Making Memory Matter: Strategies of Remembrance in Contemporary Art* (Chicago: University of Chicago Press, 2006).

55. Nicholas De Oliveira, Nicola Oxley, and Michael Petry, *Installation Art in the New Millennium: The Empire of the Senses* (London: Thames and Hudson, 2003), 9.

56. Michel Foucault, *The Archaeology of Knowledge and the Discourse on Language*, trans. A. M. Sheridan Smith (New York: Pantheon Books, 1972), 7.

57. Michel Foucault, *Language, Counter-Memory, Practice: Selected Essays and Interviews*, ed. Donald F. Bouchard (Ithaca, NY: Cornell University Press, 1977), 160.

58. Michel Foucault, "Of Other Spaces," *Diacritics* 16, no. 1 (Spring 1986): 23.

59. Doane, *Emergence of Cinematic Time*, 3.

Chapter 1: Expanding the Frame

1. See also Reiss, *From Margin to Center*, 109–31.

2. Hal Foster, *Compulsive Beauty* (Cambridge, MA: MIT Press, 1997), xii.

3. Brian O'Doherty, "Inside the White Cube, Part I: Notes on the Gallery Space," *Artforum* 14, no. 7 (March 1976): 25.

4. O'Doherty, "Inside the White Cube, Part I," 25.

5. Brian O'Doherty, "Inside the White Cube, Part II: The Eye and the Spectator," *Artforum* 14, no. 8 (April 1976): 27.

6. O'Doherty, "Inside the White Cube, Part II," 33–34.

7. Jacques Derrida, *The Truth in Painting*, trans. Geoff Bennington and Ian McLeod (Chicago: University of Chicago Press, 1987), 59.

8. John C. Welchman, "In and Around the 'Second Frame,'" in *The Rhetoric of the Frame: Essays on the Boundaries of the Artwork*, ed. Paul Duro (Cambridge: Cambridge University Press, 1996), 213.

9. Derrida, *Truth in Painting*, 61.

10. Linda Blumberg, program director of PS1, statement in *Rooms*, PS1, Institute for Art and Urban Resources catalog, designed and edited by Stephen Alexander and Eugenie Diserio (New York: The Institute, 1977), 133.

11. Martin Beck, "Alternative: Space," in *Alternative Art, New York, 1965–1985*, ed. Julie Ault (Minneapolis: University of Minnesota Press, 2002), 257.

12. Nancy Foote, "Apotheosis of the Crummy Space," *Artforum International* 15, no. 2 (October 1976): 28–37.

13. José Bélisle, *David Rabinowitch* (Montreal: Musée d'art contemporain de Montréal, 2003), 10.

14. Rosalind Krauss, "Sculpture in the Expanded Field," *October* 8 (Spring 1979): 30–44. In this article, Krauss mapped a field of sculptural practice based on

the fixed cultural categories of architecture and landscape, from which she derived sculpture, site construction, marked sites, and axiomatic structures. In these new categories, Krauss could fit site-specific earthworks, outdoor sculptural arrangements, and other sculptural practices, plotting their positions relative to the category of sculpture. The idea of a field of relationships is based on this idea.

15. Quoted in Stephen Alexander and Eugenie Diserio, eds. and designers, "Richard Tuttle on Richard Serra," in *Rooms*, PS1, Institute for Art and Urban Resources catalog (New York: The Institute, 1977), 69.

16. Quoted in Alexander and Diserio, *Rooms*, 123, 126.

17. Quoted in Alexander and Diserio, *Rooms*, 124.

18. Doane, *Emergence of Cinematic Time*, 76–77. She cites Henri Bergson, who indicates that consciousness occurs as a result of perception, and, therefore, the mind is aware of only a moment that has passed and never experiences the present moment as it happens. There is always a lag between perceptual stimulus and the mind's conscious awareness.

19. Doane, *Emergence of Cinematic Time*, 102.

20. Doane, *Emergence of Cinematic Time*, 10.

21. Krauss, "Notes on the Index," 69.

22. Krauss, "Notes on the Index, Part 2," 70.

23. Doane, *Emergence of Cinematic Time*, 95.

24. Doane, *Emergence of Cinematic Time*, 219.

25. Derrida, *Of Grammatology*, 304.

26. Krauss, "Notes on the Index, Part 2," 65.

27. Krauss, "Notes on the Index, Part 2," 69.

28. Doane, *Emergence of Cinematic Time*, 10–11.

29. Doane, *Emergence of Cinematic Time*, 63.

30. Quoted in Alexander and Diserio, *Rooms*, 122.

31. Foote, "Apotheosis," 37.

32. See the useful summary of the uses of photography in Matta-Clark's work in Christian Kravagna's chapter "It's Nothing Worth Documenting If It's Not Difficult to Get: On the Documentary Nature of Photography and Film in the Work of Gordon Matta-Clark," in *Gordon Matta-Clark*, ed. Corinne Diserens (London: Phaidon, 2003).

33. Pamela M. Lee, *Gordon Matta-Clark: Object to Be Destroyed* (Cambridge, MA: MIT Press, 2000), 36–38.

34. Moure, *Gordon Matta-Clark*, 252.

35. Martin Jay, *Downcast Eyes: The Denigration of Vision in Twentieth Century French Thought* (Berkeley: University of California Press, 1993), 85, 160–64.

36. David Summers, *Real Spaces: World Art History and the Rise of Western Modernism* (London: Phaidon, 2003), 559.

37. See, for instance, Amelia Jones, *Self/Image: Technology, Representation, and the Contemporary Subject* (London: Routledge, 2006), 4–5. Amelia Jones connects this notion of knowledge directly to photography.

38. Summers, *Real Spaces*, 603.

39. Summers, *Real Spaces*, 603.

40. Summers, *Real Spaces*, 458–66.

41. Moure, *Gordon Matta-Clark*, 21.

42. Bergson, *Creative Evolution*, 305.

43. Bergson, *Creative Evolution*, 306.

44. Mary Jane Jacob, *Gordon Matta-Clark: A Retrospective* (Chicago: Museum of Contemporary Art, 1985), 20–23.

45. Mary Warner Marien, *Photography and Its Critics: A Cultural History, 1839–1900* (Cambridge: Cambridge University Press, 1997), 3–5.

46. Marien, *Photography*, 3.

47. Tina Kukielski, "In the Spirit of the Vegetable: The Early Works of Gordon Matta-Clark (1969–71)," in *Gordon Matta-Clark: You Are the Measure*, ed. Elisabeth Sussman (New York: Whitney Museum of American Art), 36–37.

48. Kukielski, "In the Spirit," 43.

49. Jeffrey Meikle, *American Plastics: A Cultural History* (New Brunswick, NJ: Rutgers University Press, 1995), Kindle edition, chap. 1.

50. Lee, *Gordon Matta-Clark*, 67–68.

51. Anne M. Wagner, "Splitting and Doubling: Gordon Matta-Clark and the Body of Sculpture," *Grey Room* 14 (Winter 2004): 35.

52. For more, see Lee, "Holes of History," in *Object to Be Destroyed*.

53. Craig Owens, "Earthwords," in *Beyond Recognition*, ed. Scott Bryson et al. (Berkeley: University of California Press, 1992), 41; and James Meyer, "Nostalgia and Memory: Legacies of the 1960s in Recent Work," in *Painting, Object, Film, Concept: Selections from the Herbig Collection* (New York: Christie's, 1998), 26–27.

54. Moure, *Gordon Matta-Clark*, 61.

55. Karl Marx, *Early Writings*, ed. T. B. Bottomore (New York: McGraw-Hill, 1963), 124–25.

56. Moure, *Gordon Matta-Clark*, 142.

57. Moure, *Gordon Matta-Clark*, 253.

58. Al Brunelle, "The Great Divide: Anarchitecture by Gordon Matta-Clark," *Art in America* 62, no. 5 (September–October 1974): 92.

59. Gordon Matta-Clark, *Splitting* (New York: Loft Books, 1974).

60. Wagner, "Splitting and Doubling," 35. For more comments on Matta-Clark's photo-collages, see Simon Morrissey, "Gordon Matta-Clark," *Creative Camera* 337 (December 1995/January 1996): 40; Lisa Le Feuvre, "The W-hole Story," *Art Monthly* 255 (April 2002): 12–15; Judith Russi Kirshner, "Non-uments," *Artforum* 24, no. 2 (October 1985): 102–8.

61. Moure, *Gordon Matta-Clark*, 252.

62. Gilles Deleuze, *Bergsonism*, trans. Hugh Tomlinson and Barbara Habberjam (New York: Zone Books, 1966, 1988), 70.

63. Deleuze, *Bergsonism*, 32.

64. Julie Ault, "Chronology," in *Alternative Art, New York, 1965–1985*, ed. Julie Ault (Minneapolis: University of Minnesota Press, 2002), 35.

65. Claudia Gould and Valerie Smith, eds., *5000 Artists Return to Artists Space* (New York: Artists Space, 1998), 58.

66. Janelle Reiring, press release from Artists Space, summer 1978.

67. Janelle Reiring, interview with author, June 24, 2009.

68. Adrian Piper, *Adrian Piper: A Retrospective* (Baltimore: University of Maryland, 1999).

69. Louise Lawler, *Louise Lawler and Others* (Basel, Switzerland: Kunstmuseum Basel, Hatje Cantz Verlag, 2004), 20–21.

70. In addition to this work, Lawler designed a logo for the exhibition that appeared in the catalog and throughout Lower Manhattan, extending her work outside the traditional exhibition space.

71. Gould and Smith, *5000 Artists*, 101.

72. Louise Lawler, questionnaire prepared by author, June 30, 2009.

73. Quoted in Gould and Smith, *5000 Artists*, 97.

74. Janelle Reiring, ___________, *Louise Lawler, Adrian Piper and Cindy Sherman Have Agreed to Participate in an Exhibition Organized by Janelle Reiring at Artists Space, September 23 to October 28, 1978* (New York: Committee for the Visual Arts, 1978), 13–14.

75. Gwyn Prins, "The Battle for Control of the Camera in Late Nineteenth-Century Western Zambia," in *Anthropology and Photography, 1860–1920*, ed. Elizabeth Edwards (New Haven, CT: Yale University Press, 1992), 221.

76. These works include Allan Sekula's "The Body and the Archive," in *The Contest of Meaning: Critical Histories of Photography*, ed. Richard Bolton, 344–89 (Cambridge, MA: MIT Press, 1989); "On the Invention of Photographic Meaning," *Artforum* 13, no. 2 (January 1975): 36–45; Martha Rosler's "In, Around and Afterthoughts: Notes on Documentary Photography," in *The Contest of Meaning: Critical Histories of Photography*, ed. Richard Bolton (Cambridge, MA: MIT Press,

1989), 303–41; and Roland Barthes, "The Rhetoric of the Image," in *Image, Music, Text*, ed. and trans. Stephen Heath (New York: Hill and Wang, 1977).

77. Lawler, questionnaire.

78. Reiring, interview.

79. April Kingsley, "Art Goes Underground," *Village Voice*, October 18, 1978, 122.

80. Lawler also says that these images were never printed. Lawler, questionnaire.

81. Douglas Crimp, "Pictures," *October* 8 (Spring 1979): 75–88.

82. Derrida, *Truth in Painting*, 59.

83. Derrida, *Truth in Painting*, 61.

84. Derrida, *Truth in Painting*, 61.

Chapter 2: The Politics of Representation

1. Renée Green, Alexander Alberro, Nora M. Alter, and Nuria Enguita Mayo, *Shadows and Signals* (Barcelona: Fundácio Antoni Tapies, 2000), 46–47. Most of the descriptions of these pieces were derived from Alex Alberro's descriptions in this catalog.

2. Part of the material in this chapter was published previously in "The Family Slide Show as Critical History in Renée Greene's Video Partially Buried Continued," *Third Text* 21, no. 4 (July 2007): 441–50.

3. Hal Foster, *The Return of the Real* (Cambridge, MA: MIT Press, 1996), 184.

4. Rosalind Krauss, *A Voyage on the North Sea: Art in the Age of the Post-Medium Condition* (London: Thames and Hudson, 1999), 26–29. Krauss labels this relationship the phenomenological vector of the work.

5. Benjamin H. D. Buchloh, "Warburg's Paragon? The End of Collage and Photomontage in Postwar Europe," in *Deep Storage: Collecting, Storing, and Archiving in Art*, ed. Ingrid Schaffner and Matthias Winzen (Munich: Prestel, 1998), 54.

6. Buchloh, "Warburg's Paragon?" 59.

7. Hal Foster, "An Archival Impulse," *October* 110 (Fall 2004): 3–6. Foster includes Green among the group, although he does not elaborate on her work.

8. Lev Manovich, *The Language of New Media* (Cambridge, MA: MIT Press, 2001), 214–15.

9. Elizabeth A. Brown, "Social Studies: 4 + 4 Young Americans," *Allen Memorial Art Gallery Bulletin* 44, no. 1 (1990): 51.

10. See James Meyer, "Artist as Nomad," in *Space, Site, Intervention: Situating Installation Art*, ed. Erika Suderberg (Minneapolis: University of Minnesota Press, 2000), 27.

11. Sekula, "On the Invention," 36.

12. Foucault, *Archaeology of Knowledge*, 6–7.

13. Alex Alberro notes that Green practices a form of Foucaultian genealogy in her work. Green et al., *Shadows and Signals*, 25.

14. Nora, "Between Memory and History," 12–14.

15. Hollis Frampton, *Circles of Confusion: Film Photography and Video Texts, 1968–1980* (Rochester, NY: Visual Studies Workshop Press, 1983), 75.

16. Quoted in Marien, *Photography*, 77–78.

17. Doane, *Emergence of Cinematic Time*, 82.

18. Stephen Kern, *The Culture of Time and Space, 1880–1918* (Cambridge, MA: Harvard University Press, 1983), 39.

19. Elizabeth Edwards, "Photographs as Objects of Memory," in *Material Memories*, ed. Marius Kwint, Christopher Breward, and Jeremy Aynsley (Oxford, UK: Berg, 1999), 221.

20. Louis-Jacques Mandé Daguerre, "Daguerreotype," in *Classic Essays on Photography*, ed. Alan Trachtenberg (New Haven, CT: Leete's Island Books, 1980), 12.

21. Prins, "The Battle for Control," 221.

22. Barbara Kirshenblatt-Gimblett, "Objects of Ethnography," in *Exhibiting Cultures: The Poetics and Politics of Museum Display*, ed. Ivan Karp and Steven D. Laine (Washington, DC: Smithsonian Institution Press, 1991), 388.

23. Christian Metz, "Photography and Fetish," *October* 34 (Fall 1985): 84. Allan Sekula also discusses the fetishism of photographs. See Sekula, "On the Invention," 38.

24. For more on this subject, see Richard Bolton, ed., *The Contest of Meaning: Critical Histories of Photography* (Cambridge, MA: MIT Press, 1989).

25. See Edward Steichen, "A Special Portfolio of Photographs by Ezra Stoller of the Family of Man Exhibition on the Walls of the Museum of Modern Art, New York," in *The Family of Man* (New York: Museum of Modern Art, 1955), 195–207.

26. Steichen, "A Special Portfolio," 4.

27. Roland Barthes, *Image, Music, Text*, ed. and trans. Stephen Heath (New York: Hill and Wang, 1977), 24.

28. Svetlana Alpers, "Museums as a Way of Seeing," in *Exhibiting Cultures: The Poetics and Politics of Museum Display*, ed. Ivan Karp and Steven D. Laine (Washington, DC: Smithsonian Institution Press, 1991), 26.

29. Jennifer A. González, "Siting Histories: Material Display and the Politics of Display in the Work of Fred Wilson, Pepón Osorio, and Amalia Mesa-Bains, 1985–1995," PhD diss., University of California, Santa Cruz, 1996.

30. Mary Ann Staniszewski, *The Power of Display: A History of Exhibitions at the Museum of Modern Art* (Cambridge, MA: MIT Press, 1998), 18–22.

31. Conceptual artists in the 1960s took up nonaesthetic, document-like form in their photo work in a critique of institutions that upheld formalist aesthetic photography conventions. Jeff Wall has argued that such practices were a critique of the modernist photographic aesthetics that overvalued technical skill, uniqueness, and serious subject matter. Jeff Wall, "Marks of Indifference: Aspects of Photography in or as Conceptual Art," in *Reconsidering the Object of Art, 1965-75*, ed. Ann Goldstein and Anne Rorimer (Cambridge, MA: MIT Press, 1995), 258–65.

32. Sekula, "On the Invention," 36.

33. Foucault, "Of Other Spaces," 22.

34. Renée Green, questionnaire prepared by author, November 2008.

35. Jennifer A. González, *Subject to Display: Reframing Race in Contemporary Installation Art* (Cambridge, MA: MIT Press, 2008), 245–49.

36. Fred Wilson, *The Museum: Mixed Metaphors* (Seattle: Seattle Art Museum, 1993), 29–32.

37. Robert Morris, "Notes on Sculpture, Part III: Notes and Nonsequitors," in *Art in Theory: 1900–1990: An Anthology of Changing Ideas*, ed. Charles Harrison and Paul Wood (Oxford, UK: Blackwell, 1992), 819.

38. Susan Krane and Bruce Jenkins, *Hollis Frampton: Recollections and Recreations* (Buffalo, NY: Albright-Knox Art Gallery, 1984), 10.

39. Rachel Moore, *Hollis Frampton: Nostalgia* (London: Afterall Books, 2006).

40. Doane, *Emergence of Cinematic Time*, 23.

41. Green et al., *Shadows and Signals*, 51. Please see, in particular, Nora Alter's chapter "Beyond the Frame: Renee Green's Video Practice."

42. Yvonne Rainer, *Journeys from Berlin*, DVD (New York: Zeitgeist Films, 1980).

43. This is excluded in Rainer's version. Walter Benjamin, *Reflections*, ed. Peter Demetz (New York: Schocken Books, 1978), 182.

44. Green et al., *Shadows and Signals*, 145.

45. Renée Green, *World Tour* (Los Angeles: Museum of Contemporary Art, 1993), E57.

46. Manovich, *Language of New Media*, 240.

47. Renée Green, "Partially Buried in Three Parts: Extract," in *Ruins in Reverse: Time and Progress in Contemporary Art*, ed. Grant Kester, *CEPA Journal* (Buffalo, NY: Center for the Exploratory and Perpetual Arts [CEPA], September 1998–March 1999), 34.

48. Renée Green, *Between and Including* (Vienna: Secession, 2001), 61.

49. Darsie Alexander et al., *Slide Show: The Projected Image in Contemporary Art* (University Park: University of Pennsylvania Press, 2005), ix.

50. Frampton, *Circles of Confusion*, 111.

51. Renée Green, questionnaire prepared by author, May 2006.

52. Douglas Collins, *The Story of Kodak* (New York: Abrams, 1990), 263.

53. Eastman Kodak Company, *Adventures in Outdoor Color Slides* (Rochester, NY: Kodak Sales Division, 1962), 44.

54. Pierre Bourdieu, *Photography: A Middle-Brow Art*, trans. Shaun Whiteside (Stanford, CA: Stanford University Press, 1990), 24.

55. Fred Davis, *Yearning for Yesterday: A Sociology of Nostalgia* (New York: Free Press, 1979), 14.

56. Svetlana Boym, *The Future of Nostalgia* (New York: Basic Books, 2001), 42–43.

57. Nancy Martha West, *Kodak and the Lens of Nostalgia* (Charlottesville: University of Virginia Press, 2000), 5.

58. The piece is "Mirror Displacement on a Compost Heap," 1969, Düsseldorf, Germany. Guglielmo Bargellesi-Severi, ed., *Robert Smithson: Slideworks* (Milan, Italy: Carlo Frua, 1997), 125.

59. Owens, "Earthwords," 40–41.

60. Robert Smithson, *Robert Smithson: The Collected Writings* (Berkeley: University of California Press, 1996), 119.

61. Robert Smithson, "Hotel Palenque, 1969–72," *Parkett* 43 (March 1995): 117–32.

62. Kwon, *One Place after Another*, 51.

63. See also González, *Subject to Display*, 241–49.

64. Rosalind Krauss, "Photography's Discursive Spaces: Landscape/View," *Art Journal* 42, no. 4 (Winter 1982): 316–18.

Chapter 3: The Poetics of Experience

1. Ann Hamilton, e-mail message to author, August 21, 2001.

2. Siegfried Kracauer, *The Mass Ornament: Weimar Essays*, trans. and ed. Thomas Y. Levin (Cambridge, MA: Harvard University Press, 1995), 47–63.

3. Roland Barthes, *Camera Lucida*, trans. Richard Howard (New York: Hill and Wang, 1981), 92.

4. Ann Hamilton, Tomoaki Kitagawa, Bernhart Schwenk, and Takao Ueda, *the picture is still* (Ostfildern, Germany: Hatje Cantz Publishers, 2003).

5. Hamilton, e-mail message.

6. Ann Hamilton, personal communication, 2011.

7. Joan Simon, *Ann Hamilton* (New York: Abrams, 2002), 256.

8. Simon, *Ann Hamilton*, 11.

9. Ireland, *Subaltern Appeal*, 63–66.

10. John Dewey, *Art as Experience* (New York: Perigee Books, 1934), 246.

11. Hans-Robert Jauss, *Question and Answer: Forms of Dialogic Understanding*, as quoted in Ireland, *Subaltern Appeal*, 44.

12. Martin Jay, *Songs of Experience: Modern American and European Variations on a Universal Theme* (Berkeley: University of California Press, 2005), 7. See footnote 33.

13. Ireland, *Subaltern Appeal*, 199–200.

14. Ireland, *Subaltern Appeal*, 44.

15. Jay, *Downcast Eyes*, 24–31, 69–82.

16. Robert Morris, "The Present Tense of Space," in *Continuous Project Altered Daily: The Writings of Robert Morris* (Cambridge, MA: MIT Press, 1993), 182.

17. Rosalind Krauss, "The Cultural Logic of the Late Capitalist Museum," *October* 54 (Autumn 1990): 9–11.

18. Jeff Kelley, *Childsplay: The Art of Allan Kaprow* (Berkeley: University of California Press, 2004), 7.

19. Allan Kaprow, *Essays on the Blurring of Art and Life*, ed. Jeff Kelley (Berkeley: University of California Press, 1996), 9.

20. Krauss, "Cultural Logic," 7.

21. Krauss, "Cultural Logic," 15–16.

22. Kate Mondloch, *Screens: Viewing Media Installation Art* (Minneapolis: University of Minnesota Press, 2010), 56–59. Mondloch refers to Krauss's assessment of the "late-capitalist museum" as a place to experience "experience."

23. Chrissie Iles, Shamim M. Momin, and Debra Singer, *Whitney Biennial 2004* (New York: Whitney Museum of American Art, 2004), 243.

24. Mary Jane Jacob and Lynn Gumpert, *Christian Boltanski: Lessons of Darkness* (Los Angeles: Los Angeles Museum of Contemporary Art, 1988), 54.

25. Jacob and Gumpert, *Christian Boltanski*, 71.

26. Hugh M. Davies and Lynda Forsha, "A Conversation with Ann Hamilton," in *Ann Hamilton* (San Diego: Museum of Contemporary Art, 1991), 70.

27. Ann Hamilton, personal communication, 2011.

28. Ann Hamilton, unpublished lecture notes, 2001.

29. Anna Chave, "Sculpture, Gender, and the Value of Labor," *American Art* 24, no. 1 (Spring 2010): 26–29.

30. Davies and Forsha, "A Conversation with Ann Hamilton," 70.

31. Jay, *Songs of Experience*, 331.

32. E. P. Thompson, *The Essential E. P. Thompson*, ed. Dorothy Thompson (New York: New Press, 2001), 62.

33. Thompson, *Essential E. P. Thompson*, 61.

34. Eileen Boris, *Art and Labor: Ruskin, Morris, and the Craftsman Ideal in America* (Philadelphia: Temple University Press, 1986), xi.

35. Herbert Marcuse, *One-Dimensional Man* (Boston: Beacon Press, 1964), 98.

36. Bruce Kaiper, "The Human Object and Its Capitalist Image," *Left Curve*, no. 5 (Fall–Winter 1975): 43.

37. Frank B. Gilbreth, *Motion Study: A Method for Increasing the Efficiency of the Workman* (1911; repr., Easton, PA: Hive Publishing, 1972), 6–7.

38. Gilbreth, *Motion Study*, 62–63.

39. Quoted in Jonathan Crary, *Suspensions of Perception: Attention, Spectacle, Modern Culture* (Cambridge, MA: MIT Press, 1999), 15.

40. Reesa Goldberg, "The Exhibited Redistributed: A Case for Reassessing Space," in *Thinking about Exhibitions*, ed. Reesa Goldberg (London: Routledge, 1996), 350–53; also cited in Richard J. Williams, *After Modern Sculpture: Art in the United States and Europe, 1965–70* (New York: Manchester University Press, 2000), 101–2.

41. Ann Hamilton, notes to author, 2011.

42. Thibault Jeanson, interview with author, December 2006.

43. Ann Hamilton, interview with author, November 2006.

44. Mary Katherine Coffey, "Histories That Haunt: A Conversation with Ann Hamilton," *Art Journal* 60, no. 3 (Fall 2001): 22–23. Hamilton gave me a revised version of this quotation, which is what appears in this text. Ann Hamilton, personal communication, 2011.

45. Bernard Comment, *The Painted Panorama* (New York: Abrams, 2000), 1–18.

46. Wolf Prix, "The Imaging of Reality," *Architecture California* (May 1992): 14.

47. Craig Hodgetts, "Heretical Thoughts on Architecture and Photography," *Architecture California* (May 1992): 61.

48. Robert Hopkins, *Picture, Image, and Experience: A Philosophical Inquiry* (Cambridge: Cambridge University Press, 1998), 17.

49. Hamilton et al., *the picture is still*.

50. Quoted in Kelley, *Childsplay*, 130–31.

51. Buskirk, *Contingent Object*, 212–58.

52. Ann Hamilton, interview with author, November 2006.

53. Morris, "The Present Tense," 182.

54. Morris, "The Present Tense." Morris is using the work of Herbert Mead as a reference.

55. Judith Rodenbeck, "Foil: Allan Kaprow before Photography," in *Experiments in the Everyday: Allan Kaprow and Robert Watts, Events, Objects, Documents*, by Benjamin H. D. Buchloh et al. (New York: Columbia University, 1999), 58.

56. Barthes, *Camera Lucida*, 10.

57. Le désir de photographier est le contraire du désir de signifier à tout prix; de témoigner ou d'informer. Il est de l'ordre de la sidération et de l'illusion. De l'ordre de la disparition aussi, car si quelque chose veut devenir image, ce n'est pas pour durer, c'est pour mieux disparaître.

58. Tendance Floue and Jean Baudrillard, *Sommes-Nous?* (Paris: Naïve, 2006).

59. Ann Hamilton, notes to the author.

60. Amelia Jones, *Self/Image: Technology, Representation, and the Contemporary Subject* (London: Routledge, 2006), 6.

61. Jones, *Self/Image*, 56.

62. Jones, *Self/Image*. Jones borrows this term from Laura U. Marks.

63. Barthes, *Camera Lucida*, 8.

64. Barthes, *Camera Lucida*, 51.

65. Barthes, *Camera Lucida*, 14.

66. Helène Cixous, "Coming to Writing," in *"Coming to Writing" and Other Essays*, ed. Deborah Jenson, trans. Sarah Cornell et al. (Cambridge, MA: Harvard University Press, 1991), 4.

67. Doane, *Emergence of Cinematic Time*, 102.

68. Ann Hamilton has a photographic archive of her works in her studio, and her works up to 2000 have been described in detail and cataloged in the catalogue raisonné by Joan Simon.

Chapter 4: Camera Obscura

1. Quoted in Doane, *Emergence of Cinematic Time*, 4.

2. Sherry Turkle, ed., *Evocative Objects: Things We Think With* (Cambridge, MA: MIT Press, 2007), 5.

3. James Quandt gives them a European genealogy by describing them as "Moholy-Nagy" compositions. James Quandt, "Tacita Dean, Schaulager Basel," *Artforum* 3 (November 2006): 287.

4. Jean-Christophe Royoux uses the term in his work about Dean's work in Jean-Christophe Royoux, Marina Warner, and Germaine Greer, *Tacita Dean* (London: Phaidon, 2006), 50–101.

5. Royoux, Warner, and Greer, *Tacita Dean*, 8.

6. Tacita Dean, *Floh* (Göttingen, Germany: Steidl Publications, 2001).

7. Royoux, Warner, and Greer, *Tacita Dean*, 98.

8. Royoux, Warner, and Greer, *Tacita Dean*, 64.

9. Royoux, Warner, and Greer, *Tacita Dean*, 17.

10. Susan Buck-Morss, *The Dialectics of Seeing: Walter Benjamin and the Arcades Project* (Cambridge, MA: MIT Press, 1989), 98.

11. Foster, "An Archival Impulse," 4.

12. Jennifer Uhrhane, "Timeline," Photographic Resource Center at Boston University, accessed June 14, 2011, www.godowskycolorawards.org/2009/timeline.html.

13. Quandt, "Tacita Dean," 287–88.

14. Mondloch, *Screens*, 2.

15. Laurent Mannoni, *The Great Art of Light and Shadow: Archaeology of the Cinema* (Exeter, UK: University of Exeter Press, 2000), 6–7.

16. Doane, *Emergence of Cinematic Time*, 108.

17. Saltzman, *Making Memory Matter*. Lisa Saltzman also refers to this artwork in her book.

18. Margaret Morse, "Video Installation Art: The Body, the Image, and the Space In-Between," in *Illuminating Video: An Essential Guide to Video Art*, ed. Doug Hall and Sally Jo Fifer (New York: Aperture, 1990), 154.

19. *Image of Absalon to Be Projected until It Vanishes*, 2001, accessed May 11, 2011, www.matthewbuckingham.net/Image%20Absalon.html.

20. Mark Godfrey, "Artist as Historian," *October* 120 (Spring 2007): 140–72. This essay is a useful source for information on Buckingham's work.

21. Raymond Fielding, ed., *A Technological History of Motion Pictures and Television* (Berkeley: University of California Press, 1967), 119, 130.

22. Fielding, *A Technological History*, 132–33.

23. Doane, *Emergence of Cinematic Time*, 22.

24. Jean Baudrillard, *The System of Objects*, trans. James Benedict (1968; repr., London: Verso, 1996), 135–40.

25. Benjamin, *Illuminations*, 159–60.

26. Kern, *Culture of Time*, 39.

27. Doane, *Emergence of Cinematic Time*, 63.

28. Godfrey, "Artist as Historian," 159–62.

29. Theodor Adorno and Walter Benjamin, *The Complete Correspondence: 1928–1940*, ed. Henri Lonitz, trans. Nicholas Walker (Cambridge, MA: Harvard University Press, 1999), 321.

30. Royoux, Warner, and Greer, *Tacita Dean*, 17.

31. Quandt, "Tacita Dean," 287.

32. Debra Singer, "The Way Things Never Were: Nostalgia's Possibilities and the Unpredictable Past," in *Whitney Biennial 2004*, by Chrissie Iles, Shamim M. Monim, and Debra Singer, 22–33 (New York: Whitney Museum of American Art, 2004).

33. Malcolm Turvey et al., "Roundtable: The Projected Image in Contemporary Art," *October* 104 (Spring 2003): 75.

34. F. R. Ankersmit, *Sublime Historical Experience* (Stanford, CA: Stanford University Press, 2005), 121.

35. Foucault, "Of Other Spaces," 22–25.

36. Chrissie Iles and Philippe Vergne, *Whitney Biennial 2006: Day for Night* (New York: Whitney Museum of American Art, 2006), 244.

37. Davis, *Yearning for Yesterday*, 31.

38. Tony Cokes, questionnaire prepared by author, September 2007.

39. Fred Barnum, "His Master's Voice," in *America: Ninety Years of Communications Pioneering, and Progress: Victor Talking Machine Company* (Camden, NJ: General Electric, 1991), 251, 318–19.

40. Patrick McGeehan, "Vinyl Records and Turntables Are Gaining Sales," *New York Times*, December 6, 2009.

41. Elizabeth E. Guffey, *Retro: The Culture of Revival* (London: Thames and Hudson, 2006), 44.

42. Davis, *Yearning for Yesterday*, 90.

43. Jameson, *Postmodernism*, 290.

44. Baudrillard, *Simulacra and Simulation*, 43.

45. Jameson, *Postmodernism*, 156.

46. Jameson, "Postmodernism and Utopia," 14.

47. Jameson, "Postmodernism and Utopia," 70.

48. Eduardo Cadava, *Words of Light: Theses on the Photography of History* (Princeton, NJ: Princeton University Press, 1997), xx.

49. Doane, *Emergence of Cinematic Time*, 30.

50. Philip Rosen, quoted in Doane, *Emergence of Cinematic Time*, 221.

Conclusion

1. James Atlee and Lisa Le Feuvre, *Gordon Matta-Clark: The Space Between* (London: Nazraeli Press, 2003), 7.

2. Craig Owens, "The Allegorical Impulse: Toward a Theory of Postmodernism," in *Beyond Recognition*, ed. Scott Bryson et al. (Berkeley, CA: University of California Press, 1992), 77.

3. Owens, "Allegorical Impulse," 56–58.

4. The Dia Art Foundation has an ongoing effort to document *Spiral Jetty* in order to preserve it. There are concerns about the work because of not only interventions by people who visit the site and take rocks but also encroaching development. Randy Kennedy, November 17, 2009.

5. Ellen Handy, "Installations and History," *Arts Magazine*, February 1989, 62.

6. Allan Kaprow, "The Legacy of Jackson Pollock," *ArtNews* 57, no. 6 (1958): 56.

7. I use this term keeping Mary Ann Doane's and Martha Buskirk's work in mind.

8. Lisa G. Corrin, "Installing History," *Art Papers* 18, no. 4 (July–August 1994): 6.

9. Marcuse, *One-Dimensional Man*, 98.

bibliography

Adorno, Theodor, and Walter Benjamin. *The Complete Correspondence: 1928–1940*. Edited by Henri Lonitz. Translated by Nicholas Walker. Cambridge, MA: Harvard University Press, 1999.

Alexander, Darsie, et al. *Slide Show: The Projected Image in Contemporary Art*. University Park: University of Pennsylvania Press, 2005.

Alexander, Stephen, and Eugenie Diserio, eds. and designers. *Rooms*, PS1, Institute for Art and Urban Resources catalog. New York: The Institute, 1977.

Alpers, Svetlana. "Museums as a Way of Seeing." In *Exhibiting Cultures: The Poetics and Politics of Museum Display*, edited by Ivan Karp and Steven D. Laine. Washington, DC: Smithsonian Institution Press, 1991.

Alter, Nora. "Beyond the Frame: Renee Green's Video Practice." In *Shadows and Signals*, by Renée Green, Alexander Alberro, Nora M. Alter, and Nuria Enguita Mayo. Barcelona: Fundació Antoni Tàpies, 2000.

Ankersmit, F. R. *Sublime Historical Experience*. Stanford, CA: Stanford University Press, 2005.

Atlee, James, and Lisa Le Feuvre. *Gordon Matta-Clark: The Space Between*. London: Nazraeli Press, 2003.

Ault, Julie. "Chronology." In *Alternative Art, New York, 1965–1985*, edited by Julie Ault. Minneapolis: University of Minnesota Press, 2002.

Bargellesi-Severi, Guglielmo, ed. *Robert Smithson: Slideworks*. Milan, Italy: Carlo Frua, 1997.

Barnum, Fred. *America: Ninety Years of Communications Pioneering, and Progress: Victor Talking Machine Company*. Camden, NJ: General Electric, 1991.

Barthes, Roland. *Camera Lucida*. Translated by Richard Howard. New York: Hill and Wang, 1981.

——. *Image, Music, Text.* Edited and Translated by Stephen Heath. New York: Hill and Wang, 1977.

Baudrillard, Jean. *Simulacra and Simulation.* Translated by Sheila Faria Glaser. 1981. Reprint, Ann Arbor: University of Michigan Press, 1994.

——. *The System of Objects.* Translated by James Benedict. 1968. Reprint, London: Verso, 1996.

Beck, Martin. "Alternative: Space." In *Alternative Art, New York, 1965–1985*, edited by Julie Ault. Minneapolis: University of Minnesota Press, 2002.

Bélisle, José. *David Rabinowitch.* Montreal: Musée d'art contemporain de Montréal, 2003.

Benjamin, Walter. *Illuminations.* Translated by Harry Zohn. New York: Schocken Books, 1969.

——. *Reflections.* Edited by Peter Demetz. New York: Schocken Books, 1978.

Bergson, Henri. *Creative Evolution.* Translated by Arthur Mitchell. 1911. Reprint, New York: Henry Holt, 1926.

Bishop, Claire. "Antagonism and Relational Aesthetics." *October* 110 (Fall 2004): 51–79.

——. *Installation Art: A Critical History*. New York: Routledge, 2005.

Blumberg, Linda. Statement. In *Rooms*, PS1, Institute for Art and Urban Resources catalog, designed and edited by Stephen Alexander and Eugenie Diserio. New York: The Institute, 1977.

Bolton, Richard, ed. *The Contest of Meaning: Critical Histories of Photography.* Cambridge, MA: MIT Press, 1989.

Boris, Eileen. *Art and Labor: Ruskin, Morris, and the Craftsman Ideal in America.* Philadelphia: Temple University Press, 1986.

Bourdieu, Pierre. *Photography: A Middle-Brow Art.* Translated by Shaun Whiteside. Stanford, CA: Stanford University Press, 1990.

Bourriaud, Nicolas. *Relational Aesthetics.* Dijon, France: Le Presses du Réel, 1998.

Boym, Svetlana. *The Future of Nostalgia.* New York: Basic Books, 2001.

Brown, Elizabeth A. "Social Studies: 4 + 4 Young Americans." *Allen Memorial Art Gallery Bulletin* 44, no. 1 (1990).

Brunelle, Al. "The Great Divide: Anarchitecture by Gordon Matta-Clark." *Art in America* 62, no. 5 (September–October 1974): 92–93.

Buchloh, Benjamin H. D., et al. *Experiments in the Everyday: Allan Kaprow and Robert Watts, Events, Objects, Documents.* New York: Columbia University, 1999.

——. "From Factura to Factography." In *The Contest of Meaning: Critical Histories of Photography*, edited by Richard Bolton. Cambridge, MA: MIT Press, 1989.

———. "Warburg's Paragon? The End of Collage and Photomontage in Postwar Europe." In *Deep Storage: Collecting, Storing, and Archiving in Art*, edited by Ingrid Schaffner and Matthias Winzen. Munich: Prestel, 1998.

Buck-Morss, Susan. *The Dialectics of Seeing: Walter Benjamin and the Arcades Project*. Cambridge, MA: MIT Press, 1989.

Buckingham, Matthew. "Image of Absalon to Be Projected Until It Vanishes." Accessed May 11, 2011. www.matthewbuckingham.net/Image%20Absalon.html.

Buskirk, Martha. *The Contingent Object of Contemporary Art*. Cambridge, MA: MIT Press, 2005.

Cadava, Eduardo. *Words of Light: Theses on the Photography of History*. Princeton, NJ: Princeton University Press, 1997.

Chave, Anna. "Sculpture, Gender, and the Value of Labor." *American Art* 24, no. 1 (Spring 2010): 26–30.

Cixous, Helène. *"Coming to Writing" and Other Essays*. Edited by Deborah Jenson. Translated by Sarah Cornell et al. Cambridge, MA: Harvard University Press, 1991.

Clausen, Barbara, et al. *After the Act: The (Re)Presentation of Performance Art*. Vienna: Museum Moderner Kunst Stiftung Ludwig Wien, 2007.

Coffey, Mary Katherine. "Histories That Haunt: A Conversation with Ann Hamilton." *Art Journal* 60, no. 3 (Fall 2001): 10–23.

Collins, Douglas. *The Story of Kodak*. New York: Abrams, 1990.

Comment, Bernard. *The Painted Panorama*. New York: Abrams, 2000.

Cooke, Lynne. "The Site of Memory." In *Doubletake: Collective Memory and Current Art*, by Lynne Cooke, Brian Curiger, and Greg Hilty. New York: Parkett, 1992.

Cooke, Lynne, Brian Curiger, and Greg Hilty. *Doubletake: Collective Memory and Current Art*. New York: Parkett, 1992.

Corrin, Lisa G. "Installing History." *Art Papers* 18, no. 4 (July–August 1994): 6–14.

Crary, Jonathan. *Suspensions of Perception: Attention, Spectacle, Modern Culture*. Cambridge, MA: MIT Press, 1999.

Crimp, Douglas. "Mourning and Militancy." *October* 51 (Winter 1989): 3–18.

———. "Pictures." *October* 8 (Spring 1979): 75–88.

Daguerre, Louis-Jacques Mandé. "Daguerreotype." In *Classic Essays on Photography*, edited by Alan Trachtenberg. New Haven, CT: Leete's Island Books, 1980.

Davies, Hugh M., and Lynda Forsha. *Ann Hamilton*. San Diego: Museum of Contemporary Art, 1991.

Davis, Douglas. "Performance Photography." *Connoisseur* (March 1985): 144–45.

Davis, Fred. *Yearning for Yesterday: A Sociology of Nostalgia.* New York: Free Press, 1979.

Dean, Tacita. *Floh.* Göttingen, Germany: Steidl Publications, 2001.

Deitcher, David, William Olander, and Abigail Solomon-Godeau. *The Art of Memory: The Loss of History.* New York: New Museum of Contemporary Art, 1985.

Deleuze, Gilles. *Bergsonism.* Translated by Hugh Tomlinson and Barbara Habberjam. New York: Zone Books, 1966, 1988.

De Oliveira, Nicholas, Nicola Oxley, and Michael Petry. *Installation Art in the New Millennium: The Empire of the Senses.* London: Thames and Hudson, 2003.

Derrida, Jacques. *Of Grammatology.* Translated by Gayatri Spivak. Baltimore: Johns Hopkins University Press, 1978.

———. *The Truth in Painting.* Translated by Geoff Bennington and Ian McLeod. Chicago: University of Chicago Press, 1987.

Dewey, John. *Art as Experience.* New York: Perigee Books, 1934.

Doane, Mary Ann. *The Emergence of Cinematic Time: Modernity, Contingency, the Archive.* Cambridge, MA: Harvard University Press, 2002.

Eastman Kodak Company. *Adventures in Outdoor Color Slides.* Rochester, NY: Kodak Sales Division, 1962.

Edwards, Elizabeth, ed. *Anthropology and Photography, 1860–1920.* New Haven, CT: Yale University Press, 1992.

———. "Photographs as Objects of Memory." In *Material Memories*, edited by Marius Kwint, Christopher Breward, and Jeremy Aynsley. Oxford, UK: Berg, 1999.

Fielding, Raymond, ed. *A Technological History of Motion Pictures and Television.* Berkeley: University of California Press, 1967.

Floue, Tendance, and Jean Baudrillard. *Sommes-Nous?* Paris: Naïve, 2006.

Foote, Nancy. "Apotheosis of the Crummy Space." *Artforum International* 15, no. 2 (October 1976): 28–37.

Foster, Hal. "An Archival Impulse." *October* 110 (Fall 2004): 3–22.

———. *Compulsive Beauty.* Cambridge, MA: MIT Press, 1997.

———. *The Return of the Real.* Cambridge, MA: MIT Press, 1996.

Foucault, Michel. *The Archaeology of Knowledge and the Discourse on Language.* Translated by A. M. Sheridan Smith. New York: Pantheon Books, 1972.

———. *Language, Counter-Memory, Practice: Selected Essays and Interviews.* Edited by Donald F. Bouchard. Ithaca, NY: Cornell University Press, 1977.

———. "Of Other Spaces." *Diacritics* 16, no. 1 (Spring 1986): 22–27.

Frampton, Hollis. *Circles of Confusion: Film Photography and Video Texts, 1968–1980*. Rochester, NY: Visual Studies Workshop Press, 1983.

Francbline, Catherine. "Interview with Jean Baudrillard." *Flash Art* 130 (October–November 1986): 54–55.

Fried, Michael. "Art and Objecthood." In *Art and Objecthood: Essays and Reviews*. Chicago: University of Chicago Press, 1998.

Gibbons, Joan. *Contemporary Art and Memory: Images of Recollection and Remembrance*. London: I.B. Tauris, 2009.

Gilbreth, Frank B. *Motion Study: A Method for Increasing the Efficiency of the Workman*. 1911. Reprint, Easton, PA: Hive Publishing, 1972.

Godfrey, Mark. "Artist as Historian." *October* 120 (Spring 2007): 140–72.

Goldberg, Reesa, ed. *Thinking about Exhibitions*. London: Routledge, 1996.

Goldstein, Ann, and Anne Rorimer, eds. *Reconsidering the Object of Art, 1965–75*. Cambridge, MA: MIT Press, 1995.

González, Jennifer A. "Siting Histories: Material Display and the Politics of Display in the Work of Fred Wilson, Pepón Osorio, and Amalia Mesa-Bains, 1985–1995." PhD diss., University of California, Santa Cruz, 1996.

———. *Subject to Display: Reframing Race in Contemporary Installation Art*. Cambridge, MA: MIT Press, 2008.

Gott, Ted. *Don't Leave Me This Way: Art in the Age of AIDS*. London: Thames and Hudson, 1994.

Gould, Claudia, and Valerie Smith, eds. *5000 Artists Return to Artists Space*. New York: Artists Space, 1998.

Green, Renée. *Between and Including*. Vienna: Secession, 2001.

———. "Partially Buried in Three Parts: Extract." In *Ruins in Reverse: Time and Progress in Contemporary Art*, edited by Grant Kester. *CEPA Journal*. Buffalo, NY: Center for the Exploratory and Perpetual Arts [CEPA], September 1998–March 1999.

———. *World Tour*. Los Angeles: Museum of Contemporary Art, 1993.

Green, Renée, Alexander Alberro, Nora M. Alter, and Nuria Enguita Mayo. *Shadows and Signals*. Barcelona: Fundació Antoni Tàpies, 2000.

Greenberg, Clement. *Art and Culture: Critical Essays*. 1961. Reprint, Boston: Beacon Press, 1989.

Guffey, Elizabeth E. *Retro: The Culture of Revival*. London: Thames and Hudson, 2006.

Hall, Doug, and Sally Jo Fifer, eds. *Illuminating Video: An Essential Guide to Video Art*. New York: Aperture, 1990.

Hamilton, Ann, Tomoaki Kitagawa, Bernhart Schwenk, and Takao Ueda. *The picture is still.* Ostfildern, Germany: Hatje Cantz Publishers, 2003.

Handy, Ellen. "Installations and History." *Arts Magazine*, February 1989.

Heiss, Alanna. "Introduction." In *Rooms*, PS1, Institute for Art and Urban Resources catalog, designed and edited by Stephen Alexander and Eugenie Diserio. New York: The Institute, 1977.

Hodgetts, Craig. "Heretical Thoughts on Architecture and Photography." *Architecture California* (May 1992): 57–63.

Hopkins, Robert. *Picture, Image, and Experience: A Philosophical Inquiry.* Cambridge: Cambridge University Press, 1998.

Howell, John, and Lisa Liebmann. "Forum: Retro/Trends." *Artforum* 22 no. 3 (November 1983): 73.

Iles, Chrissie, Shamim M. Momin, and Debra Singer. *Whitney Biennial 2004.* New York: Whitney Museum of American Art, 2004.

Iles, Chrissie, and Philippe Vergne. *Whitney Biennial 2006: Day for Night.* New York: Whitney Museum of American Art, 2006.

Iles, Chrissie, et al. *Into the Light: The Projected Image in American Art, 1964–77.* New York: Whitney Museum of American Art, 2001.

Ireland, Craig. *The Subaltern Appeal to Experience: Self-Identity, Late Modernity, and the Politics of Immediacy.* Montreal: McGill-Queen's University Press, 2004.

Jacob, Mary Jane. *Gordon Matta-Clark: A Retrospective.* Chicago: Museum of Contemporary Art, 1985.

———. *Places with a Past: New Site-Specific Art at Charleston's Spoleto Festival.* New York: Rizzoli Publications, 1991.

Jacob, Mary Jane, and Lynn Gumpert. *Christian Boltanski: Lessons of Darkness.* Los Angeles: Los Angeles Museum of Contemporary Art, 1988.

Jameson, Fredric. *Postmodernism, or the Cultural Logic of Late Capitalism.* 1984. Durham, NC: Duke University Press, 1991.

———. "Postmodernism and Utopia." In *Utopia/Post-Utopia.* Boston: Institute of Contemporary Art, 1988.

Jay, Martin. *Downcast Eyes: The Denigration of Vision in Twentieth-Century French Thought.* Berkeley: University of California Press, 1993.

———. *Songs of Experience: Modern American and European Variations on a Universal Theme.* Berkeley: University of California Press, 2005.

Jones, Amelia. *Body Art: Performing the Subject.* Minneapolis: University of Minnesota Press, 1998.

———. *Self/Image: Technology, Representation, and the Contemporary Subject.* London: Routledge, 2006.

Kaiper, Bruce. "The Human Object and Its Capitalist Image." *Left Curve*, no. 5 (Fall–Winter 1975): 40–60.

Kaprow, Allan. *Essays on the Blurring of Art and Life.* Edited by Jeff Kelley. Berkeley: University of California Press, 1996.

———. "The Legacy of Jackson Pollock." *ArtNews* 57, no. 6 (1958): 24–26, 55–57.

Karp, Ivan, and Steven D. Laine, eds. *Exhibiting Cultures: The Poetics and Politics of Museum Display.* Washington, DC: Smithsonian Institution Press, 1991.

Kaye, Nick. *Site-Specific Art: Performance, Place, and Documentation.* London: Routledge, 2000.

Kelley, Jeff. *Childsplay: The Art of Allan Kaprow.* Berkeley: University of California Press, 2004.

Kern, Stephen. *The Culture of Time and Space, 1880–1918.* Cambridge, MA: Harvard University Press, 1983.

Kester, Grant. "The Rise and Fall of Baudrillard." *New Art Examiner* 15, no. 3 (November 1987): 20–23.

———, ed. *Ruins in Reverse: Time and Progress in Contemporary Art. CEPA Journal.* Buffalo, NY: Center for the Exploratory and Perpetual Arts (CEPA), September 1998–March 1999.

Kingsley, April. "Art Goes Underground." *Village Voice*, October 18, 1978.

Kirshenblatt-Gimblett, Barbara. "Objects of Ethnography." In *Exhibiting Cultures: The Poetics and Politics of Museum Display*, edited by Ivan Karp and Steven D. Laine. Washington, DC: Smithsonian Institution Press, 1991.

Kirshner, Judith Russi. "Non-uments." *Artforum* 24, no. 2 (October 1985): 102–8.

Kracauer, Siegfried. *The Mass Ornament: Weimar Essays.* Translated and edited by Thomas Y. Levin. Cambridge, MA: Harvard University Press, 1995.

Krane, Susan, and Bruce Jenkins. *Hollis Frampton: Recollections and Recreations.* Buffalo, NY: Albright-Knox Art Gallery, 1984.

Krauss, Rosalind. "The Cultural Logic of the Late Capitalist Museum." *October* 54 (Autumn 1990): 3–17.

———. "Notes on the Index: Seventies Art in America." *October* 3 (Spring 1977): 69.

———. "Notes on the Index: Seventies Art in America, Part 2." *October* 4 (Autumn 1977): 70.

———. "Photography's Discursive Spaces: Landscape/View." *Art Journal* 42, no. 4 (Winter 1982): 311–19.

———. "Sculpture in the Expanded Field." *October* 8 (Spring 1979): 30–44.

———. *A Voyage on the North Sea: Art in the Age of the Post-Medium Condition.* London: Thames and Hudson, 1999.

Kravagna, Christian. "It's Nothing Worth Documenting If It's Not Difficult to Get: On the Documentary Nature of Photography and Film in the Work of Gordon Matta-Clark." In *Gordon Matta-Clark*, edited by Corinne Diserens. London: Phaidon, 2003.

Kukielski, Tina. "In the Spirit of the Vegetable: The Early Works of Gordon Matta-Clark (1969–71)." In *Gordon Matta-Clark: You Are the Measure*, edited by Elisabeth Sussman. New York: Whitney Museum of American Art.

Kwint, Marius, Christopher Breward, and Jeremy Aynsley, eds. *Material Memories.* Oxford, UK: Berg, 1999.

Kwon, Miwon. "One Place after Another: Notes on Site-Specificity." In *Space, Site, Intervention: Situating Installation Art*, edited by Erika Suderberg. Minneapolis: University of Minnesota Press, 2000.

———. *One Place after Another: Site-Specific Art and Locational Identity.* Cambridge, MA: MIT Press, 2002.

Lawler, Louise. *Louise Lawler and Others.* Basel, Switzerland: Kunstmuseum Basel, Hatje Cantz Verlag, 2004.

Lawson, Thomas. "Forum: Generation In Vitro." *Artforum* 23, no. 1 (September 1984): 99.

Lee, Pamela M. *Gordon Matta-Clark: Object to Be Destroyed.* Cambridge, MA: MIT Press, 2000.

Le Feuvre, Lisa. "The W-hole Story." *Art Monthly* 255 (April 2002): 12–15.

Linker, Kate. "From Imitation, to the Copy, to Just Effect: On Reading Jean Baudrillard." *Artforum* 22, no. 8 (April 1984): 44–47.

Mannoni, Laurent. *The Great Art of Light and Shadow: Archaeology of the Cinema.* Exeter, UK: University of Exeter Press, 2000.

Manovich, Lev. *The Language of New Media.* Cambridge, MA: MIT Press, 2001.

Marcuse, Herbert. *One-Dimensional Man.* Boston: Beacon Press, 1964.

Marien, Mary Warner. *Photography and Its Critics: A Cultural History, 1839–1900.* Cambridge: Cambridge University Press, 1997.

Marx, Karl. *Early Writings.* Edited by T. B. Bottomore. New York: McGraw-Hill, 1963.

Matta-Clark, Gordon. *Splitting.* New York: Loft Books, 1974.

Matta-Clark, Gordon, and Mary Jane Jacob. *Splitting.* New York: Holly Solomon Gallery, 1990.

McGeehan, Patrick. "Vinyl Records and Turntables Are Gaining Sales." *New York Times*, December 6, 2009.

Meikle, Jeffrey. *American Plastics: A Cultural History*. New Brunswick, NJ: Rutgers University Press, 1995. Kindle edition.

Melchionne, Kevin. "Rethinking Site-Specificity: Some Critical and Philosophical Problems." *Art Criticism* 12, no. 2 (1997): 36–49.

Metz, Christian. "Photography and Fetish." *October* 34 (Fall 1985): 81–90.

Meyer, James. "Artist as Nomad." In *Space, Site, Intervention: Situating Installation Art*, edited by Erika Suderberg. Minneapolis: University of Minnesota Press, 2000.

———. "The Functional Site; or, The Transformation of Site-Specificity." In *Space, Site, Intervention: Situating Installation Art*, edited by Erika Suderberg. Minneapolis: University of Minnesota Press, 2000.

———. "Nostalgia and Memory: Legacies of the 1960s in Recent Work." In *Painting, Object, Film, Concept: Selections from the Herbig Collection*. New York: Christie's, 1998.

Mondloch, Kate. *Screens: Viewing Media Installation Art*. Minneapolis: University of Minnesota Press, 2010.

Moore, Rachel. *Hollis Frampton: Nostalgia*. London: Afterall Books, 2006.

Morris, Robert. *Continuous Project Altered Daily: The Writings of Robert Morris*. Cambridge, MA: MIT Press, 1993.

———. "Notes on Sculpture, Part III: Notes and Nonsequitors." In *Art in Theory: 1900–1990: An Anthology of Changing Ideas*, edited by Charles Harrison and Paul Wood. Oxford, UK: Blackwell, 1992.

Morrissey, Simon. "Gordon Matta-Clark." *Creative Camera* 337 (December 1995/January 1996): 40.

Morse, Margaret. "Video Installation Art: The Body, the Image, and the Space In-Between." In *Illuminating Video: An Essential Guide to Video Art*, edited by Doug Hall and Sally Jo Fifer. New York: Aperture, 1990.

Moure, Gloria, ed. *Gordon Matta-Clark: Works and Collected Writings*. Barcelona: Ediciones Poligrafia, 2006.

Nora, Pierre. "Between Memory and History: Les Lieux de Mémoire." *Representations* 26 (Spring 1989): 7–24.

O'Doherty, Brian. "Inside the White Cube, Part I: Notes on the Gallery Space." *Artforum* 14, no. 7 (March 1976): 25.

———. "Inside the White Cube, Part II: The Eye and the Spectator." *Artforum* 14, no. 8 (April 1976): 27.

Owens, Craig. *Beyond Recognition*. Edited by Scott Bryson et al. Berkeley, CA: University of California Press, 1992.

Piper, Adrian. *Adrian Piper: A Retrospective.* Baltimore: University of Maryland, 1999.

Prins, Gwyn. "The Battle for Control of the Camera in Late Nineteenth-Century Western Zambia." In *Anthropology and Photography, 1860–1920*, edited by Elizabeth Edwards. New Haven, CT: Yale University Press, 1992.

Prix, Wolf. "The Imaging of Reality." *Architecture California* (May 1992): 14–22.

Quandt, James. "Tacita Dean, Schaulager Basel." *Artforum* 3 (November 2006): 287–88.

Rainer, Yvonne. *Journeys from Berlin.* DVD. New York: Zeitgeist Films, 1980. 125 min.

Reiring, Janelle. ___________, *Louise Lawler, Adrian Piper and Cindy Sherman Have Agreed to Participate in an Exhibition Organized by Janelle Reiring at Artists Space, September 23 to October 28, 1978.* New York: Committee for the Visual Arts, 1978.

Reiss, Julie. *From Margin to Center: The Spaces of Installation Art.* Cambridge, MA: MIT Press, 1999.

Rodenbeck, Judith. "Foil: Allan Kaprow before Photography." In *Experiments in the Everyday: Allan Kaprow and Robert Watts, Events, Objects, Documents*, by Benjamin H. D. Buchloh et al. New York: Columbia University, 1999.

Rosler, Martha. "In, Around and Afterthoughts: Notes on Documentary Photography." In *The Contest of Meaning: Critical Histories of Photography*, edited by Richard Bolton, 303–41. Cambridge, MA: MIT Press, 1989.

Saltzman, Lisa. *Making Memory Matter: Strategies of Remembrance in Contemporary Art.* Chicago: University of Chicago Press, 2006.

Schaffner, Ingrid, and Matthias Winzen, eds. *Deep Storage: Collecting, Storing, and Archiving in Art.* Munich: Prestel, 1998.

Sekula, Allan. "The Body and the Archive." In *The Contest of Meaning: Critical Histories of Photography*, edited by Richard Bolton, 344–89. Cambridge, MA: MIT Press, 1989.

———. "On the Invention of Photographic Meaning." *Artforum* 13, no. 2 (January 1975): 36–45.

Simon, Joan. *Ann Hamilton.* New York: Abrams, 2002.

Singer, Debra. "The Way Things Never Were: Nostalgia's Possibilities and the Unpredictable Past." In *Whitney Biennial 2004*, by Chrissie Iles, Shamim M. Monim, and Debra Singer, 22–33. New York: Whitney Museum of American Art, 2004.

Smithson, Robert. "Hotel Palenque, 1969–72." *Parkett* 43 (March 1995): 117–32.

———. *Robert Smithson: The Collected Writings*. Berkeley: University of California Press, 1996.

Staniszewski, Mary Ann. *The Power of Display: A History of Exhibitions at the Museum of Modern Art*. Cambridge, MA: MIT Press, 1998.

Steichen, Edward. *The Family of Man*. New York: Museum of Modern Art, 1955.

Suderberg, Erika, ed. *Space, Site, Intervention: Situating Installation Art*. Minneapolis: University of Minnesota Press, 2000.

Summers, David. *Real Spaces: World Art History and the Rise of Western Modernism*. London: Phaidon, 2003.

Thompson, E. P. *The Essential E. P. Thompson*. Edited by Dorothy Thompson. New York: New Press, 2001.

Trachtenberg, Alan, ed. *Classic Essays on Photography*. New Haven, CT: Leete's Island Books, 1980.

Turkle, Sherry, ed. *Evocative Objects: Things We Think With*. Cambridge, MA: MIT Press, 2007.

Turvey, Malcolm, et al. "Roundtable: The Projected Image in Contemporary Art." *October* 104 (Spring 2003): 71–96.

Uhrhane, Jennifer. "Timeline." Photographic Resource Center at Boston University. Accessed June 14, 2011. www.godowskycolorawards.org/2009/timeline.html.

Wagner, Anne M. "Performance, Video, and the Rhetoric of Presence." *October* 91 (Winter 2000): 59–80.

———. "Splitting and Doubling: Gordon Matta-Clark and the Body of Sculpture." *Grey Room* 14 (Winter 2004): 26–45.

Wall, Jeff. "Marks of Indifference: Aspects of Photography in or as Conceptual Art." In *Reconsidering the Object of Art, 1965–75*, edited by Ann Goldstein and Anne Rorimer. Cambridge, MA: MIT Press, 1995.

Royoux, Jean-Christophe, Marina Warner, and Germaine Greer. *Tacita Dean*. London: Phaidon, 2006.

Welchman, John C. "In and Around the 'Second Frame.'" In *The Rhetoric of the Frame: Essays on the Boundaries of the Artwork*, edited by Paul Duro. Cambridge: Cambridge University Press, 1996.

West, Nancy Martha. *Kodak and the Lens of Nostalgia*. Charlottesville: University of Virginia Press, 2000.

Williams, Richard J. *After Modern Sculpture: Art in the United States and Europe, 1965–70*. New York: Manchester University Press, 2000.

Wilson, Fred. *The Museum: Mixed Metaphors*. Seattle: Seattle Art Museum, 1993.

index